The Courage
to Collaborate

The Courage
to Collaborate

*The Case for Labor-Management
Partnerships in Education*

Ken Futernick

HARVARD EDUCATION PRESS
CAMBRIDGE, MASSACHUSETTS

Library of Congress Control Number: 2015951063

Paperback ISBN 978-1-61250-892-4
Library Edition ISBN 978-1-61250-893-1

Published by Harvard Education Press,
an imprint of the Harvard Education Publishing Group

Harvard Education Press
8 Story Street
Cambridge, MA 02138

Cover Design: Ciano Design
Cover Graphic: iStock.com/toniaver
The typefaces used in this book are Scala and ITC Stone Sans.

Contents

Foreword   ix
  Adam Urbanski

Preface   xv

INTRODUCTION   *Changing the Narrative*   1

CHAPTER 1   *What Is Labor-Management Collaboration?*   23

CHAPTER 2   *The Impact of Labor-Management Collaboration*   47

CHAPTER 3   *Obstacles to Collaboration*   71

CHAPTER 4   *Cultivating Collaboration, Part I: Strategies*   91

CHAPTER 5   *Cultivating Collaboration, Part II: Tactics*   113

CHAPTER 6   *Needed Reforms for Management and Unions*   135

EPILOGUE   *The Future We Choose*   155

APPENDIX   *A Guide to Resources on Labor-Management Collaboration in Education*   163

Notes   179
Acknowledgments   197
About the Author   201
Index   203

If you want to go fast, go alone.
If you want to go far, go together.

—AFRICAN PROVERB

Foreword

After a quarter of a century of education reforms, schools today remain more like yesterday's than we'd like to admit. Many of the reforms that have been promoted are wrong-headed. They ignore the collective wisdom of teachers, are imposed on schools and teachers unilaterally, emphasize testing over teaching and learning, punish rather than support neglected schools, and divert resources from public schools to charters and privatization schemes. They discourage collaboration and even hijack the language: "reforms" are really deforms; "shared decision making" means we'll make all the decisions and then share it with you; and what sounds good is more important than what is good and sound.

Understandably, even teachers who would be inclined to collaborate are reluctant to do so because of this climate. This is a time to fight, not collaborate, they are told by some of their leaders. This is especially true for teachers in urban districts, where student "performance" is worst, starved for resources and struggling with the impediments presented by concentrated poverty. They find themselves in a dilemma: do we accept these wrong-headed reforms just to get the desperately needed funds attached to them? Or do we resist those reforms at the risk of the sanctions that often follow?

All is not lost, however, for there is a way out of this dilemma.

As a union leader for thirty-four years, I have learned that no single constituency in education can succeed by itself in making our public schools effective for all students. It's tough enough even if we all work together—impossible if we do not. That is why labor-management collaboration is indispensable to the success of reform efforts. And that is also why both unions and management must support change and seek improvement.

Ken Futernick's timely and important book makes this case. He identifies the major opportunities for collaboration; provides actual and specific examples of districts that practice it; and describes the needed policies, strategies and practices to implement it. And while Futernick elaborates on how teachers can make their unions even more responsible and more responsive to students' needs, he also informs school managers how they must change and how they can support the progressive impulses of teachers and their unions. Such a shift in relationships can lead to the kind of culture change that would result in a more hospitable environment for continuous improvement and sustained progress.

Futernick also explains why we need to build better relationships in tandem with building better systems, how to distinguish between collaboration and collusion, and how to both depolarize and contextualize reform efforts. He also takes on one of the most daunting challenges in education reform: how to make authentic collaboration the norm in education. And he provides real specifics and substance where, until now, there had been mostly rhetoric. He calls for more collaboration at all levels of the system—not just at the central office but at school sites as well as between union leaders and policy makers at the state and national level.

The time for collaboration is now. Many educators, policy makers, and others are reaching the conclusion that reforms can be effective only if they are done—to quote American Federation of Teachers President Randi Weingarten—*with* teachers and not *to* teachers. And teachers and their unions are increasingly recognizing that they must become agents of reform, or they will surely remain the targets of reform.

There is also a growing body of evidence that when management and labor at the local level learn how to collaborate, reforms have been adopted that teachers consider fair to them and good for their students. But labor-management collaboration does not guarantee positive results in every instance. Even when they're working together, local stakeholders may not select the most effective reform strategies or, if they do, may not implement them well. Other variables, like funding and state and federal education policies, over which local labor and management have little control, also play a central role in determining success. Without better systems, better relationships will merely heighten the level of comfort among the adults; and without better relationships, it will be difficult to build and sustain better systems, and positive reforms will be unattainable. And while neither good systems nor good relationships are likely to thrive in a milieu of polarized debates and closed minds, both are achievable if we seek common ground and contextualize our initiatives within the realities that exist for students, teachers, and schools.

Teacher unions and school management across America must work together to promote the kinds of reforms that reflect the collective experience and wisdom of educators. This can best happen if teacher unionists and school managers themselves recognize not only the need for change but also that it is in their own interest to welcome the evolution of teacher unions and school management. Such collaborations as in Montgomery County, Cincinnati, and the ABC Unified district in California, highlighted in this book, serve as good examples of what is possible. But we should also be willing to learn from other countries, such as Finland and Singapore. As Futernick rightfully points out, it is disingenuous for policy makers to celebrate the achievements in these places but not to acknowledge, much less advocate for, the kinds of reforms they implemented—many of which are diametrically opposite to those being imposed here.

Here in Rochester, New York, through a collaborative relationship, we have sought to move even beyond the interest-based model of collective bargaining—one of the major strategies for collaboration described in this book. Together, the district and the teacher union developed strategic objectives and engaged in joint problem solving. By changing the negotiations process, and by expanding the scope of collective bargaining to include educational and instructional issues, we have negotiated "living contracts" that include a shared commitment to view collective bargaining as collaboration rather than a time for positional and adversarial fights. We have adopted "what's best for students" as the shared value, the common denominator, and the litmus test for every specific proposal advanced by either the district or the union. We now conduct ongoing negotiations as timely problem solving rather than an exercise relegated to a once-in-a-while fight. And we have incorporated standards, benchmarks, and formulae that continue to guide us beyond the life of any individual contract. Essentially, we have decided to use the collective bargaining process as a vehicle for building a more genuine profession for teachers and more effective schools for all our students.

Yet, Rochester is a good example of the reality that labor-management collaboration, while necessary, is not sufficient to substantially improve student learning, especially in America's urban school districts. After more than three decades of commitment to labor-management collaboration, Rochester's students still ranked last in New York State in student learning as measured by state-mandated tests. And while there's good reason not to accept these tests as a necessarily accurate reflection of learning, other indicators such as graduation rates, attendance, and literacy and numeracy proficiency are also woefully disappointing.

We can certainly speculate as to the reasons for this. Clearly, concentration of poverty is the most important impediment to learning. Rochester ranks as the proportionately poorest school district in New York State and the fifth poorest in the nation. And while individual poverty does not have a deterministic impact on learning, concentrated poverty has a predictable impact—especially when policy makers do too little to address the effects of poverty. With half of students in America's public schools now living at or below poverty level, it should be increasingly difficult to ignore this tragic impediment to learning.

Still, labor-management collaboration remains our best hope for addressing and resolving impediments to better student learning. Blaming each other is not the answer, since we're all in the same boat. And if we're all in the same boat, it matters little which end leaks. Only together can we access the needed resources and persuade others—the public, the politicians, and our communities—that we'll make good use of the resources we seek. And only together can we nurture collaboration at the school level, where it matters most. Besides, if the adults in the lives of children cannot get their act together, why should we expect that the students could? And if we, educators, cannot forge a compelling agenda, why would we be surprised that others would fill the void? So, our options are to reform or to be reformed.

Many years ago, with six brothers and parents whose formal education did not extend beyond elementary grades, I escaped communist Poland in search of freedom and a better life. After hiding in several countries for nearly four years, we finally reached our new homeland. And if it were not for the opportunities that I received through public schools, I would not have been able to build a better life for myself and for my family. Public schools still represent the best hope for opportunity and upward mobility for millions of children who otherwise would have none. Many of these are foreign born for whom English is not a native language—as was the case for me. Most were born here but are nevertheless strangers in their own land, and our schools have never served them well. That's the main reason why we must collaborate as equal partners to improve, not abandon, public schools for all our students.

—*Adam Urbanski*
   President, Rochester Teachers Association
   Vice President, American Federation of Teachers
   Rochester, NY

Preface

In the Montgomery County Public Schools in Maryland, just northwest of Washington, DC, in the year 2000, only 59 percent of kindergarteners could read a simple story. For Latinos and African Americans, the percentages were much lower. Meanwhile, a slowing economy was reducing tax revenues, forcing district leaders to make painful cuts to an already-dwindling budget.

At the time, the district's two hundred schools were serving one hundred forty-four thousand students, making it the nation's sixteenth largest district. Although the county was perhaps best known for its affluence, its population was actually quite diverse by way of income and racial makeup. Close to half of students were Latino or African American and, for several years by then, district leaders had faced intense pressure from the community and from state and national education officials to close a persistent achievement gap between poor and more affluent students.

All in all, conditions were ripe for protracted battles between the district's managers and its teachers union. As tensions rose, no one would have been surprised if administrators and union leaders had pointed fingers at one another, issued threats, and competed with one another for public backing. After all, that's exactly what leaders in so many other districts across the country were doing at the time as they faced similar challenges.

Montgomery County's education leaders, however, did something unusual. They decided to face the crisis as partners rather than adversaries. In a new compact between the district and its three labor unions to close the achievement gap, which they titled "R.E.S.P.E.C.T.," they agreed that "[t]here must be an end to the culture of blame. A new environment had to be created, one that valued risk-taking, recognition, and shared accountability." In addition, "[p]olicy makers could not mandate change. Change could only come about through local capacity and local will. To that end, resources had to be reorganized to help all instructional staff—teachers, support staff, and administrators—to act in new ways."[1]

The seeds of collaboration had been planted several years earlier. Starting with contract negotiations in 1997–1998, management and labor replaced the confrontational bargaining process with interest-based bargaining (IBB)—a way for each side to seek mutually agreeable solutions based on common interests. The resulting contract, signed in 1998, stated that it was "more than a contract that describes the wages, hours, and working conditions of the unit members covered by it. This negotiated Agreement describes a relationship of collaboration being forged between the teachers' union and the school system, dedicated to the continuous improvement of the quality of education in Montgomery County Public Schools. For the union, taking responsibility for the improvement of the quality of teaching and learning represents an expanded role, and for the administration, forging a partnership with the union over ways the system and schools can improve is also new."[2] Management and unions still represented the interests of their respective constituents, but with this new partnership, their main goal was to ensure that every student received the opportunity to learn at high levels.

This compact marked the start of one of the most dramatic turnarounds that a school district of this size has ever produced. By a decade later, academic achievement had risen significantly among not just white and Asian American students but also among Latinos and African Americans, and the gap between the groups had narrowed. Far more students were graduating from high school and going to college, and more of the collegians were graduating. For its extraordinary achievements, the district received the Malcolm Baldrige National Quality Award in 2010, the highest presidential honor for performance excellence by US organizations. Montgomery County was only the sixth public school system to receive it.

Moreover, Montgomery County isn't the only place where educators chose collaboration over confrontation. Similar partnerships emerged in such places as Toledo and Cincinnati, Ohio; Rochester, New York; and Sacramento, California. Many of those partnerships were supported by the Teacher Union Reform Network (TURN), founded in 1995 and composed of union locals of the two big national teacher unions, the American Federation of Teachers (AFT) and National Education Association (NEA). TURN promoted a progressive unionism based on collaboration and, since its founding, it has grown significantly; it now includes more than two hundred AFT and NEA locals, and it has six regional chapters that stretch from California to the East Coast.

Through such collaboration, Montgomery County was not the only district to achieve positive outcomes. In Cincinnati, the high school graduation rate rose dramatically from 51 percent in 2000 to 82 percent in 2010, and the achievement gap between whites and African Americans was eliminated.[3]

Despite these developments, management and labor are not collaborating in most of America's school districts. Most educational leaders, from principals and union representatives at individual schools to education officials and labor leaders on the national level, continue either to operate as adversaries or to remain disengaged from one another. That approach is not serving students well.

My Thesis

Effective collaboration between management and unions is essential to creating an education system in which *all* students have an opportunity to attend good schools. Such factors as adequate funding and declining poverty are also critical to ensuring that all students have that opportunity, but effective collaboration is a *sine qua non* of good schools; without it, good school systems won't become great and struggling systems will continue to struggle.

Moreover, evidence shows, labor-management collaboration can improve student learning in a way that solves many other problems that schools face, including high teacher turnover rates, poor teaching conditions, poorly conceived and implemented education policy, and so on. To pave the way for more of these productive partnerships, teacher unions *and* management will have to implement specific reforms in how they operate.

While not all management and union leaders have the dispositions and skills of the collaborative education leaders in Montgomery County, many are already open to collaboration and capable of cultivating the dispositions and skills of collaborative leadership. This is no small job, however, and education leaders at all levels must commit real time and effort to it. Administrators and union leaders will need professional development in collaborative leadership, which most currently do not receive; districts will need to recruit and select leaders who embrace a collaborative approach; and federal, state, and district leaders will need to design polices to encourage collaboration rather than foment disunity and isolation (as many currently do).

Despite the time and effort required, however, I firmly believe that this is the only approach that will produce the schools we want for our students. The current carrot-and-stick approach, resting on the belief that most educators cannot work as partners and need outside levers to motivate them, will at best produce small, short-term gains in test scores for a few outliers. At worst, large numbers of committed educators will continue to flee dysfunctional environments that do little to educate students. Teachers will spend too much time preparing students to take tests rather than generating deep knowledge of their subjects. Core subjects like science, social studies, and art, which are less subject to testing, will receive less attention. And, most ominously, students—even many who score well on tests—will remain disengaged and miss the genuine opportunities, rewards, and joys that come with a truly high-quality education.

Why I Wrote This Book

Because I believe that labor-management collaboration is essential to the success of America's public school systems, I wrote this book to relay its benefits to educators across the nation and to explain how they can best put it to use. Several important books have been written on this topic, including *United Mind Workers* in 1997 and *Win-Win Labor-Management Collaboration in Education* in 2005. More recently, a few writers have chronicled the recent rise in interest in labor-management collaboration, and researchers have begun to study its impact on school systems and student outcomes. As you will read, collaboration is often misunderstood, leading some to criticize it, but the evidence in favor of what I call "authentic collaboration" is strong. In the pages that follow, I hope to address at least two critical questions that remain unanswered:

- Why, despite the evidence, are collaborative labor-management partnerships not more widespread?
- How can we overcome the obstacles to collaboration to make such partnerships the rule rather than the exception?

I draw from the emerging case study literature of districts engaged in labor-management collaboration and from numerous interviews I have conducted with labor and management leaders who are engaged in this practice.

About Me

I taught elementary school for several years in California and then joined the faculty at California State University, Sacramento, in 1988, teaching courses in education and supervising teachers in the field. I have researched teacher retention, teacher preparation, and school reform and advised state and federal lawmakers on education policy.

In 2008, I left Cal State and helped found the School Turnaround Center at WestEd, a national nonprofit educational research and service organization based in San Francisco. The Center partnered with some of the nation's lowest performing schools, and this work enabled me to experience—firsthand—the frayed relationships, incivility, lack of trust, and absence of collaboration that fueled the dysfunction in virtually every circumstance. I discovered that successful turnarounds always begin with a turnaround in adult relationships. In most struggling school systems, one of the few things on which people can agree is that they don't enjoy their work or the professional relationships with most of their colleagues. Fortunately, most everyone in these dysfunctional systems is open to trying things to address the problem.

My WestEd colleagues and I wrote two research reports on labor-management collaboration. One examined the impact of the first national conference on labor-management collaboration, cosponsored by the leading management and labor organizations in education and the US Education Department, in 2011.[4] The other analyzed case study research on districts that engaged in labor-management collaboration.[5] The positive findings from these studies inspired me to write this book, but it was my work on the ground with teachers, administrators, parents, and school board members that really convinced me that collaboration held the power to transform public schools.

Most recently, I served as an expert witness for the state in *Vergara v. State of California*, the landmark 2014 court case that struck down tenure laws and other teacher protections in California. My testimony focused on teacher effectiveness and the conditions in schools, especially schools with high concentrations of poor students and students of color, that often diminish it. I left WestEd in 2014 and am now helping education leaders who are involved in California's new Labor Management Initiative, a joint effort by the state's teacher unions, the administrator's association, the school board's associations, and California's Department of Education to promote collaboration and to implement sensible education reforms.

My Audience

I hope to reach teachers, district administrators, school board members, and labor leaders, of course, but also those who have been ignored in discussions about labor-management collaboration—school principals, local union site representatives, community leaders, and parents. I also want to reach state and national education officials and their union counterparts whose interactions influence collaboration at the local level in powerful ways. Education leaders throughout the system have a role to play, and their absence from the conversation about collaboration is one reason it has floundered.

To improve teaching and enhance student outcomes, we need well-designed collaborative partnerships between management and labor. Education leaders at all levels should know how to create such partnerships. The purpose of this book is to show them how they can—and why they should.

Changing the Narrative

"WE CAN HOPE TO SERVE every child by committing to whole-district transformation—and Montgomery County is one of the examples that is showing us the way," US Education Secretary Arne Duncan said in praising the 2009 book *Leading for Equity: The Pursuit of Excellence in Montgomery County Schools.*[1] Two years later, Michelle Rhee, the controversial former chancellor of Washington, DC's school system, said of her Montgomery County counterpart who engineered the improvements, "Jerry Weast took the Montgomery County schools to a new level. His work and leadership made MCPS a model for the nation."[2]

Though Montgomery County's education leaders surely welcomed the praise from Duncan and Rhee, they must have found it more than a little ironic. That's because for years by then, Duncan, Rhee, and others had promoted "reform" strategies that stood in sharp contrast to those that produced the very results in Montgomery County that they hailed.

Jerry Weast, who retired in 2011 after more than a decade as Montgomery County's Superintendent of Schools, refused to take $12 million from Race to the Top, Duncan's signature federal school reform program, because it required districts to use standardized test scores to evaluate teachers. By then, Weast and other district leaders had adopted an effective way to increase teaching quality, and they believed standardized tests were an unreliable way to evaluate teachers. Weast worried, he said, that taking Race to the Top money would turn his district into a "test factory."[3]

Joshua Starr, Weast's successor who was finishing his term in early 2015 and who had supported the district's successful reform strategies, was a strong and outspoken critic of the test-heavy reform agenda of not just Duncan and Rhee but of such other reform leaders as Joel Klein, the former chancellor of New York City's public schools. Starr had called for a three-year moratorium on standardized tests.

Along with a heightened focus on standardized tests, such reformers as Klein and Rhee have opted not for more labor-management cooperation but, instead, for more overt confrontation. In fact, a key component of a "manifesto" for fixing schools that Klein, Rhee, and many other like-minded reformers published in 2010 is policy changes that would make it easier to fire teachers.[4] (To his credit, Duncan instead has promoted labor-management collaboration, although some believe his motivation for doing so has been to get unions to go along with his reform agenda.) In pursuing those policy changes, Klein, Rhee, and the others have fostered dissension, distrust, and confrontation.

"Collaboration is the elixir of the status-quo crowd," Klein said shortly after he resigned as New York City's chancellor in 2011.[5] Rhee also disparaged the idea of nourishing a culture of trust between teachers and administrators. "If there is one thing I have learned over the last 15 months," she said in 2008, "it's that collaboration and consensus building are way overrated."[6]

Declining Support for Teacher Unions

Klein and Rhee are not pushing their agenda in a vacuum. Quite the contrary, their efforts reflect a pervasive strain of thinking about America's teacher unions that appears in the writings of mainstream journalists, the films of documentary makers, and the findings of academicians.

"Teachers are great, a national treasure," *Newsweek's* Jonathan Alter stated in a telling salvo that reflects this viewpoint. "Teachers' unions are, generally speaking, a menace and an impediment to reform."[7] In the 2010 documentary *Waiting for Superman*, which *New York* magazine called "a paean to reformers" like Rhee,[8] filmmaker Davis Guggenheim showcased charter schools as a panacea for underperforming schools, demonized teacher unions, praised Rhee's efforts to change union rules that govern teachers, and described the backlash that she generated.

Meanwhile, researchers Frederick Hess and Martin West offered this gloomy perspective about a new collaborative role for teacher unions, as advocated by the Teacher Union Reform Network (TURN) and others: "In reality, sustained attempts to instill new unionism have occurred in just a handful of districts," they wrote, referring to the movement to focus unions more on student achievement, "and the results have been fairly disappointing. This bleak track record should be no surprise. Union leaders are elected by current members to protect their interests, and most teachers remain highly satisfied with their unions' conduct of collective bargaining."

Consequently, Hess and West wrote, management needs to "negotiate hard" and "[in] the short run schools may need more, fiercer, and uglier contract disputes." Management must also "rally the public," even if that means "upsetting the apple cart." Referring to parent groups and community leaders, they added, "These stakeholder groups need to rethink their belief that labor unrest is uniformly a sign of leadership failure. Labor unrest can be a good thing when the alternative is to continue to accept an anachronistic, stifling, and perversely constructed status quo."[9]

The False Promise of an Adversarial Approach

Had the reform agenda of Klein, Rhee, and the others—top-down change, test-based evaluations, merit pay, and so on—produced significantly better student outcomes in New York and Washington, some might be tempted to say that the conflicts and acrimony were worth the effort—and the calls from Klein, Rhee, Hess and West, and others for more confrontation would be harder to refute. Despite the boasts of Klein and Rhee, however, student outcomes didn't improve under their leadership.[10] In fact, I can't find evidence from any US school district that labor-management confrontation generated positive, long-term student outcomes like those in the Montgomery County Public Schools or the Cincinnati Public Schools.

Klein boasted of significant improvements in academic achievement under his leadership, particularly for poor students and students of color. "We are closing the achievement gap faster than ever," he said in 2009.[11] If true, such improvements would give pause to our notion that collaboration is essential to reform. But, a year later, results from a redesigned test (which state officials said more accurately reflected students' abilities) showed a 25 percentage point decline in passing rates, virtually canceling out the achievement gap improvements about which Klein had boasted a year earlier. Because the tests that New York City uses have changed, we can't know for sure whether Klein's claims are true. But in 2015, 237 New York City schools participated in the National Assessment of Educational Progress (NAEP), which many consider the gold standard of academic tests. When the results are published, they will provide a much clearer picture of whether achievement gaps under Klein's leadership have narrowed.

Meanwhile, Rhee is an ardent, outspoken critic of teacher unions. Her toughness, confrontational style, and willingness to fight the unions to advance her agenda garnered her lavish praise from political leaders (conservatives and liberals alike) as well as the national media; she appeared on the covers of *Time* and *Newsweek* and, as noted previously, was a key figure in *Waiting for Superman*. She pushed hard to provide merit pay for teachers and fire those who didn't raise student test scores. Montgomery County's leaders not only didn't employ her strategies; they publicly criticized them.

Rhee predicted that, under her leadership, Washington, DC, would become the nation's highest performing urban district. But as with New York City's schools under Klein, the results in Washington, DC, did not meet her lofty expectations. For one thing, a cheating scandal raised questions about some of the gains in test scores on her watch.[12] For another, a US Department of Education analysis of the district's reading and math scores under NAEP found, "DC's NAEP scores had already steadily improved under [Rhee's] two predecessors, Superintendent Paul Vance and Clifford Janey. Moreover, the rates of DC score gains under Rhee were no better than the rates achieved by Vance and Janey."[13]

The Battle in San Diego

A situation similar to that of New York and Washington, DC, unfolded years earlier in San Diego, although it didn't start off that way.

"The usual story concerning the San Diego reform is that a confrontational, hard-line, top-down superintendent refused to back down from the teachers union and took no prisoners," Alan Bersin, San Diego's superintendent for seven years starting in 1998, recalled his efforts to implement a reform agenda titled *The Blueprint for Student Success in a Standards-Based System.* "This isn't an entirely inaccurate or a completely unfair description. But it was not that way at the beginning."

"This was a war I did not choose and would not fight," he went on, "until it became crystal clear that there really was no middle ground to be reached with the union leadership in place, and its two allies on the school board. In my previous career," said Bersin, who earlier served as California's Secretary of Education and, before that, as an Assistant United States Attorney. "I assembled coalitions, built consensus, and resolved lawsuits. But I also had to try lawsuits when settlements failed. So, when the fight came, I didn't shy away from what I believed in. And goodness knows, there was a fight to be had in San Diego over school reform. Conflict was unavoidable because the issues were real and the differences unbridgeable at the time and in the context. The price of getting along here was simply too high."[14]

Like Klein and Rhee, Bersin later cited academic achievements on his watch that others have questioned. He pointed to academic gains at the elementary level and said that, due to his reforms, teachers and principals were better equipped to teach and lead. He cited San Diego's second-place finish in 2014 for the Broad Prize, which recognized academic excellence among large, urban districts across the nation, to prove that his district was flourishing.

A study of Bersin's reforms by Stanford University researchers, however, found that while San Diego students made some gains during his tenure, the rate of change "lagged slightly behind the rate of change statewide."[15] A separate study by the American Institutes for Research concluded that teacher resistance was key to the disappointing results. "The fact that teachers have not 'bought in' sufficiently is likely to be impeding the effects of professional development, peer coaching, principal leadership, and other reform strategies," the authors wrote. "While dissatisfaction of teachers might be expected with any change at the outset, the continued dissatisfaction of San Diego teachers with certain *Blueprint* features, and with the district change process could ultimately undermine the long-term success of the *Blueprint*."[16] After studying San Diego's experience, educational historian Diane Ravitch acknowledged that Bersin's *Blueprint* had enthusiastic supporters but concluded that the plan was doomed. "You can't lead your troops," she said, "if your troops do not trust you."[17]

While Ravitch and others paint Bersin as an autocratic, untrustworthy leader who refused to collaborate with the union, Richard Lee Colvin, who studied Bersin's tenure in San Diego, believes the teacher union bore much of the responsibility for the poor relationship between them and the *Blueprint's* ultimate failure. "To [Marc] Knapp (the union leader at the time), collaboration meant conversation and getting along. It did not mean compromise or real change," Colvin wrote.[18] Bersin himself viewed collaboration this way: "There are times we agree and times when we disagree. Collaboration enables the concerned parties to explore, discuss, and debate ideas and proposals together. But the default position cannot invariably be inaction and stagnation."[19]

Perhaps Bersin acted in ways that caused teachers and the union to distrust him. Perhaps the union was unwilling to really collaborate with *any* superintendent unless he or she met each of its conditions. That's not how real collaboration works. With real collaboration, both sides strive to find common ground, to compromise on programs and policies without compromising their core educational values. If the union or management cannot engage in this kind of collaboration or seek assistance from the outside to do so, then hopes for significant improvement in student learning—what surely must be their most important core value—are doomed from the start. Regardless of what actually happened in San Diego, the point is this: creating school systems that provide a quality education to all students is possible only when both sides engage in *authentic collaboration.*

Rising Antiunion Activity

Despite their questionable achievements in improving student performance, no one should doubt the determination of Klein, Rhee, and others to pursue their antiunion reform agenda or underestimate the obstacle that these efforts pose for labor-management collaboration.

In 2010, Rhee founded StudentsFirst—a Sacramento-based nonprofit group that is "fighting for one purpose: to make sure every student in America has access to great schools and great teachers"—and she planned to raise $1 billion to promote an antiunion agenda that includes abolishing teacher tenure and promoting charter schools and voucher programs.[20]

In 2013, Klein and others joined Rhee to form StudentsFirstNY and pledged to raise $10 million a year to offset the influence of New York City's teacher unions and preserve the approaches that Klein and then-mayor Michael Bloomberg began to implement. The group comprised, according to the *New York Times*, "some of the most well-known and polarizing figures in public education."[21]

The effort to confront the teacher unions and eschew collaboration extends far beyond disgruntled former chancellors and superintendents to include other educational figures and well-heeled financial interests. Geoffrey Canada, who founded the Harlem Children's Zone, which operates charter schools in New York City, supported the efforts of StudentsFirstNY. So, too, did several hedge fund managers and venture capitalists who agreed to finance its lobbying effort. Canada, who also was featured in *Waiting for Superman,* acknowledges that some educators favor a more congenial approach to addressing the problems of public education, but he agrees with Klein and Rhee that solutions will emerge only through battles.

"Folks are genuinely looking for opportunities to make peace and not war," he said. "And I think that's terrific. But someone has to make war."[22]

Wariness About Collaboration

Along with growing antiunion sentiment, those who promote collaboration face a series of other obstacles.

For starters, a call for collaboration is far more than a call for one more reform strategy; it's a call for something more fundamental—a paradigm shift that dramatically redefines the roles of management and unions and the relationship between them. Paradigm shifts don't come often or easily. Powerful forces stand in the way, even when the evidence points to a brighter future. Educators resist change for the same reasons that others do—comfort in what's familiar, fears of what change will bring, and cultural inertia.

Another formidable obstacle to collaboration is a fundamental misconception about what it means. Some administrators and labor leaders worry that, in a highly politicized environment in which resources are limited, overly cozy relations with the other side amount to "sleeping with the enemy." Blurring the lines, each side fears, inevitably leads to collusion or capitulation.

Still another obstacle to collaboration is the absence of a robust support system to help administrators and union leaders transition to a partnership model. Most professional development programs for new leaders devote little or no attention to the skills required for effective collaboration. Education conferences and research reports that feature partnership success stories are inspiring, but for most leaders who want to transition to collaboration, they raise more questions than they answer. How do we begin? What are the risks? What if we face resistance? Hearing what some districts have accomplished through their partnerships doesn't explain to other districts how they, in particular, can make the difficult shift to collaboration.

One more obstacle to collaboration looms as well: highly prescriptive, often ill-advised, federal, state, and local education policies. Management and labor often question the point of collaboration when prescriptive policies already set the agenda for what they must do. In fact, some of those policies themselves create tensions and, in some cases, fierce labor-management conflict.

That's what happened with each of the last two major federal education reform efforts: the No Child Left Behind (NCLB) Act of 2001 under President George W. Bush that Congress passed with bipartisan support and Duncan's Race to the Top program under President Barack Obama. In many states and districts, administrators felt they had no choice but to comply with these programs, even when they disagreed with them. At the same time, some unions resisted them because they believed that some of their requirements were unsound and didn't serve students well. As a result, administrators accused unions of resisting change while unions accused management of selling out.

To be sure, some federal or state educational policies invariably will generate labor-management conflict, but the policy makers who design them and require administrators and teachers to implement them should weigh the potential benefits of these policies against the potential harm that may come from more conflict. Moreover, policy makers could avoid a lot of unnecessary conflict if they collaborated with unions and administrators when they developed the policies in the first place.

Confrontation Can't Work

Everyone who seeks to improve education would be wise to push back against simplistic solutions and confrontational approaches that don't work. Common sense and experience show that school systems can't thrive if administrators and teachers are fighting with one another, with each side focused only on its own interests.

"Adversarial relationships between teachers and school management significantly impede change efforts required to improve student achievement," researcher Linda Kaboolian explained in her book, *Win-Win Labor-Management Collaboration in Education.* "Adversity is expensive and hinders a clear focus on students, using up resources—money, time, energy, and leadership attention—which could be put to better use."[23]

Persistent and intense adversity among educators creates a toxic environment that prompts strikes and costly employee grievances. It breeds cynicism, ill will, hostility, and mistrust that invariably seep into the classroom, teaching students exactly what we don't want them to learn about how people should work with one another. In addition, it prompts finger pointing first between administrators and teachers and then inevitably at students and parents for poor school performance. It also causes many of the best educators to leave the profession altogether or seek work in other districts, where colleagues are more supportive and where they can make a difference in the lives of their students.

In short, when trust and civility vanish and educators reach a point where all they can do is fight with one another, they lose any chance to create good schools. Making matters worse, parents and the greater community—critical allies for educators—lose confidence in their schools and grow less willing to support them.

Consider the bitter battle that unfolded in 2012 between the office under Chicago Mayor Rahm Emanuel that manages the city's schools and the Chicago Teachers Union. It prompted twenty-six thousand teachers to strike for nine days over school closures, teaching conditions, and certain school reforms. Teachers returned to the classroom after both sides offered compromises, but tensions between the mayor's administration and the union have persisted—and, as of this writing, nothing remotely resembling a partnership has emerged.

Consider also what unfolded in San Diego after Superintendent Bersin resigned. Carl Cohn, who replaced him, said, "I inherited a district in which the driving philosophy over the previous six years had, similarly, been to attack the credibility of any educator who spoke out against a top-down education reform model. These attacks allowed those in charge to portray themselves as the defenders of children, to justify any means to promote their model of improving student achievement, and to view their critics through the same apocalyptic lens of good and evil that has characterized many of our recent national debates. At any level of governance, this perspective is counterproductive. In San Diego, it produced a climate of conflict that is only now beginning to improve."[24]

Authentic Collaboration

Even if administrators and teachers aren't fighting, that doesn't mean they're collaborating.

Instead, in many cases, they are simply disengaged from one another. Union leaders get what they can for their members in terms of "bread-and-butter" rewards—wages, benefits, and worker protections—but outside of the formal bargaining process, management and labor have little interaction with one another. Management makes all of the key decisions related to policies, programs, budgets, personnel, curriculum, and professional support. This scenario may sound idyllic, with the adults avoiding public battles and ugly politics—and it would be if all of the students in a district like this were receiving a quality education.

I don't know of any school systems that succeed this way, however, with disengaged parties who nevertheless achieve better student outcomes. Even the most capable, respectful, and well-intended management leaders can't run schools well without the active, responsible participation of teachers *and* their unions. It's hard enough when these groups *are* working together. In the absence of authentic collaboration among those who face the extraordinary complexities of running a school system, management can't make good decisions, solve problems, innovate, or secure the necessary buy-in from teachers and other stakeholders.

What, then, is real, authentic collaboration that will make a difference in the educational experience of students?

The first chapter explores this concept in depth but, for now, suffice it to say that it's much more than a label or slogan. Indeed, collaborative partnerships will have no impact if they exist in name only—if they appear merely in superficial vision statements in which stakeholders declare their willingness to work as partners but don't really do so. Authentic collaboration, the kind that leads to substantive change, is about improving practices and policies that then, in turn, improve the educational experiences of students. In fact, authentic collaboration affects everything—from the way unions and management negotiate their contracts, to the way they discuss curriculum and increase student engagement in learning.

"The promise of collaborative bargaining is not simply in changing the tenor of the discussion, in increasing the level of civility," researchers Daniel Humphrey and Julia Koppich pointed out. "The promise of collaborative bargaining lies in altering the substance of labor-management discussions and agreements. It lies in management and unions being willing to examine the previously unexamined, doing the hard work together of confronting tough, high-stakes issues, and reaching accord on how to proceed when decisions carry real and human consequences."[25]

Fortunately, the constituency for collaboration is growing, presaging what could be a brighter future for America's public schools.

The Call for Change

The roots of change date back nearly two decades, and the leaders of the movement for change emerged from both the teacher unions and the world of academic research.

"Teacher unions must be reformed," Adam Urbanski wrote back in 1998, shortly after he helped found the Teacher Union Reform Network, or TURN, which consists of local unions of the two national teacher unions—the American Federation of Teachers (AFT) and National Education Association (NEA). "This can best happen if teacher unionists themselves recognize not only the need for change but also that it is in the enlightened self-interest of their unions to welcome the next logical stage in their unions' evolution.

"Certainly," Urbanski continued, "forces and threats from the outside can play a role. In fact, much hinges on the capacity of teacher union leaders to understand the changing environment and to interpret it for their members. Such a proactive mode would ensure that the changes are not merely a begrudging accommodation but rather a purposeful fulfillment of our own vision for our institution and our members.

"But unless it is voices from within the teacher union movement who are driving the call for reforms, there is a great risk that the voices from outside would be viewed as hostile 'bashing.' So it does matter a great deal who is calling for teacher union reform. In a sense, unions are more likely to change if the unionists are agents of reform. Ironically, if unionists do not become agents of reform, they will remain targets of reform."[26]

Around the time of TURN's founding, researchers Charles Kerchner, Julia Koppich, and Joseph Weeres called for a new, postindustrial unionism in which teachers work with management on all matters related to teaching and learning—not just on the traditional bread-and-butter issues of hours, wages, and benefits. "Teachers care about changes in teaching and learning," they wrote in their 1997 book, *United Mind Workers: Unions and Teaching in the Knowledge Society*. "They know more about how children think and learn—and the conditions that promote thinking and learning—than do governors, business leaders, and most college professors."

Historically, the authors explained, teachers were not part of conversations about how best to run school systems. "Collective bargaining legitimated teachers' economic interests, but it never recognized them as experts about learning," they wrote. "The idea of *knowledge workers* who create, synthesize, and interpret information dominates the literature on modern workplaces, but teaching is still organized around the industrial-era assumption that teachers are essentially manual workers, pouring curriculum into passive minds."[27]

Kerchner and his colleagues argued that schools and unions must be reorganized around three core ideas:

- *Organize around quality*: Advocate, implement, and enforce standards for student learning and standards for teaching. Back these up with adequate professional development and strong peer review systems.
- *Organize around schools*: Slim the district contract and create individual school compacts covering resource allocation, hiring, quality assurance, and how teachers take joint responsibility for reforms.
- *Organize around an external labor market*: Create modern hiring halls that allow teachers to switch jobs more easily. Make pensions and benefits portable, and shape a career ladder that allows people to enter education as classroom aides and advance through education and experience to teaching.[28]

Nearly two decades after Kerchner and his colleagues outlined their vision, their ideas are slowly coming to life in new labor-management arrangements across the country, with the two sides organizing around quality, promoting innovation, and producing better outcomes for students.

Union Reforms Emerge

In *Win-Win Labor Management Collaboration*, Linda Kaboolian and Paul Sutherland described some of the first peer assistance and review (PAR) programs across the country that allowed accomplished teachers to evaluate their peers and provide intense support to those who are struggling.[29] After the Toledo, Ohio district first developed PAR in the early 1980s, several other districts, including Montgomery County, Maryland, adopted it. The benefits are well documented.[30] Most participating teachers improve their practice and those who don't improve leave voluntarily or are dismissed without grievances and expensive lawsuits.

In Toledo, Ohio; Rochester, New York; and Eugene, Oregon, new contracts gave local educators more flexibility and control over their schools. Career lattice programs, alternative compensation programs, teacher-led schools, extended day and year programs, and numerous other innovations have emerged in districts that embraced the postindustrial unions that Kerchner and his colleagues promoted in 1997. The innovations have, in turn, spurred greater teacher retention as well as more and better learning time for students.

The concept of collaboration between administrators and teachers reached an important milestone in 2011 when, under Duncan, the US Department of Education joined with leading national education organizations to cosponsor the first national conference on labor-management collaboration in education. Teams of superintendents, labor leaders, and board presidents from 150 school districts attended the event, hearing firsthand stories of collaboration from their counterparts in Montgomery County and about a dozen other exemplary districts.

A year later, a follow-up study of conference participants revealed that many were impressed with what they heard, and nearly half were trying to implement new strategies to promote collaboration. The success of this event and strong demand for future events of this kind from education leaders who could not attend convinced the same cosponsors to conduct two additional conferences—one in 2012 whose theme was "Transforming the Teaching Profession" and another in 2014 that focused on implementing college- and career-ready standards.[31]

Undoubtedly, powerful voices will continue to oppose teacher unions and dismiss the calls for collaborative partnerships. Nonetheless, there is reason for optimism that more such partnerships will emerge and one day become the norm rather than the exception. The reason is that the critics of collaboration will find it increasingly hard to resist the pressures for change since they're now seeing the benefits of collaboration and the pressures are coming from a host of influential constituencies within the education sector—the broad community, unions, teachers, and union critics.

Broad community. The critics of collaboration will face growing pressure from the broad community of educators and other interested parties, especially if the critics can't point to any success stories of real system change and better student outcomes in the absence of collaboration. Again, I see no evidence that the alternative to collaboration—management and unions that fight with, or ignore, one another—will improve the status quo.

Unions. The critics will face growing pressure from the unions themselves. Teacher unions in recent years have faced an unprecedented assault from political leaders and journalists, even liberals who once offered unconditional support.[32] As the nation has grown increasingly impatient with the pace of reform, unions have borne much of the blame. A 2013 poll by Harvard University and the journal *EducationNext* found that 43 percent of Americans believe unions have a negative effect on schools, up from 31 percent just two years earlier.[33] Union membership and revenues have dropped precipitously in recent years, partly due to such criticism.[34] As unions increasingly fight for relevance, and perhaps survival, they can't forever be known for what they oppose; they need to articulate a positive agenda that explains what they're *for* and lead the effort to make it happen.

"We are a union of professional educators," former Massachusetts Teachers Association President Paul Toner wrote in the spring of 2014, "and we must be the voice of public education and the profession. We absolutely should continue to advocate for good salaries, working conditions and benefits, but if we are to remain relevant to our members, we need to listen to what they have to say about education policies and advocate for the time, tools and resources they need to do their jobs well. If we are to remain relevant to the public, we need to listen to their concerns and show them, not just tell them, that we have the best interest of their students at heart. We must be advocates for the profession and for taking charge of quality. We must put forward our best ideas for meeting the needs of our students and communities. We must be more proactive and promote student centered, union-led change."[35]

In 2012, the AFT and NEA signed a shared vision statement with other national organizations, including those representing administrators and school boards, to support more collaboration and commit that student learning would guide all of their decisions.[36] While the statement was just that—a statement—it signaled that unions and other key stakeholder groups were willing to change, to work together, and to collectively accept responsibility for educational results.

Teachers. Beyond unions, a growing number of teachers want their unions to play a greater role in education reform. "Today's teachers want more than just bread and butter basics from their unions," according to Sarah Rosenberg and Elena Silva, authors of a 2011 Education Sector report. "They expect that unions will not only protect them, but also will engage in some of the reforms aimed at transforming their profession." A survey that Rosenberg and Silva conducted for this report found that 43 percent of union members wanted their unions to "put more focus than they currently do on issues such as improving teacher quality and student achievement." Just four years earlier, only 32 percent responded that way.[37]

Union critics. Even union critics, such as *New York Times* columnist Nicholas Kristof, are beginning to see the benefits of labor-management partnerships. After learning of new reforms in New Haven, Connecticut, that management and labor developed collaboratively, he wrote: "Teachers' unions are here to stay, and the only way to achieve systematic improvement is with their buy-in. Moreover, the United States critically needs to attract talented young people into teaching. And that's less likely when we're whacking teachers' unions in ways that leave many teachers feeling insulted and demoralized. The breakthrough experiment in New Haven offers a glimpse of an education future that is less rancorous."[38]

Collaboration Is No Silver Bullet

Finally, it's time to put the concept of collaboration in its proper context: However fervently one might believe it's critical to improving teacher quality and student outcomes, one should have no illusions that, by itself, it can create great schools and close achievement gaps. Collaboration is necessary, but it's not sufficient.

In their books and policy papers on education reform, all too many others have offered silver bullet solutions that, they promised, would revolutionize education. When, not surprisingly, these strategies did not fulfill the inflated boasts of their proponents, observers were quick to criticize or dismiss what very well might have been useful, even vital, avenues to pursue.[39]

Here, then, are a few of the critical conditions that must be in place to create and sustain good schools.

Adequate funding. Few issues in public education generate more debate than funding. Some argue that money doesn't matter and, in some cases, that's true. If districts do not spend money on the right things, or if they do not wisely use the books and technology they have bought with their money, then the money will make little difference. But, in fact, money *does* matter. Like collaboration, money is essential, but it's not sufficient.

Just how much money do districts need? That's debatable. In recent years, most states have been home to lawsuits related to inadequate or inequitable funding. In 2014, such litigation was pending against eleven states. However the courts decide these cases in the coming years, we obviously cannot create good schools in the absence of adequate resources.

Declining poverty. Nothing poses a greater threat to the nation's ability to provide high-quality, equitable education than poverty. No matter how much we adopt authentic collaboration or how well we fund schools, many schools will continue to lag far behind as long as the practices and policies that perpetuate poverty persist at such a high level in America.[40]

Education experts often point to Finland as a model that offers important lessons for America. But, as researchers David Berliner and Gene Glass noted, "Finland boasts the best education system in the world . . . but has a child poverty rate of less than 5%. . . . In the United States, if we looked only at the students who attend schools where child poverty rates are under 10%, we would rank as the number one country in the world, outscoring countries like Finland, Japan, and Korea."[41]

Those who dismiss poverty will point to the exceptions—poor students who become extraordinarily successful or schools in poor neighborhoods that do better than expected. Yes, those high achieving students and high performing schools are out there, and we should do everything we can to ensure that *every* child (rich, poor, and in between) can get a good education.

At the same time, we shouldn't base our public policy on a small number of outliers. Instead, we have a moral obligation to reduce poverty, and we can move forcefully in the right direction by reducing unemployment and assuring living wages. The question is whether we have the will to do it.

A Roadmap for the Book

In the chapters that follow, I walk you through the concept of labor-management collaboration and offer ways to bring it to life in school districts around the country.

Chapter 1 explains that authentic labor-management collaboration is about far more than better interpersonal relations. It's about building structures that promote trust, convincing stakeholders to own decisions and share responsibility, and investing time and changing habits. It's about not only tolerating but also inviting constructive debate in the search for better solutions. Specifically, this chapter explains that effective collaboration has eight essential features: (1) both sides depend on one another; (2) both sides address their differences constructively; (3) both sides assume joint ownership of decisions; (4) both sides assume joint responsibility for results; (5) both sides collaborate on everything that affects teaching and learning; (6) both sides collaborate at all levels of the education system; (7) both sides rely on collaboration when bargaining contracts; and (8) both sides collaborate on ways to attract and retain good teachers.

Chapter 2 describes the impact of labor-management collaboration on educational outcomes. It discusses how best to measure results when evaluating educational practices and how labor-management collaboration can help produce better results. The chapter then looks closely at the successes that labor-management collaboration generated in large school districts in Montgomery County, Maryland; Los Angeles; and Cincinnati. It then shows how labor-management collaboration, or the lack thereof, helps explain why some states, such as California and Massachusetts, are implementing the new Common Core State Standards without significant problems, whereas others, such as New York, have been torn apart by the experience.

Chapter 3 pinpoints six major obstacles that have dissuaded many districts across the country from following the lead of Montgomery County, Los Angeles, and Cincinnati and bringing labor-management collaboration to their own school systems. These obstacles that are preventing labor-management collaboration from becoming the norm, rather than the exception, are (1) resistance to change; (2) the myth of consensus; (3) the myth of collusion; (4) skepticism about unions; (5) a shortage of technical support; and (6) misguided education policy.

Chapter 4—the first of two chapters that provides technical advice to help would-be partners get started—explains that real collaboration means that school boards and superintendents, union leaders and teachers, community leaders and parents, and state and local educational associations invest the requisite time and effort to make it happen. It further explains that educators of all kinds can pursue six strategies to bring effective collaboration to life: (1) develop new mindsets; (2) develop the capacity for collaboration; (3) go slow to go fast; (4) build trust through better relationships; (5) pursue sound education policy; and (6) bargain better.

Chapter 5 recommends six specific tactics for educators of all kinds that flow from the six strategies of the previous chapter: (1) start with yourself; (2) pitch it first; (3) commit publicly to collaborative norms and monitor progress; (4) strengthen collaboration through safe, anger-free dialogue; (5) find personal spaces to promote reflection and dialogue; and (6) seek solutions to solvable problems. In addition, this chapter outlines another set of tactics that apply to particular groups of educators—school board members, superintendents, union leaders, teachers, community leaders, parents, and state organizations.

Chapter 6 explains that, while adopting strategies and tactics to change their interactions with one another, management and labor also need to adopt reforms within their own spheres. Management needs to accept unions as equal partners in providing education to students, build the capacity of teachers, conduct meaningful teacher evaluations, and provide meaningful professional development for them. Unions need to put the interests of students first; articulate more clearly what they're for and not just what they're against; help address such controversial issues as teacher tenure, seniority regulations, and compensation systems; and give voice to teachers by promoting autonomy for local union chapters.

Finally, the Epilogue explains why it's so important that we get education reform right, suggests that we look not only to the few successful labor-management partnerships in America that are making a real difference but to a notable example from abroad, and calls for the courageous leadership in management and unions that's required to bring collaboration to far more places.

Now that you know where we're headed in the chapters that follow, let's begin by turning to eight essential features of labor-management collaboration.

CHAPTER 1

What Is Labor-Management Collaboration?

A SKED TO DEFINE *collaboration*, most people would say it's a process in which people get along, cooperate, and act respectfully toward one another. But this simple description does not begin to capture what teachers, administrators, and education officials do when they really collaborate to improve the quality of education for students. If getting along was all it took to improve schools, many schools would be much better than they are today.

If the call for collaboration sounds too idealistic and even sentimental, here are two points in response. First, "deep collaboration," as change theorist Michael Fullan described it, isn't easy. Yes, people must get along, listen to one another, and resolve conflicts respectfully. But beyond that, collaboration is about building structures and creating routines that promote trust and effective communication, convincing stakeholders at all levels to own decisions and share responsibility. The stakeholders need to invest significant time, and they often need the help of outside facilitators.

They need to change their habits and also to address their fears that overly friendly relations with the other side will prompt unnecessary concessions.

Second, collaboration doesn't eliminate disagreement. In fact, leaders in highly collaborative districts still disagree, often vehemently, because the best solutions are not always obvious. But they learn how to work through their disagreements, preserve trust, and continue to craft solutions on the other problems they face. "[Labor-management collaboration] is not about unions and districts being more cordial to one another for the sake of cordiality," labor-management expert Julie E. Koppich explained. "The goal of labor-management collaboration is not to alter the tenor of the discourse but to change the substance of the conversation and, ultimately, the quality of decisions."[1]

In Maryland's Montgomery County Public Schools, where collaboration is the cornerstone of district improvement efforts, leaders defined collaboration within their collective bargaining agreement itself as

> a process in which partners work together in a meaningful way and within a time frame that provides a real opportunity to shape results. The purpose of the process is to work together respectfully to resolve problems, address common issues, and identify opportunities for improvement. To be successful, the collaborative process must be taken seriously and be valued by both parties. The process must be given the time, personal involvement and commitment, hard work, and dedication that are required to be successful. The partners will identify and define issues of common concern, propose and evaluate solutions, and agree on recommendations.[2]

This definition pinpoints the purposes of collaboration and describes some of the conditions required to achieve it, including a genuine commitment to it by labor *and* management.

Collaboration is complex, so this chapter explores its core dynamics and identifies eight essential features of effective collaboration. The first three are based on the work of Barbara Gray, an organizational theorist who has written extensively on collaboration. In her book *Collaborating: Finding Common Ground for Multiparty Problems*, she illustrated how these three features function within any organization.[3] I add five other features that are essential for labor-management collaboration to have a positive impact in educational settings.

Here, then, are the eight essential features of effective collaboration to improve educational outcomes:

Feature 1: Both sides depend on one another.

Feature 2: Both sides address their differences constructively.

Feature 3: Both sides assume joint ownership of decisions.

Feature 4: Both sides assume joint responsibility for results.

Feature 5: Both sides collaborate on everything that affects teaching and learning.

Feature 6: Both sides collaborate at all levels of the education system.

Feature 7: Both sides rely on collaboration when bargaining contracts.

Feature 8: Both sides collaborate on ways to attract and retain good teachers.

How do these features manifest themselves in the context of labor-management collaboration?

Feature 1: Both Sides Depend on One Another

In school districts in which labor and management view one another as adversaries, the two sides draw clear lines of authority and fiercely protect their autonomy. They resent demands from the other side and often give only what's required, not necessarily what's needed. They are quick to blame each other when things go wrong and seldom praise each other when thing go right. Some even celebrate when the other side fails because, in an "us versus them" world, "their" missteps make "us" look good.

In districts that truly embrace collaboration, however, labor and management build a unique relationship based on trust, and each understands that it cannot educate well without the other. They pull for one another and celebrate one another's successes because they know that if one side struggles, so, too, will the other. They take a "systems approach" to their work, which Richard DuFour, an expert on professional learning communities, said "represents the antithesis of a culture based on individual isolation and independence."[4]

"We don't let each other fail." That's a guiding principle for California's ABC Unified School District in Los Angeles County, a national model for collaboration and the host of the annual West Coast Labor Management Institute. Far from viewing his union counterpart as an impediment to progress, as top educational administrators around the country often do, former ABC Superintendent Gary Smuts said at the time, "I am a better superintendent because I have a strong union president."[5]

Management and union leaders from nearby Culver City Unified attended an ABC Institute several years ago and then committed themselves to follow ABC's lead and create their own collaborative culture. Dave LaRose, Culver City's superintendent, and Dave Mielke, its local teacher union president, told me they're constantly looking for ways to support one another. LaRose described a situation in which a small but vocal group of teachers were frustrated by a feature in the district's salary schedule that underpaid some teachers when raises were allotted. "They personalized the attack against the union leaders for not supporting them," LaRose said. "I told Dave [Mielke] to stay strong and assured him that we would look into the matter together and correct it if indeed there was a problem."[6]

Together with the district's business manager, they solved the problem and then met with teachers to explain how they would do so. "The fact that the assistant superintendent for business services agreed to come to a union meeting to help explain the technical side of the salary schedule adjustment was great," Mielke said. "You don't see that every day."[7]

Feature 2: Both Sides Address Their Differences Constructively

Effective collaboration does more than tolerate a diversity of perspectives; it demands it. Only when the parties are encouraged to share different points of view will decision makers have the diverse set of ideas needed to solve difficult problems. *How* they do so, however, is critical. With true collaboration, parties that are fundamentally committed to the same core values learn to disagree without being disagreeable. They don't speak disparagingly about one another (at least publicly), and they remain open to other perspectives, new solutions, and compromises that most people can support. And, as their disagreements continue on some issues, they nevertheless work together on others.

Even those working in the most collaborative districts will appreciate Gray's astute observation that "[r]espect for differences is an easy virtue to champion verbally and a much more difficult one to put into practice in our day-to-day affairs."[8] Differences of opinion, and the difficult conversations that result, are a fact of life even in districts in which collaboration is working. But when the parties manage their disagreements poorly and incivility becomes the norm, they lose trust and let other important issues go unresolved. Without trust, conversations will never move to the issues that matter and collaboration will stall.

"Of course, labor-management collaboration does not mean unions and districts do not fight," Koppich wrote. "They do, sometimes disagreeing vehemently. But they do not live in a state of permanent hostility. Neither are these disputes over workaday issues. Rather, points of labor-management contention center on matters critical to the preservation of public education. They are at least as much about the public good—what is right for students—as they are about teacher interests."[9]

Tom Alves, codirector of the Teacher Union Reform Network (TURN) and executive director of the teacher union in California's San Juan Unified School District, has spent decades learning to manage conflict effectively with district management. "First we had to understand that we have markedly different organizational cultures and structures," he said. "We still have serious differences, but to sustain the strong partnership we have with management, we've had to learn how to fight better with each other." "Fighting well," he said, means that neither party ever "blindsides" the other. Whenever a problem arises, no matter how serious, each party goes directly to the other to resolve it. "This does not mean that either party ever gives up their right to advocate strongly for their constituency. But sometimes we discover something important that we did not know," Alves explained. "We always listen, argue our points, and, if needed, try to find a satisfactory agreement. In the end our purpose is the same—improve the learning for adults and students."[10]

The union resolves most disputes with management privately, Alves said, but occasionally it has decided to disseminate leaflets, walk picket lines, and deploy other old-school tactics. "Whatever actions we decide to take, management is always informed," he explained. "They know what we are going to do and why. Management does the same thing. When they cannot convince us of something, they bring it to the board or we go to arbitration and allow an outside party to give us an objective decision." Alves sees two important benefits when parties learn to "fight well": (1) both sides more likely will get what they want, and (2) they preserve their professional relationships with one another so they can make progress on other important problems. In terms of the needed paradigm shift discussed in the introduction, "fighting well" has great potential to transform the interactions between labor and management.

Shortly after Culver City's leaders returned from ABC Unified's Institute, they hit their first bump in the road when contract negotiations began and management's initial salary offer was "really crummy," Mielke recalled. "I sent out an e-mail with details about the offer, and when teachers got wind of it, they said, 'So much for collaboration and good will.' I, too, was very disappointed because I thought that things really would be different with the new superintendent. They are now, but at that moment it seemed like the same old story." Mielke's subsequent conversations with LaRose, the superintendent, were heated at first, but they improved when the two agreed to listen to one another, applying a key strategy for resolving differences called "fierce conversations" that they had learned at the Institute.[11]

"His e-mail to all staff did surprise and upset me," LaRose said. "I did not think the district's offer acknowledged our positive intent. I drafted a long response that I never sent, but shared with Dave [Mielke]. He and I met with other leaders of the district partnership, processed what had happened, gained some trust and appreciation for each other's position, and committed to meet every other week. Dave [Mielke] quickly sent out a more positive, encouraging e-mail to staff that I very much appreciated." Reflecting on their first bump in the road as partners, LaRose said, "The whole mess could have been avoided had we been meeting more regularly, as the leaders from ABC Unified had urged us to do."

Engaging constructively in conflict is not easy, and it's especially hard when trust is low or nonexistent. But education leaders can and do break these dysfunctional patterns, often with the help of experienced facilitators who can convince parties to reflect on their actions and consider whether those actions advance their mutual goals. When labor and management break old patterns, the impact is often significant.

Feature 3: Both Sides Assume Joint Ownership of Decisions

With joint ownership of decisions, Gray wrote, "the participants in a collaboration are directly responsible for reaching agreement on a solution. Unlike litigation or regulation, in which intermediaries . . . devise solutions that are imposed in the stakeholders, in collaborative agreements the parties impose decisions on themselves. They set the agenda; they decide what issues will be addressed; they decide what the terms will be."[12]

Effective collaboration extends well beyond wages, hours, and working conditions—the core issues that the two sides typically negotiate at the bargaining table. Collaborative districts really do set their own agendas and make joint decisions on a wide variety of topics that affect teaching and learning, even when the teacher contract or other local policies do not require it.

In Ohio's Columbus City School District, for instance, management joined with the Columbus Education Association to address low graduation rates and poor student outcomes in one of its high schools. They cocreated a new curriculum that emphasized critical thinking and content in science, technology, engineering, and math (STEM), according to Abigail Paris, who studied the district.[13] The union led a conversation about the changes with over three hundred parents and other community members. Just a year after the district implemented the STEM curriculum, graduation rates at the high school rose from 53 to 63 percent.

Make no mistake—some district leaders can find joint ownership threatening. Robert Kosienski, a veteran Board of Education member for Connecticut's Meriden public schools, was skeptical that district administrators could work closely and effectively with the teacher union, and he heard warnings from others that "[w]hen you start being collaborative with the union, you're going to be beholden to the union."[14] Nevertheless, wrote Jennifer Dubin, who studied labor relations in Meriden, Kosienski saw the virtues of collaboration after studying the results of an extended learning program that the district staff and the Meriden Federation of Teachers had codeveloped.

"[Kosienski] has begun to realize," Dubin wrote, "that student achievement in the district has steadily increased because teachers, administrators, and the board of education 'have all bought into the fact that we need to work together.'"[15] From 2012 to 2013, proficiency rates among district sixth graders rose from 73 to 78 percent in math and among seventh graders from 70 to 79 percent in reading—at a time when these rates were falling statewide. That outcome is particularly impressive because the student poverty rate in Meriden is twice the state average.

On the union side, members who lack an appreciation for meaningful collaboration sometimes worry that friendly administrators will use the process simply to convince unions to endorse their preset agenda. These skeptics fear that collaboration will lead to *capitulation*, even *collusion*, with their leaders cozying up to management and forgetting about those they represent.

On both sides, the qualms about joint ownership are widespread, and they help explain why effective collaboration has been slow to spread. Consequently, school boards hire hard-nosed superintendents who can "take on the unions" while teachers refuse to elect collaborative union leaders because they appear too "soft." Fortunately, individuals on all sides can overcome the fears about joint ownership, as Kosienski did when he witnessed its benefits first hand.

Feature 4: Both Sides Assume Joint Responsibility for Results

Effective collaboration often prompts both sides to create governance structures (e.g., committees, communication systems) that guide how they communicate and coordinate their activities. Indeed, these structures appear in virtually every district in which leaders have adopted a collaborative approach.

In New York's Plattsburgh City School District, collaboration and joint responsibility have been strategic priorities for decades. "[A]ll stakeholder groups, including teachers, administrators, the board, parents, students, and the voting public share responsibility for student achievement," according to researcher Jonathan Eckert. One formal structure is the District Wide Educational Improvement Council (DWEIC), which "recommends changes in current education policies, discusses educational changes in the district prior to implementation, and provides for dialogue between the union, the administration and the board, allowing input by the professional staff on district wide matters."[16] Among many important programs that emerged from the DWEIC is a mentor program for new teachers and administrators, a comprehensive educator evaluation system, and a peer assistance and review (PAR) program for teachers.

Meanwhile, Eckert said, joint responsibility is promoted informally through Superintendent Jake Short, who "encourages decisions to be made at the level where they will be implemented to the extent possible while monitoring results and providing support. This builds the capacity of the district and creates a pool of leadership talent with experience in problem solving, taking advantage of the professional expertise of teachers."[17]

In California's Poway Unified District, where union and district leaders created a peer assistance and review program that's a national model, they also established an Interest Based Problem Solving (IBPS) team that consists of four union members and four administrators, with an external consultant who facilitates their meetings. Among the team's many accomplishments is a districtwide professional learning program, called the Teaching and Learning Cooperative (TLC). Candy Smiley, president of the Poway Teachers Association, explained that, under TLC, teachers submit their own professional proposals that must be approved by a union-district governing board, which determines whether a proposal meets the district's professional learning standards. Teachers who complete approved professional learning activities are eligible for salary increases. Smiley said the TLC has been so successful that the district's classified staff bargaining unit is developing a similar program with the district.[18]

In Cincinnati, where collaboration has helped to dramatically improve high school graduation rates and virtually eliminate an achievement gap between white and African American students, collaborative practices are explicitly included in the district's collective bargaining agreement with teachers. "Its most recent three-year agreement," said Greg Anrig, a researcher who studied the district, "builds on previous contracts with a multitude of provisions ensuring that teachers have a strong voice in decision-making processes.

"Those structures," he continued, "range from districtwide committees that focus on budgets, employee benefits, school performance oversight, peer review, and disciplinary issues, to school-based teams. Each school is governed by a local decision-making committee comprising three teachers, three parents, and three community members along with the principal. The contract also requires the creation of instructional leadership teams, which include elected leaders of teacher groups who work together on a daily basis, as well as parents, leaders of community service providers, and the principal."[19]

Feature 5: Both Sides Collaborate on Everything That Affects Teaching and Learning

In most districts, labor and management interact exclusively on contractual matters. The leaders on each side do not innovate with one another, and they rely on formal grievance procedures, rather than informal dialogue, to solve contract disputes.

In highly collaborative districts and states, however, labor and management work together on a far broader range of issues that affect teaching and learning. For example:

- In Maryland's Montgomery County Public Schools, labor and management codeveloped a comprehensive professional growth system for teachers and administrators.
- In Florida's Hillsborough County Public Schools, the board, administrators, and union developed an intensive, two-year induction program for new teachers, and expert mentor teachers work full time to assist their novice colleagues.[20]
- In Tennessee's Hamilton County, labor and management replaced a seniority-based teacher transfer policy to ensure that accomplished teachers would be working in high-need schools; several factors now determine teacher transfers, not just seniority.[21]
- In Chelsea, a Boston suburb, teams from elementary schools (including building union representatives and administrators) voluntarily developed detailed proposals to extend learning time in their schools as a way to enrich learning and close the achievement gap.[22]
- In Cincinnati's public schools, community leaders, administrators, and union leaders codeveloped thirty-four Community Learning

Centers to provide comprehensive support services to students and their families—including health care, social and recreational services, early childhood education, and arts programs.[23]

- In Massachusetts, over thirty schools expanded learning time for students as part of the Mass 2020/National Council on Time and Learning initiative developed in collaboration with unions. Over fifty schools have become Innovation Schools, which are in-district charter schools that unions and school administrators developed to improve student achievement.

In highly collaborative districts, administrators and labor leaders have frequent informal conversations to address problems when they first emerge and to consider innovative ways to strengthen leadership and teaching. At ABC Unified in Los Angeles, Superintendent Mary Sieu and union president Ray Gaer meet each week for this purpose. They also focus directly on the quality of collaboration among various constituencies within the district, and they develop strategies to address challenges when they arise. Similarly, in Sacramento's San Juan Unified School District, union leaders and district administrators have regular off-site "check-in" meetings to ensure that their relationships remain strong.

The list of teaching-related issues on which administrators and unions could collaborate is a long one. Even in collaborative districts, educators often avoid "undiscussable" issues such as differentiated pay, teacher and principal evaluation, and accountability because many fear that raising them would jeopardize the trust and positive working relationships that collaboration has established. That, however, leaves those important issues unresolved, and it leaves educators with unpopular programs that don't work—until, of course, policy makers or the courts step in and impose solutions that often are even more distasteful.

Take teacher evaluation. Broken evaluation systems have become a lightning rod for the media and other outsiders who say they prevent administrators from firing incompetent teachers.[24] Teachers and unions, on the other hand, have long complained about "drive-by" observations, superficial evaluation checklists, and the absence of follow-up support to help teachers improve. Administrators say they lack the time or training to evaluate teachers appropriately.

Because most states and school districts have not developed sensible evaluation systems, the US Department of Education (through programs like Race to the Top and School Improvement Grants) has forced many of them to adopt high-stakes teacher evaluation systems that I and many others believe are flawed. Most problematic, many states and districts adopted systems that lean heavily on standardized tests to evaluate teachers, though the research suggests that such tests cannot be used reliably for this purpose.[25] Two exceptions are Massachusetts and California, which chose not to use standardized test scores for high-stakes decisions but, instead, as one of several indicators to promote continuous improvement.

Among other teacher-related issues on which labor and management should collaborate are the following:

- How can districts use experience, extraordinary accomplishments, and additional responsibilities to differentiate compensation?
- How can districts ensure that transfer, layoff, and other personnel decisions are fair and that they recognize experience and accomplishments?
- How will districts support struggling teachers?
- How can teacher termination proceedings protect teachers' due process rights and not prove excessively time-consuming or costly?
- How should districts allocate their budgets to ensure that all students have an adequate opportunity to learn?
- How can teachers and administrators develop a complete curriculum that includes culturally relevant social studies, science, and the arts?
- How can teachers and administrators provide professional development for teachers in using pedagogies that engage students in interdisciplinary learning?
- How can teachers and administrators engage parents in the instructional process?

Feature 6: Both Sides Collaborate at All Levels of the Education System

Studies of labor-management collaboration focus mostly on interactions at the district level—that is, between administrators and school board members on one hand and leaders of local teacher unions on the other. To be sure, these are critical players because they negotiate contracts, address districtwide problems, and set a tone through their interactions that affects other stakeholders.

But collaboration between unions and management and with other stakeholders is just as important at other levels of the education system: at individual school sites and at the state and national levels. Without meaningful interaction at these levels that brings together diverse perspectives, stakeholders will miss opportunities to develop innovative solutions, and they will make critical mistakes that adversely affect schools.

Also important are two other levels of collaboration. One is the collaboration of management and unions within their own organizations. The other is the collaboration that educators have with their counterparts in other jurisdictions (e.g., superintendents with other superintendents).

At school sites. Although it hasn't received much attention, collaboration among administrators and union leaders at a school site can generate significant benefits for everyone involved.

School administrators, site-level union representatives, parent groups, and school committees make numerous decisions that have significant implications for students. What mission and vision will a school pursue? How will the school allocate its budget? Which teachers will teach which classes? How will the school support struggling students? How will schools assess student learning? What professional learning opportunities will teachers and administrators get? How will the school address student disciplinary problems?

Meaningful collaboration at the school level improves the quality of decisions and enhances stakeholder support for them, according to growing evidence. At ABC Unified in Los Angeles, researchers Saul A. Rubinstein and John E. McCarthy found that school-level partnerships between unions and administrators were reliable predictors of improved student performance. These improvements arose from formal and informal interactions between union building representatives and principals and from more communication among teachers working on curriculum, integrating subjects across grade levels, and sharing instructional practices.[26]

At the state level. Also receiving relatively little attention is the collaboration that must occur between state education officials on one side and state union leaders on the other. Here, too, the impacts can be significant.

In California, recent state-level collaboration has better positioned the state to successfully implement several reforms, notably the transition to Common Core State Standards. By contrast, in the absence of such collaboration, New York State has found it much harder to implement Common Core and other reforms because state education officials and union leaders focused their attention on contentious debates over using high-stakes tests for teachers and students.

California's state-level success set the stage for a promising Labor Management Initiative that brought together the state Department of Education, state teacher unions, and the state's administrator and school board associations to learn about labor-management partnerships and help local districts pursue them. In that way, California is following in the footsteps of Massachusetts and Illinois, which have both created formal partnership structures among their states' leading education organizations.

At the national level. Until recently, national education officials and union leaders seldom collaborated, and they didn't view one another as education partners. But in 2011, as previously noted, these groups cosponsored three national conferences on labor-management collaboration. At the first in 2011, superintendents, labor leaders, and board presidents from 150 school districts learned first-hand how a small number of districts are leveraging collaboration to improve student learning. At the second in 2012, they signed a vision statement pledging their support for labor-management collaboration. At the third in 2014, they focused on implementing college- and career-ready standards.[27] Their continued endorsement of collaboration at the national level sends an important message to state and local stakeholders about its benefits. The resources distributed at the conferences are contributing to a new and valuable knowledge base for educators.

Nevertheless, we need to do more to promote *authentic* collaboration among those who make national education policy and those who implement it. Had these groups collaborated to develop the No Child Left Behind Act of 2001, that fundamentally flawed legislation that has guided America's education policy for well over a decade likely would have looked very different. The same goes for Race to the Top, a controversial federal funding program for a small number of states that agreed, among other things, to base teacher evaluations on standardized tests. The American Federation of Teachers (AFT) and the National Education Association (NEA) initially supported Race to the Top, but they have grown increasingly critical of it as predictions about problems with test-based evaluations have proved correct.

Policy makers and education officials have left unions out of major policy debates, undoubtedly because they believe that, for unions, the interests of their members outweigh those of students. But if we want to see authentic collaboration—collaboration that's more than a slogan or a clever ploy to convince unions to endorse a preset agenda—education officials and policy makers must suspend their beliefs and listen more carefully to the professionals on whom they depend to implement their policies. What guides the kind of collaboration that's working in a small but growing number of districts, in states like Massachusetts and in countries like Finland, is a fundamental belief that teachers and their unions have students' interests at heart and must participate as partners in educational decision making.

Within labor and management. As with relations *between* management and unions, relations *within* management and unions can be adversarial and dysfunctional. In the Rochester City School District in 2014, for example, the Association of Supervisors and Administrators of Rochester (ASAR) passed a resolution of no confidence for the district's superintendent, a fellow administrator. Just before the vote, then-ASAR president Deborah Rider cited poor communication between administrators and the superintendent, adding, "As administrators, we're not always treated with respect and our voices are not always heard."[28]

In addition, disputes among school board members are common, which you might expect with any democratically elected body but which is far from productive when disputes become rancorous and members refuse to work with one another. One chief reason for the rapid turnover of district superintendents is the conflict many of them encounter with their boards as well as the conflicts among board members themselves.[29]

Teacher unions are hardly immune from political infighting. In the nation's capital in 2008, Nathan Saunders, vice president of the Washington Teachers Union, predicted that union members would engage in civil disobedience when George Parker, their local president, was scheduled to discuss contract negotiations with then-chancellor Michelle Rhee. Union officers thought Parker had left them out of the loop and essentially colluded with Rhee by cutting private deals with her.[30]

The internal problems some unions face, however, go beyond the occasional leader who colludes with management and loses the trust of his or her members. "Unfortunately, many teachers do not perceive their unions as credible, positive and effective advocacy organizations either for themselves, their students, or the educational system itself," according to Nina Bascia, a researcher who studies what teachers want from their unions. She added, "Teachers' ambivalence, apathy, and frustration—with decision makers and with unions themselves—are rooted in part in the strategic choices unions have made about their relationships with their members, their internal organization, their strategic directions, and the discourse about teachers and teaching they promote publicly."[31]

Elsewhere, Bascia and Pamela Osmond argued that unions have to represent their members' diverse needs. "Viable teacher unions make a point of providing a range of different ways that teachers can participate in their organizations," they wrote. "Rather than emphasizing an orthodoxy in terms of the kinds of activities they sponsor, they make member interest and access a priority—for example, providing a wide assortment of different professional development formats and topics, scheduling and locating them in ways that make them accessible to busy, working teachers. They provide a range of leadership opportunities so many different teachers can develop organizational skills and become involved and known to others. They make a point of rotating the demographics of leadership so neither teachers nor outsiders develop the impression that the union is not representative of the broad teacher population."[32]

Disagreements within management and unions are inevitable, even healthy. But, if their leaders hope to retain support for their collaborative approaches, they must be able to work through internal differences and represent the diverse interests of everyone they serve. "Keeping teachers informed about the collaborative work leaders are doing on their behalf is critical," Tim Fitzgerald, a labor-management facilitator for the Massachusetts Education Partnership, told me. "Too often they are left in the dark and become suspicious of the process. They're less likely to select collaborative leaders the next time an election is held."[33]

"Outside" collaboration. I've described the characteristics of collaboration that reflect the interactions within school systems and with state and national education officials and policy makers. Michael Fullan referred to these types of interactions as "inside collaboration," but he argued that "outside collaboration"—that is, with educators outside of one's organizational sphere—is equally vital to improving school systems. "If there is anything that is underdeveloped in educational reform, it is the operational knowledge base that should be possessed and continually updated and refined by organizational members," he said.[34] Close and frequent outside collaboration exposes one to different perspectives, alternative strategies, and innovative solutions. People who tend to be skeptical about new ideas (or ideas they've only read about) are often convinced once they see them

in practice and interact with people (especially those in the same position) who have adopted them.

In the context of labor-management partnership, district leaders contemplating a shift to collaboration (and even those already pursuing it) need to learn how other districts do it. They not only must see how others operate after they establish partnerships but also must understand how others got started in the first place. District leaders who are new to collaboration will ponder some obvious questions: *What if some of my colleagues are reluctant to collaborate and don't trust the other side? What if the process bogs down and it takes forever to make decisions and implement reforms? What if the other side doesn't hold up its end of the bargain?* Individual leaders can best answer these questions when they can interact candidly, face-to-face, with their counterparts in other districts—superintendents with superintendents, union leaders with union leaders, parents with parents, and so on.

National or regional conferences that showcase highly collaborative districts provide opportunities for participants to learn, but the interactions among them are generally brief and at arm's length. Site visits to districts practicing collaboration require coordination and planning, but they allow participants to probe their questions and concerns more deeply. These visits can expand into long-term "communities of practice" with other educators that can pay dividends for years to come.

Even districts with established internal partnerships benefit from external collaboration. Many of them regularly attend conferences held by the regional chapters of TURN, the Massachusetts Education Partnership, the American Federation of Teachers, the Consortium for Educational Change, and the NEA Foundation, all of which provide opportunities for camaraderie among like-minded educators. They also allow leaders to focus together on challenges such as implementing the Common Core State Standards, developing robust educator evaluation systems, and establishing intervention programs for struggling students. Outside collaboration is a powerful way to advance organizational learning, and it often enables people to see possibilities they once thought were unachievable.

Feature 7: Both Sides Rely on Collaboration When Bargaining Contracts

Collective bargaining is the formal process by which unions and management negotiate their employment agreements. Since the 1960s, all but a few states have allowed districts and local unions to bargain for wages, benefits, and working conditions. Before collective bargaining, teachers were forced to accept the terms of employment that management gave them.

While collective bargaining helped professionalize teaching, in many districts it has become a dreaded ritual in which each side tries to exact as many concessions as it can from the other side, using whatever tactics are necessary. When practiced this way, bargaining often has two negative consequences: (1) it produces agreements that neither party likes; and (2) it damages relationships between administrators and teachers, making it harder to innovate, solve problems, and collaborate when the bargaining is over. That, Harvard researcher Susan Moore Johnson said, is why some districts have approached bargaining differently.

"Conventional bargaining, with its dissembling, distrust, and deceit, could never create conditions that would inspire teachers and administrators to work on hard problems together," Johnson said. "Moreover, the split-the-difference settlements that typically emerge from bartering were hardly the kind of creative solutions that schools needed."[35] Collective bargaining also can derail efforts to collaborate, as it did in one Massachusetts district that had been making good progress on collaboration until it came time to bargain a new contract. "The collaboration came to a halt because of the way they went about negotiations," Tim Fitzgerald told me. "Because they were unable to settle their contract, they suspended their collaboration efforts."[36]

Interest-based bargaining (IBB), a popular alternative to collective bargaining, rests on a different core assumption—that the interests of management and the union are largely aligned. That means they can seek solutions that work well for both parties rather than always settle on a middle ground compromise that nobody likes.

IBB encourages participants to expand the scope of bargaining beyond traditional bread-and-butter issues of wages, benefits, and working conditions. Districts using this approach will, for example, describe how they will deliver professional development, how they will make curriculum decisions, and how much flexibility they will give teachers to choose learning materials and decide how they want to teach.

IBB, however, can occur only when a district's contract is up for renewal, which might be every two to three years. Living contracts, which several collaborative districts use, allow leaders to modify contracts and solve problems *before* contracts expire. Some districts have even adopted school-based living contracts, which allow teachers and principals at individual schools to bargain their own contract provisions.

Whether through traditional bargaining, IBB, or living contracts, the bargaining between management and unions must be guided by the same principles of collaboration that guide partnerships away from the bargaining table. That means, most importantly, that during negotiations, both sides must be fully committed to what will benefit students and to personal interactions that are open, honest, and civil. Rather than a dreaded ritual to be endured, bargaining should be an opportunity to improve schools and strengthen relationships among the educators who are entrusted with this responsibility. Nor, in the bargaining process, should either side forget the importance of decent wages and working conditions to ensure that teaching is an attractive profession, which leads to the next and final feature.

Feature 8: Both Sides Collaborate on Ways to Attract and Retain Good Teachers

To improve educational quality and outcomes, labor and management should collaborate to strengthen teaching—a notion that's often missing in discussions about collaboration and education reform.

People like to say that schools should focus on kids, not adults. Reflecting that spirit, educational foundations adopt such names as "Just for the

Kids" and "Students First," while districts and schools almost uniformly craft vision statements that put kids first. Unfortunately, recent decades also have brought the slow erosion of professional supports, compensation, and respect for teachers that has increasingly weakened the nation's teaching profession. It's no coincidence that the number of people enrolling in teacher credential programs throughout the country dropped by nearly 30 percent from 2010 to 2014, according to the US Department of Education.[37] Teacher shortages are a problem because, in fact, quality education is *not* just about kids; it's about adults as well.

To be sure, unions and management should not worry about the interests of adults that have no connection to better teaching and learning. But education systems can't possibly be excessively catering to teachers if significant numbers of them are leaving the profession each year, if applicant pools to replace them are virtually nonexistent, or if schools routinely assign teachers to courses for which they're not qualified because they can't find qualified ones. That's true in far too many schools, especially those serving poor students and students of color—and that, in turn, has a devastating effect on student learning.

If schools can't attract, support, and retain capable and committed teachers, students won't learn. Fortunately, the path to effective recruitment and retention isn't a complicated one. Teachers want what other professionals want: fair compensation, respect as professionals, and a sense of making a difference—in this case, in the lives of students and communities. Most teachers decide to teach for special reasons, not the least of which is the inspiration they received from a great teacher.

Teaching, however, loses its allure when teachers can't make that difference because they lack the requisite support or resources, or they work in dysfunctional environments. Over time, many teachers once dedicated to their students and their profession become disillusioned, cynical, and burned out. Some transfer to schools that are more hospitable to good teaching; others—many of them highly capable educators—leave teaching altogether.[38]

Consider the Cincinnati Public Schools. For over two decades, its contract with teachers has allowed principals and teachers at school sites to make many of the operational and educational decisions. "This gave teachers a chance to address basic problems in their buildings, but it also gave them a voice in policies affecting teaching and learning," local union president Julie Sellers told me. Superintendent Mary Ronan added, "Because of this autonomy, because of the strong induction program we have for beginning teachers, and because our principals are collaborative, we don't have the teacher turnover problem that many urban districts experience. We've been able to staff our high-poverty schools with high-quality teachers."[39]

Through their collaboration in the public schools of Helena, Montana, management and the union elevated the need to strengthen the district's professional capital into a strategy priority. District leaders realized they must do more to attract and retain strong teachers in order to improve student learning. "Teachers were retiring early and going to work in Washington . . . the number of applicants for open positions was dismal," said Larry Nielsen, a field consultant for the Montana Education Association/ Montana Federation of Teachers (MEA-MFT).[40] For this district, the problem was less about teaching conditions and more about compensation. As board member Don Jones put it, "Having the best teachers is key to student performance. . . . Generally to get the best, you need to be willing to pay for the best."[41]

To address the issue, administrators and the union codeveloped the Professional Compensation Alternative Plan (PCAP). Rather than letting seniority determine one's salary, teachers opting into PCAP can move up the ladder based on career development plans, professional service, and positive evaluations from supervisors. Teachers atop that ladder could earn $10,000 more than those who chose the traditional compensation plan. Teachers initially balked at PCAP because they assumed it was the kind of merit pay that tied compensation to student test scores. However, they eventually embraced the plan once they understood that salary increases would be based on additional responsibilities and a more comprehensive assessment of their teaching. By 2011, 93 percent of Helena's teachers had opted into PCAP. Districts in Baltimore, Maryland, and in Lawrence and Springfield, Massachusetts, have adopted similar systems.

At all levels of the educational system, collaborative efforts should focus on maintaining a profession that attracts and retains great teachers. Wherever turnover rates are high and applicant pools are thin, labor, management, education officials, and policy makers should identify and address the particular factors that are causing those problems. Maintaining a strong and attractive teaching profession helps to ensure high-quality outcomes for students.

To be sure, the eight features outlined here assume a serious commitment on all sides to make labor-management collaboration a success. On the other hand, the impact that it can generate in the form of positive results for students is substantial.

CHAPTER 2

The Impact of Labor-Management Collaboration

I N ASSESSING an educational practice like labor-management collaboration, we need to both ask the right questions and seek the right answers. The most fundamental question, of course, is: Does it work? How
we seek the answer, though, matters enormously.

Educational researchers usually urge educators to adopt practices that
will produce concrete, measurable results. In recent decades, researchers
have sought such results in standardized tests largely because they're easy
to analyze and because federal and state accountability systems rely almost exclusively on them. That's problematic, however.

Evaluating the controversial top-down management style of former
San Diego Superintendent Alan Bersin (as described in the Introduction),
Diane Ravitch mused, "Did the get-tough policy produce results? Did it
lead to higher student test scores? These may not be the right questions.
It makes more sense," she explained, "to ask whether a policy of coer-
cion can create good schools. Can teachers successfully educate children

to think for themselves if teachers are not treated as professionals who think for themselves? Can principals be inspiring leaders if they must follow orders about the most minute details of daily life in classrooms? If a get-tough policy saps educators of their initiative, their craft, and their enthusiasm, then it is hard to believe that the results are worth having."[1]

The top-down approach of Bersin, along with New York's Joel Klein, Washington's Michelle Rhee, and Chicago's Rahm Emanuel, not only didn't produce higher-performing schools, but also generated much antipathy and low morale among district educators. This chapter discusses how collaborative leadership based on a foundation of trust among educators can create good schools—those with students who learn to think for themselves, who are taught well in all subject areas (not just language arts and math), who learn to interact well with their peers, and who perform well on a range of academic assessments. It also looks more closely at how labor-management collaboration produced positive results in three large districts: Montgomery County, Maryland; Los Angeles; and Cincinnati. The chapter then looks at how labor-management collaboration, or the lack thereof, helps explain why some districts implemented the new Common Core State Standards without significant problems, whereas others were torn apart by the experience.

Let me be clear: We shouldn't dismiss all types of test scores as one legitimate indicator of school performance. The National Assessment of Educational Progress (NAEP), for example, provides useful information about what students know in various subjects and at various grade levels. And since these tests are not used for high-stakes purposes, they don't have the harmful side effects associated with other commonly used standardized tests.[2]

Standardized test scores, however, typically reflect performance only in English language arts and math, so researchers and educational leaders should seek a broader perspective on the impact of labor-management collaboration. A more accurate appraisal of school quality would provide rich information on how students are doing in *all* subject areas, whether they can think critically and apply what they've learned in real life situations, and how they're progressing socially and emotionally.

The Wide-Ranging Benefits of Collaboration

Labor-management collaboration not only can have a direct impact on student learning, but, as researchers have demonstrated, it has important *intermediary* effects that themselves can bring positive results for students.

One of the most important intermediary effects, which is critical to educational progress, is that both sides have more capacity to innovate and solve problems that affect teaching and learning. "Union-management partnerships, because they are problem focused, can . . . help drive thinking about ways to increase student learning," Rubinstein and McCarthy explained. "These types of partnerships are designed to use collaboration among educators to find solutions to gaps in student achievement and then effectively implement those solutions because those closest to the problem—with tacit knowledge of it—are key stakeholders in the improvement process."[3]

Improving relationships among educators is not the ultimate purpose of collaboration, but it's a critical by-product that indirectly affects student learning. In 2011, University of Pittsburgh researcher Carrie Leana examined how "human capital" and "social capital" affected student achievement in 130 elementary schools in New York City. Human capital refers to the qualifications and capabilities of individual teachers. Social capital refers to the quality of professional relationships between teachers. Leana said the prevailing approach to reform presumes that human capital must be nurtured through professional development, coaching, and incentives that motivate teachers to do their best.

As expected, Leana found that students assigned to better teachers (i.e., those with more professional education, experience, and pedagogical knowledge) performed better on standardized tests, but teachers who had the greatest impact on academic achievement were those with more ability *and* stronger professional connections with their colleagues (i.e., more social capital). The reverse was also true. Teachers with little ability *and* weak connections with their peers had the least impact on their students.

These results highlight the very real impact of collaboration: "[Even] low-ability teachers can perform as well as teachers of average ability *if* they have strong social capital," Leana concluded from her research. "Strong social capital can go a long way toward offsetting any disadvantages students face when their teachers have low human capital."[4]

Granted, Leana was focused on the effects of social capital among teachers, not between district managers and union leaders. But more social capital among these individuals as well would generate better decision making, greater innovation, and fewer distracting battles. Indeed, social capital likely accounts for the improved student outcomes that, as we will see later, Saul Rubinstein and John McCarthy observed in the elementary schools of the ABC Unified School District of southeastern Los Angeles.

Another benefit of collaboration that's essential for building social capital, problem solving, and innovation is more trust. "Teachers must take on new practices that may not work," researchers Tony Bryk and Barbara Schneider wrote in their groundbreaking book, *Trust in Schools.*[5] "Principals must commit substantial personal effort to an uncertain change process. In addition, school reform movements often are accompanied by external pressure to improve quickly and considerable external scrutiny as well. In short, the stakes suddenly are high and the demands for change great. The presence of relational trust, however, moderates the sense of uncertainty and vulnerability that individuals feel as they confront such demands. When trust is strong, individual engagement with reform does not feel like a call for heroic action. In this sense, relational trust is a catalyst for innovation."[6] Trust reduces the "transaction costs" that are common in organizations with intense decision making, Bryk and Schneider wrote. "[W]hen arguments arise over the merits of some reform effort, these disagreements are more likely to be resolved in a straightforward fashion, again because of the assumed good intentions all around."[7]

Leaders who trust each other will less likely devote time and resources to battles that seldom, if ever, mean victories for children and too often leave leaders and their colleagues weary, dispirited, and cynical. Without the distractions and costs that are typical in an adversarial environment, educators who work together can better craft effective solutions and garner critical support from those who must implement them.

That was a key finding of a meta-analysis, in which I participated, of case study research on fifty-five districts that practice labor-management collaboration. "[I]n nearly all of the district cases," I wrote with my fellow researchers Dennis Shirley, Sara McClellan, and Scott Vince, "stakeholders described improved professional relationships and trust as the foundation for effective problem solving and the development of policies that support student learning."[8]

The amount of trust coworkers have for one another is largely a function of the level of civility that exists among them. Disagreements are unavoidable, but when they get played out with rude, hostile, disrespectful behavior (including, for example, angry, "reply-all" e-mail messages), loss of trust is often the greatest casualty. Again, civility is not the ultimate goal of collaboration, but it is a critical contributor to effective partnerships, and it has a significant impact on workers' productivity. Christine Porath and Christine Pearson, experts in organizational leadership, studied the cost of incivility and found these effects for workers on the receiving end of it:

- 48% intentionally decreased their work effort.
- 47% intentionally decreased the time spent at work.
- 38% intentionally decreased the quality of their work.
- 80% lost work time worrying about the incident.
- 63% lost work time avoiding the offender.
- 66% said that their performance declined.
- 78% said that their commitment to the organization declined.
- 12% said that they left their job because of the uncivil treatment.
- 25% admitted to taking their frustration out on customers.[9]

Granted, the subjects in their study were not educators (but they did work in seventeen different industries), it's not hard to imagine how the harmful effects of incivility would play out in school settings and ultimately harm students. Nor should we be surprised that students would treat one another uncivilly after witnessing the adults in their midst acting this way. Part of the problem here is the questionable belief systems of some leaders. "Many are skeptical about the returns of civility," according to Porath. Among the leaders they studied, "A quarter believe that they will be less leader-like, and nearly 40 percent are afraid that they'll be taken advantage of if they are nice at work. Nearly half think that it is better to flex one's muscles to garner power."[10] Successful labor-management partnerships are possible only when leaders on both sides fully appreciate the costs of incivility and begin to see that treating one another with respect does not weaken one's ability to lead effectively. In fact, as the case studies of successful partnerships show, it's far more likely to achieve the results they want.

In their book *Radical Collaboration*, James Tamm and Ronald Luyet highlighted yet another organizational benefit that derives from collaboration and civil relationships—"discretionary emotional energy," which they defined as "the passion, excitement, enthusiasm, and dedication that individuals choose to give freely to those causes, projects, relationships, and organizations in which they truly believe."[11]

Emotional energy is hard to quantify, but anyone who has worked in a school or any other organization can recognize it and knows how important it is. A school can have all of the resources it needs, a great reform plan, and highly qualified teachers, but it will not produce better teaching and improved student outcomes if people lack the emotional energy and passion that are present only when colleagues work well together. In fact, the absence of social capital is a leading cause of teacher turnover, driving capable educators away from schools where they're needed most.

The amount of trust and collaboration among educators determines how much emotional energy they will have to communicate, share resources, and solve problems—and the effects can be far-reaching. "The nature of relationships among the adults within a school," Harvard educator Roland Barth observed, "has a greater influence on the character and quality of that school and on student accomplishment than anything else. If the relationships between administrators and teachers are trusting, generous, helpful, and cooperative, then the relationships between teachers and students, between students and students, and between teachers and parents are likely to be trusting, generous, helpful, and cooperative. If, on the other hand, relationships between administrators and teachers are fearful, competitive, suspicious, and corrosive, then these qualities will disseminate throughout the school community."[12]

To fully appreciate the power of labor-management collaboration, let's take a closer look at what it's meant for three large school districts across America. This journey begins on the east coast, about a half-hour car ride north of Washington, DC, in Montgomery County, Maryland.

Case Study 1: Montgomery County Public Schools

In the 1990s, Mark Simon, president of the Montgomery County Education Association (MCEA, the teacher union), and his fellow union leaders explored the concept of a "new unionism" through which compensation, benefits, and job security would not dominate contract talks. Simon also wanted to use the bargaining process to reduce class sizes, improve professional development for teachers, develop a new evaluation system for teachers that would help them improve, and create a fair and efficient process to remove poor teachers.

District leaders welcomed Simon's call for collaboration. "He's sounding a conciliatory theme," Mona M. Signer, a member of the Montgomery County Public Schools (MCPS) Board of Education, said at the time, "which is certainly different than the inflammatory rhetoric we've seen in past years." Sharon Cox, the president of the Montgomery County Council of PTAs, added, "In the past, there has not been a lot of collaboration, but if this is the direction the membership is moving in, we welcome it."[13]

Then in 1999, the board chose Jerry Weast, a highly collaborative administrator who had been serving as superintendent of schools in Guilford
County, North Carolina, to fill the same job in Montgomery County. Weast
thought that partnering with the district's unions would be essential to
ensuring that the system responded effectively to the fundamental inequities affecting district students—in particular, the widening achievement
gap between the races and growing poverty rates.

To nurture trust, which was missing after years of conflict, Weast and
leaders of the district's three unions began meeting informally over breakfast and lunch. Their conversations became increasingly civil, and they
would soon sign a community-supported "aspirational goal" that 100 percent of district students would graduate and 80 percent would be prepared
for college and careers.[14] Explaining the role of collaboration in meeting
this goal, Weast said, "A large-scale reform effort such as this cannot be successful without trust and collaboration among teachers, principals, parents,
and support staff. Everyone has to be personally committed to the ideals
being sought and not merely comply with an edict from the central office."[15]

Over the next fourteen years, Montgomery County's unions and management faced daunting challenges, including painful budget cuts that
tested the partnership. During this period, however, they created some of
the nation's most innovative and successful educational initiatives, many
of them products of the collaborative, interest-based bargaining process
that the district adopted in 2000.

One of these initiatives is the district's nationally recognized Professional Growth System (PGS), which it instituted in 2000.[16] PGS was
designed to ensure continuous improvement in teaching and shared accountability for student outcomes. Teachers and administrators engage in
continuous, high-quality professional learning, and evaluations rest on a
common set of standards for teaching performance as well as evidence of
student learning that goes well beyond standardized test scores. The peer
assistance and review (PAR) element of PGS provides intensive support to

all novice teachers and to tenured veterans who are struggling. PAR is designed both to help these teachers improve and to remove those who don't.

The MCEA has taken an active role in promoting teaching quality and has developed a National Board Certification Support Program, providing scholarships, coaches, and professional development to participating teachers. As of 2014, 634 of the district's more than twelve thousand teachers who have volunteered for this rigorous, professional growth program have become board certified.[17]

Management and union leaders also created a career lattice program, modeled on the Career In Teaching Program of Rochester, New York, that enables teachers to become "lead teachers." Once a panel of administrators and teachers selects them, these highly accomplished lead teachers can serve as team leaders, consulting teachers, instructional specialists, and staff development facilitators, and they can receive annual salary supplements of up to $3,000.[18] To help lead teachers become effective leaders, the union sponsors four full-day leadership institutes.[19]

Over time, the values of equity, trust, empowerment, and collaboration spread to stakeholders throughout the district. At Viers Mill, an elementary school that serves mostly poor students and students of color, for example, efforts to build social capital among staff (by promoting collaboration and hiring team-oriented teachers) created a better working environment, reduced teacher turnover, and significantly improved the quality of instruction. Viers Mill would become one of Montgomery County's "distinguished" schools.

"Viers Mill has a culture of collaboration, support, and high commitment, in which current staff members, not just the principal, are engaged in hiring new staff," wrote Scott Thompson, a researcher who studied the school and its transformation. "Teaming is a critical success factor at Viers Mill; it's a focal point in the process of hiring new staff, and it illustrates why culture is so influential. Team participation is a key source of professional satisfaction in this school, and so it contributes to staff stability.

That continuity, in turn, contributes to a much more consistent instructional program than would otherwise have been the case."[20]

The results of Montgomery County's district- and school-level partnerships have been nothing short of extraordinary. "The best evidence of success we have thus far," Weast said in 2010, "is the recognition by teachers themselves that professional standards and expectations can be raised and improved effectively if teachers are part of the process and provide the essential leadership."[21]

The district's commitment to collaboration brought a 30 percent decline in union grievances, an important sign that teachers and administrators can resolve their differences before either side resorts to formal complaints. Fewer grievances also mean that management and union officials have more time to focus on planning, to ensure programs are implemented effectively, and to address problems proactively so they don't move to the grievance stage.

In this improved district culture, with a strong professional support system, teacher retention rates also have improved. In recent years, only 30 percent of new teachers have left the district after five years, far below a national average for urban districts (as Montgomery County is considered) that is closer to 50 percent.[22] In 2009, the district retained 95 percent of all teachers, a much higher percentage than similar districts around the country.[23] Teacher retention is important because high turnover rates are enormously costly and because they hurt the instructional programs and the relationships that teachers have with parents and each other.[24]

In terms of tangible student outcomes, the district made substantial progress toward its aspirational goals for graduation and college readiness. By 2014, 90 percent of all high school students were graduating.[25] Over the past several years, the district has consistently exceeded its expected graduation rate, based on size, poverty rates, and other demographic variables.[26] In 2013, the state's Department of Education documented that 92 percent of that year's Montgomery County high school graduates attended either a two- or four-year college.[27] Sixty percent of those who attended college graduated within six years.[28] Montgomery County's graduation rates were the highest among the nation's fifty largest school districts in 2012 and, in recent years, have consistently been among the top, according to *Education Week*.[29]

Montgomery County's collaborative reform efforts that focused on professional supports for teachers also correlated with a significant rise in academic achievement and a narrowing of the district's student achievement gap. In 2010, about 80 percent of eighth grade African American and Hispanic students and nearly 95 percent of white and Asian American students scored proficient or higher that year on the state's English Language Arts test—compared to 52 percent of African American and Hispanic students and 85 percent of white and Asian American students in 2003.[30]

For Montgomery County, the record is clear: a commitment to labor-management collaboration brought fewer union grievances, greater teacher retention, higher academic performance for all groups of students, and higher high school and college graduation rates.

Let's turn now to the west coast, to the ABC Unified School District to the southeast of downtown Los Angeles, which serves twenty-one thousand students—of whom 60 percent are students of color, 20 percent are English language learners, and nearly a quarter qualify for free or reduced lunch.

Case Study 2: ABC Unified School District

In 1993, the ABC Unified Federation of Teachers voted to strike over salaries, health benefits, and class sizes. Most of the one thousand two hundred teachers walked out on the strike's first day, and many picketed in front of their schools until the strike ended eight days later. Frustrated by the bitter fight, ABC's union president at the time, Laura Rico, approached the superintendent, Thomas Riley, and suggested they find a way to work together. Relations improved over the next few years, but it was not until Rico, several union colleagues, board members, and a new superintendent,

Ron Barnes,[31] participated in a weeklong seminar on collaboration at Harvard that they formed one of the nation's most successful labor-management partnerships.[32]

To formalize the partnership, management and the union adopted a set of guiding principles that, to this day, serve as important public reminders of the commitments that ABC's educators made to one another. The guiding principles also have helped to sustain the partnership through changes in leadership among both management and the union. They include the following:

- All students can succeed, and we will not accept any excuse that prevents that from happening in ABC. We will work together to promote student success.
- All needed support will be made available to schools to ensure every student succeeds. We will work together to ensure that happens.
- The top 5 percent of teachers in our profession should teach our students. We will work together to hire, train, and retain these professionals.
- All employees contribute to student success.
- All negotiations support conditions that sustain successful teaching and student learning.
- We won't let each other fail.[33]

ABC also agreed that all of the district's leaders were expected to follow these behavioral norms:

- We will work hard to understand the core of each other's job.
- We will respect each other.
- We will be honest with each other.
- We will not "sugar coat" difficult issues.
- We will disagree without being disagreeable.
- We will reflect on each other's comments, suggestions, and concerns.[34]

One of the partnership's first initiatives focused on improving teaching quality at the district's hardest-to-staff schools. The district raised starting teacher salaries, strengthened teacher recruitment efforts, offered $5,000 bonuses to teachers who transferred to these schools, enticed accomplished veteran teachers to the schools by ensuring they wouldn't suffer a pay cut, and beefed up professional support so that teachers wouldn't transfer away.

In another initiative, the district created a group called Proactive Problem Solvers, or PROPS, specifically to address another of its challenges—how best to serve special education students. The group, which still operates today, includes special education teachers, district administrators, and members of the union's special education advisory committee. "The consortium," a district publication says, "works together to address schools' special education issues before they escalate into larger problems."[35] In the district's publication, Dawn Hereen, the union's vice president for special education, is quoted as saying, "When we get together, we leave the titles at the door, roll up our sleeves, and honestly tackle the issues together. We speak to the 'elephants' [i.e., the most controversial issues between them] but avoid blame."[36]

One notable feature of ABC's labor-management partnership is that collaboration occurs *within* schools between principals and union site leaders, both of whom receive professional development to build and sustain their local partnerships. Union site representatives still perform their traditional roles—advocating for their members and enforcing the contract—but they're also expected to work closely with their principals on all matters that affect teaching and learning.

To sustain and strengthen partnerships throughout the district, external collaboration experts work regularly with district staff. The current superintendent, Mary Sieu, said the partnerships would fail if only she and the union president, Ray Gaer, were collaborating. "We are very intentional about providing ongoing training on collaboration for all district administrators and school board members, especially those who are new to these positions," Sieu said. "Many of them do not know coming in that this approach is key to the district's success."[37]

Likewise, Gaer said, the union provides similar professional development to all of its site-based representatives. "Most of our local union funds are used for this purpose because we want our local reps to know how to work with principals and how to communicate effectively with the teachers they represent," Gaer explained. Each year, administrators and union representatives focus on their particular partnerships at a retreat called Partnership with Administration and Labor, or P.A.L.

The partnership has profoundly influenced how the district approaches teaching conditions. For many years, teaching conditions at each school were assessed through an anonymous teacher survey in the spring. "In years past," Gaer explained, "these surveys were used as a weapon by teachers. It was a way for teachers to get back at principals they were frustrated with. In the fall, just as school was opening, principals were given the results from the surveys and many would be in tears." That's all changed, he said, with trust and collaboration serving as guiding principles. "The survey is now viewed as a tool for change. The entire staff owns the results and feels it's their responsibility to address the problems that affect teaching. They don't fall exclusively on the principal's lap. As a result, our schools are better places to teach and we have very little staff turnover."[38]

Due to ABC's success with collaboration, the district now conducts an annual West Coast Labor Management Institute, where visiting teams from other districts interact with ABC's leaders, learn about effective collaboration strategies, and watch district educators participate in collaborative activities. The event has received rave reviews by visiting teams and has inspired other districts, like nearby Culver City Unified, to launch their own collaboration efforts. For Sieu and Gaer, the annual Institutes benefit their own district just as much. "It reinforces what we do, and we learn something that helps us get better each time we do it," Sieu said.[39]

And how do ABC Unified's students benefit? Saul Rubinstein and John McCarthy responded to that question by examining the quality of partnerships among management and labor leaders in the district's school sites. "The results of this study show that the quality of union-management partnerships between teachers and administrators at the school level has had an important and significant association with educator collaboration and student achievement, as well as greater achievement gains from one year to the next," they wrote. "When partnerships are stronger, school-level collaboration is higher and so is student performance. While poverty remains a key predictor of student achievement, the data suggest that student performance can be improved through institutional union-management partnerships and the increased school-level collaboration that results from them."[40]

Schools with the strongest partnerships, as measured by the "density" of connections between educators at the school as well as the frequency of communications between site-level union representatives and their principals, had higher student scores on the state's Academic Performance Index and showed the greatest academic improvement from the 2010–2011 school year to the next one. These differences were statistically significant and accounted for student poverty, according to the researchers. The findings provide strong evidence that the intermediary benefits of collaborative partnerships—more trust, stronger communication, and better problem solving—can significantly improve student learning.

We now head to the nation's heartland, to the public schools of Cincinnati, Ohio, that serve thirty-three thousand students.

Case Study 3: Cincinnati Public Schools

In Cincinnati's public schools, management and the unions have practiced collaboration since the early 1990s—as long as any district in America. It wasn't the 1977 teacher strike that prompted the shift to collaboration, Superintendent Mary Ronan and local union president Julie Sellers told me. Instead, it was the determination of a brash, progressive union leader named Tom Mooney, president of the Cincinnati Federation of Teachers from 1979 to 2000.

Mooney convinced the district to adopt the nation's second PAR program in 1985, providing mentors to novice teachers and struggling veterans. He also negotiated a contract that established school-based committees to address operational problems. By the early 1990s, these committees were called Instructional Leadership Teams, and they included the principal and lead teachers who made most key educational decisions at their schools.

Then, about a decade ago, district management, the union, and community groups worked together to develop what are now nationally recognized Community Learning Centers, which are hubs for community services. These Centers, available to students and their families during and after school and on weekends "offer health services, counseling, after-school programs, nutrition classes, parent and family engagement programs, early childhood education, career and college access services, youth development activities, mentoring, and arts programming," according to the district website.[41]

Cincinnati's Community Learning Centers, now in thirty-four city schools, have become models for cities like New York due to their proven success. A 2011 report showed that academic growth among students in schools with Community Learning Centers outperformed those in schools without them. Absences and disciplinary referrals also have fallen in these schools.[42]

According to Ronan, some new board members need time to understand why schools have that much autonomy and why, as elected officials, board members can't tell school employees what to do. "Occasionally, Julie and I have to temper the overzealousness of the board on some issues," Ronan said. "We have to remind them that the district is bound contractually to school-based collaboration."[43] These conversations with board members are undoubtedly easier for Ronan and Sellers given the extraordinary results that the district has achieved on behalf of its students.

In particular, high school graduation rates soared from 51 percent in 2000, before the district had put all of its reforms in place, to 82 percent by 2010. Meanwhile, according to Elizabeth Holtzapple, Cincinnati Public Schools' former director of research, evaluation and testing, the achievement gap between African American and white students was eliminated.[44]

"Affirmed by student test results, improved parent involvement, stronger teacher-administrator relationships, and wraparound services provided by the community schools—which are now planned for every school in the district—Cincinnati's example clearly deserves much greater attention from struggling districts," concluded Greg Anrig, who studied the changes. "Central to Cincinnati's success has been what stakeholders there recognize as a strong degree of trust between school administrators and the teachers' union."[45] Anrig conceded that "there is no way to tease out the degree to which any particular program is most responsible for Cincinnati's impressive results," but he added, "the common thread among all the city's distinctive initiatives has been a culture that strives to overcome the barriers between teachers, administrators, parents, and service providers that prevail in many urban districts."[46]

In Cincinnati, as in Montgomery County and southeastern Los Angeles, labor-management collaboration built trust, cultivated social capital, boosted emotional energy, and reduced the number of needless and distracting battles, leaving more time for innovation and problem solving. That may well be one key factor that's helping to generate significant improvements in student learning.

Thus, those three large school districts show us the power of labor-management collaboration at the district level and within schools. To illustrate its power at the state and federal levels, the following section looks at how Common Core State Standards were implemented across the country.

Collaboration and Common Core: A Tale of Two States

In 2009, the National Governors Association and the Council of Chief State School Officers met with officials from forty-one states to develop twenty-first century academic standards to help all students become college- and career-ready. These Common Core State Standards (CCSS) initially received broad support from education stakeholder groups, including the National Education Association (NEA), the American Federation of Teachers (AFT), the National School Boards Association, and the Council of Great City Schools.

Dennis Van Roekel, president of the NEA, which represents over three million teachers, was especially optimistic about the opportunity for teacher participation in collaboration efforts. "NEA welcomes the opportunity to participate in this effort to provide manageable, high-quality standards for adoption by states to guide efforts to improve education," he wrote. "We are pleased that the voices of classroom educators will now be a part of this process."[47] AFT President Randi Weingarten expressed similar support, noting the key role that teachers played in developing the standards. "These standards . . . are essential building blocks for a better education system—not a new educational fad—and they can help prepare all children, regardless of where they live, for success in college, careers and life. Those who wrote the standards understood this, and met repeatedly with front-line educators, including AFT members from across the country, who helped turn these concepts into a reality that can make a difference in children's lives."[48]

To be sure, the standards are controversial. Conservatives view them as a federal overreach. Some liberals agree, and many also worry that national standards will bring a one-size-fits-all curriculum and more standardized testing. The NEA and AFT remain supportive, however, as do teachers across the country, based on surveys by the AFT, NEA, *Education Week,* and *Scholastic.* The standards represent a significant improvement over the ones that states were using. They also call on students to think critically and apply concepts to real-world problems. And they allow educators more flexibility to develop locally appropriate curricula. The number of standards is small, ensuring that teachers and students will still have the time to deeply explore material that lies beyond the standards.

Unfortunately, a growing number of states, districts, and schools are botching the implementation, in no small measure because they're not collaborating with the very professionals who will have to implement the standards—teachers. "Imagine that," Van Roekel said in early 2014. "The very people expected to deliver universal access to high quality standards with high quality instruction have not had the opportunity to share their expertise and advice about how to make CCSS implementation work for all students, educators, and parents."[49]

New York State's experience with the standards shows what can happen when policy makers push hard but don't consult with those who must do the implementing. To comply with the federal Race to the Top program, state lawmakers amended the education code so that standardized tests tied to the standards would play a significant role in teacher and administrator evaluations. A sharp drop in test scores after the state administered the first Common Core assessments, however, triggered a wave of resistance to the standards themselves, with many parents complaining that their students were subjected to high levels of stress because they weren't adequately prepared for the new material.[50]

Thousands of New York parents have since decided that their kids should opt out of the tests, as they're allowed to do. Teachers and administrators, whose formal evaluations were tied to test results, also complained that they did not receive ample time to transition to the standards. A third of state administrators formally objected to the new evaluation system and, in early 2014, the New York State United Teachers voted to withdraw its support for the standards as implemented. In response to growing parent and educator pressure, the state Board of Regents voted in February of 2014 to delay implementation for two years.

Strikingly, and more broadly, in June 2014 the Bill & Melinda Gates Foundation called for delaying the use of sanctions with implementation of the standards across the country. The foundation had been a strong advocate for the standards, investing over $200 million in their development. In an open letter, Foundation Director Vicki Phillips wrote, "No evaluation system will work unless teachers believe it is fair and reliable, and it's very hard to be fair in a time of transition. The standards need time to work. Teachers need time to develop lessons, receive more training, get used to the new tests and offer their feedback."[51]

Who knows whether education officials across the country will heed this advice, or whether New York's Common Core restart will ultimately allow that state to recover from its disastrous launch. Several other states have also delayed implementation, and many others have pending legislation that would reject the standards entirely.[52]

US Secretary of Education Arne Duncan, too, eventually agreed that testing related to the standards should be postponed, even though states participating in Race to the Top were required to do it. In his back-to-school comments in August of 2014, Duncan wrote, "I believe testing issues today are sucking the oxygen out of the room in a lot of schools—oxygen that is needed for a healthy transition to higher standards, improved systems for data, better aligned assessments, teacher professional development, evaluation and support, and more. [The switch to Common Core] is one of the biggest changes in education this country has ever seen, and teachers who've worked through it have told me it's allowed them to become the best teachers they've ever been. That change needs educators' full attention."[53]

On the other hand, not every state or district has felt the need to delay implementation, nor did everyone face implementation problems. In California and Massachusetts, educators overwhelmingly embraced the standards. That's a product partly of more labor-management collaboration at the district level and partly of unprecedented cooperation among education officials and union leaders at the state level.

That new spirit of cooperation first emerged in California in 2011 when a transition team formed by the newly elected state superintendent of instruction, Tom Torlakson, met over several months and produced a report titled *A Blueprint for Great Schools*. It represented a rare opportunity for a diverse group of state and local education leaders, including representatives from labor and management, to develop policy recommendations together. One recommendation was to "[l]aunch an ongoing initiative to support union-management collaboration toward high-leverage reforms in school organization, management, and instructional innovation as well as teacher, classified staff, and administrator development, support, and evaluation."[54]

Torlakson formed a task force in 2012 to focus on policies to strengthen educator effectiveness. Once again, a diverse group of education leaders (including me) spent several months wrestling with complex policy issues, eventually producing a report, *Greatness by Design*, that included recommendations on educator evaluation, peer assistance and review, equitable distribution of excellent educators, leadership development, teacher preparation, and professional learning. This report went even further than *A Blueprint for Great Schools* in advocating for labor-management collaboration because its authors recognized that many of their recommendations could be implemented only if labor and management could craft new, innovative agreements.[55]

"Implementation of many of the Task Force's recommendations will require policy changes at the state level, but some will also require innovative new agreements between labor and management at the district level," the task force wrote.[56] "The state should . . . promote labor-management collaboration to enable innovation in educator roles, responsibilities, and compensation systems. Concrete steps should include a statewide conference on labor-management collaboration to share innovative practices and to promote cross-district dialogue; creation of a comprehensive statewide agenda for improving labor-management relations in school districts across the state; and a focus in training programs for both teacher leaders and administrators on understanding strategies for labor-management collaboration and opportunities to learn new collaborative skills."[57]

State task force reports are notorious for recommending changes that never occur. But this one was different. Labor and management leaders began meeting immediately after the report's release to explore its recommendations. Two years later, the state leaders and their governing boards had agreed to cosponsor a California Labor Management Initiative, which was officially announced at a statewide symposium on labor-management collaboration in the spring of 2015. The state and school districts are implementing many other task force recommendations and, at the state level, policy makers have collaborated closely on implementation. Governor

Jerry Brown and the state legislature agreed to invest $1.25 billion in professional development on the Common Core State Standards, enacted a new school funding plan that gives more resources to students with the greatest needs, and suspended the state's high-stakes testing program to give educators time to make the transition to the Common Core assessments. With funding from philanthropic organizations in the state, the nonprofit group Californians Dedicated to Education Foundation (CDEF) has developed communication tools to help education leaders talk about Common Core with parents and community members. CDEF has also showcased district efforts to implement Common Core and provided an online forum called a Digital Chalkboard that enables California educators to share resources and collaborate about Common Core challenges.[58]

"[T]he Common Core standards in California are an engine to drive better educational practice, not a hammer to threaten children, educators, and schools with failure," Stanford education professor Linda Darling-Hammond and AFT President Randi Weingarten wrote approvingly for the *Huffington Post* in May of 2014. "This new path has been succeeding. In addition to registering the highest graduation rates in its history last year, at more than 80 percent, California had, between 2011 and 2013, the greatest growth it has ever had in student achievement on the National Assessment of Educational Progress, with gains three times larger than national averages in eighth-grade reading and math, far surpassing the improvements in most other states.

"At the end of the day," they added, "the path on which California has embarked is more likely to produce a truly accountable educational system—one that ensures all students experience engaging learning in supportive schools that help them pave a path to a productive future, not just another test."[59]

Engaging Teachers

California's success with Common Core begs an obvious question: why is this kind of collaboration between administrators and unions the exception, not the rule? Why, in all too many cases, must we see protests, threats, and boycotts before education officials will change course on misguided education policy?

To put it briefly, the education establishment (i.e., officials, policy makers, philanthropists, and much of the media) continues to believe that teachers should simply do what administrators and policy makers ask them. Teachers and their unions, which many believe care only about wages and job security, have no real place at the table where policies are made and implementation plans are charted. Clearly, the approach that excludes teachers and unions from these discussions has not worked with Common Core, and it became especially problematic in New York when parents joined the protests.

"I think Common Core is ultimately going to rise and fall on the commitment and engagement of teachers," said Jeffrey R. Henig, a professor of public policy and education at Columbia University's Teachers College. "And in that sense, I think it's cutting off your nose to spite your face to pursue a strategy of muscling this through without teacher support."[60]

Admittedly, some unions care only about the narrow interests of their members, and some have responded to education policies they don't like with extreme, sometimes untenable positions. But a growing body of evidence shows that when education officials set aside their preconceptions about unions and make genuine efforts to collaborate, unions at the national, state, and local levels are willing and able partners in creating good schools that serve all students well.

CHAPTER 3

Obstacles to Collaboration

Y OU MIGHT THINK, based on what you've read so far, that labor-management collaboration in education is spreading like wildfire. After all, it's had an extraordinary impact on student learning in districts like Montgomery County, Maryland; ABC Unified in Los Angeles County; and Cincinnati. The Education Department and leading national education organizations have cosponsored three well-attended national conferences on it, and the concept has received enthusiastic support over the past five years from the nation's leading union and management organizations.

Unfortunately, labor-management collaboration is growing far too slowly. "Success breeds success" may be a popular aphorism, but it doesn't always apply in real life—and surely not in education. All too often, the compelling success stories that we see in some schools and districts around the country are not trendsetters. Regarding labor-management collaboration in particular—and despite the growing interest in it—the number of national, state, and local leaders who have moved beyond rhetorical support and actually adopted this approach remains very small. Far too many educators don't recognize its potential.

In California, for instance, only about 4 percent of the state's roughly one thousand districts appeared to be pursuing collaborative partnerships in 2014.[1] And that's in a state with some of the nation's most successful district partnerships, which have received acclaim through the writings of educational researchers and presentations at national conferences. They include not only ABC Unified in Los Angeles but also San Juan Unified in Sacramento, Poway Unified near San Diego, and Green Dot Public Schools in Los Angeles.

In California, the proponents of labor-management collaboration have worked hard to expand it. For nearly a decade, CalTURN, the regional chapter of the Teacher Union Reform Network (TURN), has conducted biannual statewide conferences on collaboration that are open to all California districts. Meanwhile, ABC Unified has run the West Coast Labor Management Institute each year since 2009, inviting teams from other districts to watch ABC's educators engage in collaboration.

Now, finally, these efforts are starting to pay off. Leaders of California's management and labor organizations, along with the California Department of Education and support from two California-based foundations,[2] launched the California Labor Management Initiative at a two-day symposium on collaboration.[3] Over one hundred of the state's one thousand school districts signed up for the symposium, and most expressed strong interest in pursuing collaborative partnerships by the end of it.[4]

These recent developments provide important lessons about the dynamics of change, but several questions need to be addressed. Why did it take so long for California to reach this dramatic turning point? And why is labor-management collaboration rarely practiced in most other states? Unless we can pinpoint the obstacles to collaboration, we cannot develop effective strategies to overcome them.

The stakes are high. Labor-management collaboration is not just a good idea but is, in fact, a *sine qua non* of meaningful education change. If progress on collaboration slows or, worse, if administrators and teachers create partnerships that fail because they couldn't overcome the obstacles, then momentum behind this essential feature of education reform will stall, along with prospects for vastly improving the nation's schools.

The following six major obstacles are preventing labor-management collaboration from becoming the norm for America's educators:

Obstacle 1: Resistance to change

Obstacle 2: The myth of consensus

Obstacle 3: The myth of collusion

Obstacle 4: Skepticism about unions

Obstacle 5: A shortage of technical support

Obstacle 6: Misguided education policy

Let's take a closer look at each.

Obstacle 1: Resistance to Change

Real collaboration is about improvement, not just change. It's not simply about making people feel good about partaking in the conversation. It's about exploring new ideas and solving problems to create something better.

"Though we exalt [change] in principle, we oppose it in practice," organizational psychologist Robert Evans wrote in his book, *The Human Side of School Change*. "Most of us resist it whenever it comes upon us. We dislike alterations in even our smallest routines, such as the highway improvement detour on our route to work, for example, let alone in the larger aspects of our life and career, such as a major restructuring of our workplace."[5] Evans added, "Whatever we may think in the abstract about the need for change in other people's organizations, we usually look to our own for predictability."[6]

What about those who must endure the aggravations of chronically dysfunctional school systems? Wouldn't they embrace the prospects of a work environment in which healthy, supportive professional relationships were valued? You would think so, and education experts apparently think the same thing. "Indeed," Evans wrote, "many school reform proposals seem to assume that it is precisely because schools are such dispirited, ineffective institutions that fundamental change is not only necessary but welcome to teachers."[7]

Unfortunately, change is not always welcomed by teachers or their district leaders. "[P]eople get trapped by using patterns of behavior to protect themselves against threats to their self-esteem and confidence and to protect groups, intergroups, and organizations to which they belong against fundamental, disruptive change," Harvard organizational theorist Chris Argyris wrote. "As human beings become skillful in using this pattern of reasoning, they develop a defensive reasoning mind-set that they use to explain their actions and to design and implement future actions."[8]

The problem is that if education leaders resist change, they'll also resist collaboration. So, what is it about change that makes it so unappealing? Why do union and school leaders, in particular, settle for predictability, even when the status quo isn't working? The following factors play an important role.

A threat to leaders' identity and competence. Imagine that you're a tough, take-charge superintendent who's willing to confront the union if it stands in the way of your reform efforts. Then imagine how people would react if you had met with the local union president and decided that you wanted a collaborative partnership with the union. Community leaders who viewed the union negatively, some of your fellow administrators, and the board members who thought they knew what they were getting when they hired you might be skeptical, even hostile, to the idea. You'd undoubtedly be reluctant to move forward if you couldn't convince them that a collaborative partnership would bring real benefits. But even if you could, you might question your ability to pull it off, given your lack of experience with this approach. You would ask yourself any or all of the following questions: *How do I develop trust? How do I not get taken advantage of? How can we make decisions in a timely fashion? How do we resolve our differences? How do I persuade my senior staff and board members to take this leap of faith with me?*

Now imagine you're a tough-minded union leader facing the same decision. What would your fellow officers think? How would the teachers who elected you respond? Could you convince them of the advantages of collaboration over confrontation? Would you proceed if you couldn't?

These questions that superintendents and union leaders face pose very real obstacles to change, but they're not insurmountable. A number of superintendents and union leaders who were once bitter adversaries agreed to collaborate when they realized the futility of their present course. However, they had to convince others before they could move forward, and many of them had to get outside assistance to guide them through the transition.

Fear about loss of control. When leaders choose to collaborate, they often discover an interesting paradox. Relinquishing power and sharing decisions often give them more of what they wanted in the first place. For example, principals in Cincinnati's public schools used to have sole authority to select new teachers for their schools. After the district's management agreed to give schools more authority over educational decisions, teachers became part of the teacher selection process, which principals didn't like at first because they lost some of their authority. But the principals soon discovered that hiring committees were selecting excellent teachers who fit in well with the school culture. They also discovered that giving teachers a greater voice in other educational decisions improved morale and increased teacher retention rates even in the most challenging schools. Mary Ronan, Cincinnati's superintendent, and Julie Sellers, president of the Cincinnati Federation of Teachers, said this shift of power to the local schools played a key role in the district's dramatic improvement in student learning.[9]

Until leaders experience this phenomenon, however, collaboration and shared decision making can be threatening. Recall Christine Porath's findings cited in the previous chapter about organizational leaders. Of those she and her colleagues studied (albeit in noneducational settings), a significant number believe that treating their colleagues kindly diminishes their capacity to lead.[10] One of the best ways to overcome this misguided belief system is for district and union leaders to see it firsthand and speak with those who are doing it differently.

Fear of the unknown. Many of us enjoy the unpredictability of a good novel, but few of us feel the same about ambiguity in our workplaces. Collaboration promises to improve everything—policies, programs, funding, relationships, and the decision-making process. That's exhilarating to some but unsettling to reform-weary educators who have witnessed too many "promising" initiatives fail to fulfill the promises of their proponents. We should not dismiss these skeptics and their wariness about reform. We need to hear them out, and they need time to react to reform proposals—using the strategy *Go slow to go fast.*

Harder nuts to crack involve those who are not merely skeptical of something new, but who feel threatened by the possibility of change. "In business circles, this is known as the 'status quo trap:' the preference for everything to stay the same," wrote Margaret Heffernan in her book, *Willful Blindness.* "The gravitational pull of the status quo is strong—it feels easier and less risky, and it requires less mental and emotional energy, to 'leave well enough alone.'"[11]

In fact, collaboration *does* pose risks for those who have firm views or are stuck in their ways. Effective and authentic collaboration requires participants to open themselves up to new ways of framing and solving problems. To believe in collaboration, one must believe in the collective wisdom of the group and the power of vigorous debate.

Heightened accountability. Nobody likes working in a dysfunctional system, but you can tolerate it if you think others, not you, are to blame. When a school system struggles, labor and management can find comfort in blaming one another rather than taking responsibility for what's wrong. The desire to sidestep accountability and avoid blame, especially when facing rising pressures to perform, is a powerful hurdle that stands in the way of change.

The way out of this defensive reasoning is to shift the conversation from blame to reciprocal and shared responsibility. Each side can both hold the other accountable and hold *itself* accountable. That only happens in districts like Florida's Hillsborough County Public Schools, where labor and management see themselves as equal partners whose collective success depends on collaboration. Deputy Superintendent Dan Valdez, who speaks with union officials each day, said, "They hold our feet to the fire; conversely, we'll do the same for them. Sometimes, I will get a call, 'did you think this through carefully?' That probably means we didn't. This is never a negative."[12]

Lingering resentments. Change is a hard sell in districts where unions and management constantly battle. The wounds don't heal quickly. Even after they settle disputes, parties often leave dissatisfied with the compromises they've made. Leaders don't just make up and return to the business of creating great schools. Chicago's seven-day strike in 2012 by twenty-six thousand teachers is a case in point. Today, we see no signs of a rapprochement between the Chicago Teachers Union and the mayor's office that manages the district, nor evidence that the many reform efforts now underway will be implemented in ways that they will improve outcomes for the city's four hundred thousand students.

But that doesn't mean change—even the forming of a collaborative partnership—is impossible for educators who have been at war with one another. As you'll recall, protracted labor-management conflicts that culminated in teacher strikes then gave rise to partnerships in places like Montgomery County, Maryland, and Los Angeles. But as impressive as these partnerships are now, they required years to heal the wounds from earlier years. This may not occur in Chicago or other districts with similar issues unless board members, district leaders, community leaders, and parents in these districts insist on a different path.

All in all, labor-management collaboration is not merely a reform strategy. The features of deep and effective collaboration require a change in culture. And whether in education or any other realm, the components of culture—beliefs, attitudes, assumptions, and habits—don't change easily. But the cultural changes that I've witnessed in some districts give me hope for the future.

Obstacle 2: The Myth of Consensus

Experienced educators know that change never comes easily or painlessly. The problems are too complex and challenging to expect everyone to agree about how to solve them. But collaboration does not always require consensus, and the widespread view to the contrary has been a factor in preventing collaborative efforts from huge districts like New York City to tiny ones in rural Nebraska.

That misunderstanding is exemplified by some of the statements of education leaders that I've already highlighted—from Michelle Rhee ("If there is one thing I have learned over the last 15 months, it's that collaboration and consensus building are way overrated"[13]) and Joel Klein ("Collaboration is the elixir of the status-quo crowd"[14]). It's exemplified as well by a comment from the former superintendent of San Diego Unified, Alan Bersin, who said, "If you wait for consensus, reform won't happen."[15]

Collaboration, however, does not go hand-in-hand with consensus. Nor is the purpose of collaboration to nourish warm feelings among the players. "[C]ontrary to myth," Michael Fullan wrote, in an explanation of collaboration to which I subscribe, "effective collaborative cultures are not based on like-minded consensus. They value diversity because that is how they get different perspectives and access to ideas to address complex problems."[16] While consensus is a worthwhile goal, I recognize that confronting complex problems and promoting differences of opinion often heighten anxiety and conflict rather than reduce them. "Collaborative organizations fan the passion and emotions of its members because they so value commitment and the energy required to pursue complex goals,"[17] Fullan added. What makes collaborative cultures different is that they also value the quality of relationships. "Success is only possible if organizational members develop trust and compassion for each other. . . . If you understand the deep meaning of achieving diversity *and* community building, you avoid fatal mistakes."[18]

Collaborative partnerships like those in Montgomery County, Los Angeles, and Cincinnati have not avoided conflict; differences are common and emotions run high because the problems they face are extraordinarily challenging and messy. But the two sides retain confidence in their ability to manage conflict, and the cultural norms and expectations they've set preserve trust and usually allow leaders to work together until they find solutions. What leaders in these districts *don't* do when conflicts arise is resort to incivility and tactics that diminish trust. Progress continues in the face of differences. "We can argue and disagree and hopefully we come up with something better, but we don't hold grudges and we don't stop working together when this happens," Cincinnati superintendent Mary Ronan explained.[19]

To be sure, leadership like this is rare. That's true, in part, because education leaders across the country get very few opportunities to learn about effective collaboration. But it's also because, to a great extent, education leaders hold misconceptions about collaboration that dissuade them from trying it in the first place or sticking with it long enough to see it work.

Obstacle 3: The Myth of Collusion

In 2001, the Hartford, Connecticut, school district was considered a model of collaboration and successful reform. A year later, teachers became suspicious about the union's close relationship with management. After unseating union president Edwin Vargas, his successor, Tim Murphy, told the *Hartford Courant*, "I will not allow what happened to Ed Vargas to happen to me."[20]

The Hartford experience reflects concerns by both administrators and teachers, which have only grown in recent years, that labor-management collaboration inevitably leads to collusion. "You don't have to be a conspiracy theorist to wonder whether collective bargaining in education hasn't become something more like collusion," Frederick Hess and Martin West wrote in 2006, citing the decline in labor unrest and rise in collective bargaining agreements that, in their view, favored teachers' interests over students as evidence that school boards are essentially colluding with unions.[21] Hess and West argued that calls for collaboration only fuel collusion, writing,

"Superintendents in cities like San Diego, Milwaukee, and Houston have reported being urged by civic officials, business leaders, and philanthropists to seek 'consensus' and to 'partner' with the local union."

Hess and West oppose collaboration and collective bargaining because they think teacher unions don't have the best interests of children in mind. "[W]e should not expect unions at the bargaining table to be for anything but their own interests," they wrote. "Naturally enough, those interests favor existing arrangements, which protect jobs; limit the demands placed on members, including their accountability for student performance; and safeguard the privileges of senior teachers."[22]

Some teachers and union activists, meanwhile, worry that collaborative union leaders will inevitably collude with management and betray the teachers they represent. All collaborative union leaders face this balancing act—maintaining a trusting relationship with management, while assuring teachers that they will also protect their interests.

Steve Smith, the union leader in Providence, Rhode Island, faced this scenario a few years ago when he began collaborating with Tom Brady, Rhode Island's superintendent, after the two of them heard about successful labor-management partnerships around the country. Among the initiatives on which they worked together, Smith and Brady helped create a management organization called the United Providence (or UP!) Compact to oversee reform efforts of the district's lowest performing schools. But as their partnership emerged, Smith (and Brady) faced charges that they were giving away too much. "My membership felt I gave up seniority," Smith recalled. "And then I had other union leaders saying, you know, 'What the hell are you doing?' You know, Race to the Top became, oh, 'This is Steve just caving in, and it's gonna affect all of us.' That's constantly being used, even when we get into the pension reform—any issue, it's used." Speaking about the challenge that collaboration posed for himself and Brady, Smith said, "I think we both had that same risk. When you get [away from] what people expect—this is what a union president should be doing; this is what a superintendent should be doing—you get pushback. And if you go too far, you're no longer a leader; you're a crazy man."[23]

I recognize the skepticism among administrators and teachers across the country and, frankly, I agree that collaboration *can* lead to collusion. I fervently disagree, however, that collaboration *invariably* leads to collusion. There are far too many examples of labor-management collaboration in which both sides argue doggedly for their positions, compromise when necessary, and work in close concert to improve the quality of education of their students.

Hess and West do not believe that any unions push for policies that benefit students. They believe, instead, that unions inherently oppose change, and they cite examples in which unions have vigorously opposed reforms such as teacher evaluations and compensation tied to student test scores. Unions, like management, sometimes resist change, but it's wrong to assume that any time a union resists a *particular* call for change that it opposes change in general.

Indeed, the collaborative districts highlighted in the previous chapter and elsewhere have been at the forefront of programs that strengthen the teaching profession and have clear benefits for students. They include Montgomery County's Professional Growth System that strengthens teachers' pedagogical skills; the New Haven School Change Initiative that generated a comprehensive new teacher evaluation tool that has become a national model; the peer assistance and review (PAR) programs that cultivate good teaching, help struggling teachers improve, and remove those who don't; and wrap-around health and social service programs that assist students and families living in poverty.

In Springfield, Massachusetts, then-superintendent Alan Ingram appointed Timothy Collins, the district's union president, and Nancy de Prosse, a Massachusetts Teachers Association field representative, to the district's instructional leadership team (ILT). "Not everyone agreed with the decision," according to a Rennie Center case study.[24] "Ingram received criticism from some of his senior cabinet members. 'My staff thought I had lost my mind,' Ingram remembered, 'they said to me, you're going to bring him [Collins] into our meetings, where we decide what goes on in schools. What are you thinking?'"

Ingram apparently knew what he was thinking because "the ILT eventually transformed into a powerful, decision-making committee," according to the Rennie Center report. Ingram's decision to invite Collins to participate on the ILT was almost certainly influenced by the kind of leader he found in Collins, who had said publicly, "The basic idea is for teachers to stop being the objects of reform and start being the architects of reform."[25]

Hess and West and other union critics also fail to recognize that when unions advocate for decent wages, benefits, and classroom conditions that support learning, this, too, can benefit students. These tangible supports, absent in too many parts of the country, attract good candidates to the profession and prevent accomplished teachers from leaving. A weak profession is unattractive to teachers, and it's certainly not good for students.

Obstacle 4: Skepticism About Unions

Across the education sector, many leaders and experts do not see a role for teacher unions in education reform. They think the unions should stick to what they do best—advocate for their members' economic and job security—and let local administrators, state and national education officials, and others make the key decisions about educational policy. These union skeptics include conservatives and some liberals, and they include administrators and even some teachers themselves.

"[T]he highest barrier to the engagement of teachers in education reform comes from conservatives who believe that teacher unions shouldn't be involved in substantive decisions about the direction of school reform," Charles Taylor Kerchner wrote a number of years ago. "They see union involvement as an unwarranted labor intrusion into the rightful domains of school managers, school boards, or legislatures. They urge further restrictions on the scope of collective bargaining and generally seek to organize education reform around, rather than with, teacher unions."[26]

That superintendents and school board members hesitate to embrace a collaborative relationship with unions—one that gives teachers more say in shaping educational decisions—should surprise no one. For one thing, few people relinquish power voluntarily. For another, the more that superintendents and board members believe unions care only about their members, the more reluctant they'd be to embrace collaboration. As Kerchner put it, "[Union] leaders espouse values that frequently differ from those of school managers and board members. Management's adage that the shortest contract is the best one is a comfortable path. Why, after all, spend time dealing with people with whom one disagrees? Why give them the privilege of having a speaking part in the drama of school reform?"[27]

What's more surprising, however, is that resistance to a union role in education policy also comes from within some unions and from some teachers. In a 2007 survey of teachers by Education Sector, 52 percent agreed that "teachers unions or associations should mostly stick to traditional union issues such as protecting teachers' salaries, benefits, and jobs." Only 32 percent said they should "put more focus than they currently do on issues such as improving teacher quality and student achievement."[28] "There is substantial opposition," Kerchner wrote, "within unions themselves and within the ranks of teachers to the idea of teaching as a self-policing profession. Most teachers are not accustomed to judging their colleagues' performance or their fitness to remain as teachers."[29]

Union leaders in Sacramento's San Juan Unified School District found exactly this situation when they began exploring peer assistance and review programs. The San Juan Teachers Association eventually supported PAR, which is now a model program, but teachers were skeptical at first. "It was a difficult thing for some of my executive board in the beginning to believe that, as teachers, we had a responsibility to help evaluate teachers and provide them with assistance," the local union president, Steve Duditch, recalled. (Not surprisingly, San Juan Unified's administrators also resisted, Duditch said, because they did not want to relinquish power by including teachers in the evaluation process.)[30]

Fortunately, across the nation, management and unions are increasingly warming to the idea of labor-management partnerships. When Education Sector repeated its teacher survey in 2011, the percentage that thought unions should "stick to traditional issues" dropped from 52 to 42 percent, and the percentage indicating that unions should focus more on teacher quality and student achievement jumped from 32 to 43 percent.[31]

Nevertheless, we have much more work to do if we hope to convince many more administrators and teachers. Despite the improving numbers, the fact remains that fewer than half of teachers surveyed in 2011 believe that unions should focus more on teacher quality and student achievement. At the same time, many politicians and pundits continue to view teacher unions, and the policies they defend like tenure and seniority, as enemies of change. As long as these antiunion sentiments persist, unions will more likely devote more of their time, money, and energy to defending themselves than building capacity and promoting collaboration.

Meanwhile, school managers and education officials have a choice. They can adopt the antiunion narrative, push reforms without union support, and fight bitter battles with the unions along the way. If so, however, they should admit to the students, parents, and community members they serve that they lack any evidence that this adversarial approach has worked anywhere to improve teacher quality and student achievement. Or they can acknowledge the accomplishments produced by labor-management partnerships, stomach the inevitable criticisms from antiunion skeptics, and commit fully to a collaborative approach that has a real chance of working.

Obstacle 5: A Shortage of Technical Support

Collaboration doesn't happen just because management and unions accept the premise that they'll benefit by working together. Collaboration is challenging, especially when educators have spent their entire careers operating within an adversarial paradigm that eschews it. Collaboration requires significant investments in time, and many who have succeeded with it have received help from outside experts and built on it by communicating regularly with collaborative educators in other districts.

Some educators are understandably reluctant to try collaboration because they really don't know where to begin. Many who try it struggle or give up because they don't understand the process. Since collaboration hasn't been part of the culture of America's public schools, leadership development programs have not focused on the knowledge and technical skills required to do it well. A few universities offer professional development programs on aspects of collaboration, such as interest-based bargaining, but on-the-ground technical assistance is hard to come by. Education leaders who decide to embark on a collaborative path must fend for themselves.

Chapters 4 and 5 outline the strategies for management and labor leaders to pursue and the tactics to apply in order to build successful partnerships that will produce real results.

Obstacle 6: Misguided Education Policy

"To many American teachers," Dana Goldstein wrote in *The Teacher Wars: A History of America's Most Embattled Profession*, "the last decade of value-added school reform has felt like something imposed on them from outside and from above—by politicians with little expertise in teaching and learning, by corporate philanthropists who long to remake education in the mold of the business world, and by economists who see teaching as less of an art than a science."[32]

I previously argued that the benefits of collaborative partnerships—as powerful as they might be—cannot overcome other factors such as poverty and inadequate school funding. Inadequate funding—sometimes due to a struggling economy but more often due to misguided policy—also has a direct negative effect on collaboration. Labor and management essentially wind up fighting over crumbs, needlessly forcing both sides to resolve complex moral and practical dilemmas. Spend too much on teacher salaries and benefits, and not enough is left for facilities, books, technology, and other essential items that affect student learning. Spend too little on teachers, and districts find it increasingly difficult to attract and retain good ones—which, of course, has profound negative effects on students.

Even when schools are adequately funded, collaboration can occur only when the parties involved have something to collaborate about. When policy makers and education officials have already established the reform agenda, educators on the front lines understandably question the point of collaboration. In response, they often resist the agenda because they weren't invited to participate on the front end or because they simply oppose the policies. "[I]n many cases," researchers Nina Bascia and Pamela Osmond found, "the success of partnerships has been limited by the influence of fragmented, externally mandated reforms that operate in direct opposition to the collaborative goals laid out by the partnership. . . . In extreme instances, the presence of imposed school district or state requirements has actually taken over the partnership, sidelining the original purpose and becoming the new focus."[33]

Few policy initiatives have done more to thwart union-management partnerships than the No Child Left Behind (NCLB) Act of 2001, which imposed increasingly severe sanctions on the nation's lowest performing schools. Some educators, fearing their schools could be shut or converted to charter schools if their test scores didn't rise, undoubtedly thought, "Let's do whatever it takes to meet the standards." Other educators recognized that because policy makers set NCLB's goals too high and made the sanctions for not meeting them too severe, they could neither realistically meet the standards nor pursue them without compromising their values.

As NCLB's critics predicted, nearly all schools eventually would be labeled as "failing" under its strictures. In addition, NCLB's requirements would prompt teachers to "teach to the test," teachers and students to cheat, and schools to narrow their curriculum to the subjects for which NCLB would test. Even US Department of Education Secretary Arne Duncan had harsh words for the policy he inherited and was required to enforce. In 2011, he told Congress that NCLB was "fundamentally broken," "has created a dozen ways for schools to fail," and "has created very few ways to help them to succeed."[34]

As stakeholders fought to reach the unachievable goals, management and labor blamed each other more and trusted each other less. "Rather than supporting my efforts to improve student achievement, the law's unreasonable mandates and dependence on punishment are among my largest obstacles," said Carl Cohn when he was superintendent of San Diego Unified in 2007. Educators who dare to criticize the practical flaws of NCLB are, according to Cohn, "attacked as pro-union or anti-accountability and criticized for placing the needs of adults ahead of the needs of children." "In San Diego," Cohn noted, "it produced a climate of conflict that is only now beginning to improve."[35]

NCLB remains in effect and it continues to generate unnecessary tension between labor and management because the president and Congress haven't adopted better and more comprehensive education policies to replace it.

Nor did Race to the Top, an Obama Administration reform strategy, help matters. Rather than wield a "stick" to improve school performance, as NCLB did, Race to the Top offered a carrot in the form of significant funding to states that adopted federally mandated reform strategies. But like NCLB, it, too, has proven a divisive strategy, with a corrosive effect on collaboration. For the small number of states that won Race to the Top money, the most divisive element was a requirement that districts adopt new teacher and principal evaluation systems tied to student test scores.

Education officials believed the requirement would enable districts to better hold ineffective teachers accountable. Many districts began using complex value-added models (VAM), which some researchers claimed accurately reflected a teacher's impact on learning, having adjusted it for individual students' characteristics (e.g., whether they're English language learners or special needs students or impoverished). Other researchers have discovered serious flaws in VAM, concluding that it was not sound for measuring individual teacher effectiveness.

"The strategy of using value-added methods to calculate student test score gains attached to individual teachers has been found to be far less reliable and accurate than many researchers had hoped," Stanford's Linda Darling-Hammond wrote in 2013 in *Getting Teacher Evaluation Right*.[36] Conservative educators have largely supported the use of tests for teacher evaluation, but some, like Chester Finn, President Reagan's Assistant Secretary of Education, have expressed doubts. "We'll probably discover ten years from now you can't do truly quantitative achievement-based evaluation of teachers with any great reliability."[37]

Due to these controversies, education leaders in many states argued over whether to apply for Race to the Top funds. Tensions between unions, management, and education officials grew in many states that received funds. Nowhere was the negative resistance stronger than in New York. There, unions protested vehemently against the use of test scores for evaluating them because teachers were just then implementing the new Common Core State Standards. Nor, rightly, did the unions think it fair to evaluate teachers with a new test and new curriculum when they had not received any professional development to help them use the new standards.

The two national teacher unions were early supporters of Common Core, largely because they played some (albeit minor) role in its development. But when the time came to address educator development, testing, accountability, and other implementation issues, unions were largely left out, probably because education officials assumed they'd oppose testing and accountability. Now, with waning support from teacher unions and fierce opposition from teachers, parents, and even conservatives who view Common Core as government overreach, the future of national standards is very much in doubt.

What's true at the national level is sometimes also true in states and localities. Those with authority over curriculum, scheduling, professional development, and many other policies affecting instruction should think carefully about how their unilateral decisions will affect trust and teacher attitudes about the policies that emerge. The rationale for proceeding without collaboration and buy-in sometimes rests on a sense of urgency among policy makers about the need for change, the belief that "reform can't wait for consensus," as former San Diego Superintendent Alan Bersin put it. Too often, I suspect, the motivations are less noble—rooted in the belief of policy makers and school managers that they know better than teachers. Either way, without a critical mass of support from teachers, successful and sustainable reform has never materialized.

Even when administrators and unions collaborate, and when they adopt good policies, the policies can fail because the implementation is poor for any one of numerous reasons. For instance, administrators and unions spend too little time building support for them, they don't do enough professional development, and they plan inadequately. Poorly implemented initiatives don't just fail; they often also bring harmful side effects. People abandon what might be a good idea because they mistakenly conclude that the idea itself was defective, not the implementation. The failure, in turn, hurts relationships and threatens collaboration, especially when the pressure to perform and the consequences for failure are high. People point fingers; conversations grow coarse; cynicism replaces optimism; and many simply retreat to their own worlds, abandoning their hopes for collaboration.

Fortunately, we know a lot more about how to pursue effective implementation. When we apply what we know, we can significantly improve the prospects of success for new initiatives, thus avoiding the negative fallout from failure that damages relationships and thwarts collaboration.

CHAPTER 4

Cultivating Collaboration, Part I: Strategies

COLLABORATIVE DISTRICT and union leaders do not just talk a good game. They lead by example, investing the time and effort to build the relationships that make a real difference for their organization and for students.

Most school boards that are committed to collaboration hire superintendents who understand the power of partnerships and have the skills to collaborate effectively. Teachers who are similarly committed to collaboration elect the same kind of union leaders. These district and union leaders often adopt joint vision statements that reflect their commitment to trust, respect, and collaboration; translate those statements into actionable policies and practices to improve teaching and learning; create formal structures to support collaboration; and devote the necessary time to maintain strong professional relationships.

These accomplishments represent no small feat because district and union leaders work under extraordinary pressures just to conduct their day-to-day operations. They invest in collaboration over the long term, however, because they understand that they can't create and sustain successful educational programs, solve problems, and have the same impact on students without it.

The very real obstacles to collaboration explain why collaborative partnerships often emerge only after relations between a union and management have hit rock bottom—just after a strike or a particularly bitter contract negotiation. That's often when leaders recognize that their adversarial relationships do not serve anyone's interests, including the students they are trying to serve in the first place. But given the advantages—indeed the necessity—of collaboration, union-management relations should not have to hit rock bottom before the two sides seek collaboration.

This chapter and the next describe how educators of all kinds—school boards and superintendents, union leaders and teachers, community leaders and parents, state and local education organizations—can engage in real, tangible, effective collaboration. This chapter outlines the broad "strategies" they can undertake; the next details the "tactics" they can pursue to bring those strategies to life.

I offer the following six strategies for educators:

- *Strategy 1*: Develop new mindsets.
- *Strategy 2*: Develop the capacity for collaboration.
- *Strategy 3*: Go slow to go fast.
- *Strategy 4*: Build trust through better relationships.
- *Strategy 5*: Pursue sound education policy.
- *Strategy 6*: Bargain better.

Let's take a closer look.

Strategy 1: Develop New Mindsets

Most education reform initiatives promote new practices and policies. They might be different academic standards, for example, or better professional development for teachers, or more reliable assessments of student learning. Labor-management collaboration begins with something different: with the reformers themselves changing their mindsets. Leaders committed to collaboration should be willing to view themselves differently, to view leadership differently, and to view their relationships with other stakeholders differently. First and foremost, leaders must come to grips with the evidence pointing to the costs of incivility and the misguided assumptions about the virtues of mean-spirited leadership. As researchers Christine Porath and Christine Pearson have shown, this kind of leadership diminishes creativity, performance, and a sense of team spirit, all vital in a productive workplace.[1]

This task is not easy or comfortable, especially for strong leaders. As individuals, we find it reassuring to cling to our beliefs, for they help us navigate the world. That's why we admire those with strong convictions and we dislike those who are wishy-washy or who make decisions simply to win the approval of others. But strong convictions become a liability for leaders when they hold them so strongly that they stop learning, ignore opposing views, and refuse to reexamine their perceptions of others and their motivations for their own actions. Baseless convictions give rise to bias and prejudice.

Fixed, defensive mindsets are all too common in educational settings. They explain why some superintendents and school board members cast unions as greedy and self-serving, and why some union officials cast management as autocratic and exploitive. In a perverse way, however, educators with fixed views have an incentive to maneuver their adversaries into doing exactly what they, the educators, don't want. The more outrageous that their opponents' actions are, the more they can make the case that "*they, not we,*" are the culprits. "*They,* not *we,*" are the ones who must change. But in the end, these comforting mindsets are just a trap.

All successful change begins with an openness to the possibility of change, to something new and better, to what Stanford researcher Carol Dweck calls a *growth mindset.*[2] Labor-management collaboration is possible only when leaders on both sides believe that their counterparts can become trusted partners in creating good schools for students. "Leadership and organizations are best changed by asking those involved to dream and envision what might be, to dialogue about what can be, and to construct what will be," said Harvard's Chris Argyris. "The focus is on fresh perceptions and the acquisitions of new schemes that invite experimentation to overcome the rigidity created by organizational defensive routines."[3]

The key to cultivating an openness to the possibilities is convincing both labor and management to weigh the benefits of the present arrangement against the potential benefits (and risks) of something different. The three recent national conferences showcasing successful labor-management partnerships have done just that. Of the 150 labor-management teams that attended the first conference (with another hundred turned away due to space constraints), 85 percent reported that they found the experience useful. Attendees were especially pleased with the presentations by the twelve districts that the conference highlighted, and 72 percent said their team left with a plan for how to proceed.[4]

These conferences, however, did not provide any ongoing guidance or support for the teams that returned home in the hopes of implementing effective partnerships. Consequently, only 51 percent of those surveyed a year after the conference reported that they were making progress on the plans they'd made at the conference. Upon returning home, some teams undoubtedly rushed headlong into a new collaborative arrangement that people didn't understand and weren't ready to support—which brings us to our next guiding principle.

Strategy 2: Develop the Capacity for Collaboration

Successful partnerships do not happen just because management and labor leaders agree to collaborate. Yes, collaboration is a mindset. But it's also a skill. So, the leaders on both sides should commit to learning *how* to collaborate effectively. Furthermore, they should ensure that all of their key colleagues—union officers and site representatives, school board members, district administrators, principals, teachers, and parents—have an opportunity to develop these skills.

"Companies are beginning to recognize that the ability to build and maintain relationships is an essential set of skills," James W. Tamm and Ronald J. Luyet wrote with regard to collaboration in the private sector. "They recognize that the collective capital of their employees, which is the collective ability of their employees to build effective collaborative relationships, is as important as their intellectual capital and their financial capital."[5]

Educators in collaborative school districts have discovered the same thing. Administrators and union leaders in California's San Juan Unified School District have sustained their longstanding partnership by participating regularly in learning activities focused on collaboration. Management and union representatives who sit across the table from one another during contract negotiations jointly participate in training for what's known as interest-based bargaining (a concept described more fully later in this chapter). The district also uses outside facilitators to deepen management and labor leaders' knowledge about collaboration and to help them work through tough issues like budget allocations, teacher evaluation, and peer assistance and review (PAR) programs. When teachers and administrators at one of San Juan Unified's struggling high schools decided to rethink virtually everything about school operations, they hired a consulting firm that specializes in organizational transformations.[6]

Another California district, ABC Unified of southeastern Los Angeles, runs its own professional learning process to deepen knowledge about collaboration. In the early stages of the district's labor-management partnership, administrators and union leaders attended a weeklong seminar at Harvard on labor-management collaboration. The district also runs an annual retreat on collaboration for administrators and union leaders, and its seven-member board of trustees also holds a retreat each year. ABC's efforts to develop the skills to collaborate extend far beyond the district office, however. Each year, the district provides professional development on collaboration for all of its new school principals, facilitated by other district principals who have been exceptionally successful in collaborating with teachers and union representatives.

Likewise, the union provides regular professional development and support on collaboration to all of its officers and site representatives. The union and administrators also conduct an annual two-day labor-management institute for visiting teams of district and union leaders. The teams watch ABC leaders collaborate on pending issues and receive assistance from them as those teams take steps to collaborate themselves. The institutes have jump-started a number of collaborative partnerships in other districts, and they have strengthened ABC's own commitment to collaboration.

Collaborative districts sustain and strengthen their partnerships by networking with other like-minded district leaders. Many participate in regional conferences held by the Teacher Union Reform Network (TURN).[7] Others receive support from organizations such as the Massachusetts Education Partnership (MEP), the Consortium for Educational Change (CEC)[8] in Chicago, and the NEA Foundation in Washington, DC.[9] MEP's District Capacity Project (DCP), which it launched in 2012, conducts biannual Capacity Institutes to help district and state education leaders expand their knowledge of collaboration.[10] The NEA Foundation supports districts through its Institute for Innovation in Teaching and Learning, as district leaders focus on a single issue for two years with the assistance of a dedicated coach and other leaders who can strengthen the collaborative process.

Some districts receive extensive onsite assistance from experienced facilitators who help leaders build their collaborative capacity and apply what they've learned to key district initiatives such as peer assistance and review programs, early learning and literacy initiatives, Common Core State Standards implementation, and expanded learning time.[11] In fact, WestEd, the educational service organization with which I was affiliated until 2014, analyzed fifty-five case studies of labor-management collaboration and found that nearly half of the districts involved relied on outside assistance to jump-start their partnerships. That's not surprising; during the initial transition phase from confrontation to collaboration, labor and management may feel more comfortable working with a neutral third-party whose only agenda is to promote collaboration instead of working directly with one another.[12]

Strategy 3: Go Slow to Go Fast

Politicians and education leaders like to proclaim the urgent need for educational change and often receive praise for their impatience. Christopher Emigholz, the New Jersey Business and Industry Association's Director of Education Affairs, wrote approvingly in 2010 that New Jersey Governor Chris Christie "has advocated for real accountability for educational performance and outcomes, so that teachers and administrators in failing schools will have to change."[13] The only reason that Christie's "urgent solutions to [New Jersey's] urgent problems" wouldn't work, Emigholz added, is that educators are hopelessly resistant to change.

But Christie's seemingly sensible approach points up a problem that most well-intended reformers miss: the "pedal to the metal" approach is not the way to solve urgent problems. In fact, it often does more harm than good. In their study of 343 businesses, organizational researchers Jocelyn R. Davis and Tom Atkinson found that high performers consistently "slowed down to speed up." They became "more open to ideas and discussion. They encouraged innovative thinking. And they allowed time to reflect and learn. By contrast, performance suffered at firms that moved fast all the time, focused too much on maximizing efficiency, stuck to tested methods, didn't foster employee collaboration, and weren't overly concerned about alignment."[14]

One advantage of collaboration over a top-down approach is that it provides time, space, and safety to explore new ideas before educators adopt them. It enables groups to fully evaluate ideas, weed out bad ones, and develop support for the ones that educators adopt. Unless educators develop their collaborative partnerships in the same way, taking the necessary time rather than rushing to put them in place, the partnerships won't likely take hold.

As I've mentioned, many teams that left the national labor-management conferences were convinced that collaboration was *exactly* the approach they should take in their district, only to receive a cool reception from colleagues upon their return. That's a common trap for overzealous leaders; they forget that their colleagues didn't attend the conference and, thus, didn't experience what they did. For those who didn't attend, reading materials after the fact isn't the same as listening to presentations, asking tough questions, and processing information on the spot.

Moreover, collaboration can't be imposed from the outside. The parties involved should propose it themselves. As James W. Tamm and Ronald J. Luyet wrote about efforts to promote collaboration in the business world, "[Collaboration] can't be mandated, and attempts to do so will inevitably lead to either outright rebellion or passive-aggressive undermining behavior."[15] They added, "Collaborative strategies . . . are not simply another business strategy that can be imposed like a new cost-accounting scheme. Many companies learned this the hard way when they tried to create teams without first teaching employees the skills necessary for effective teamwork."[16]

The benefits of a patient, home-grown approach to collaboration come to life in the experience of Springfield, Massachusetts, the state's second largest school district. There, Superintendent Joseph Burke and Union President Timothy Collins (with support from the Rennie Center) had been meeting privately for months, even while labor and management battled to produce a union contract in 2007 that didn't thrill anyone. Through those private conversations, they eventually forged a Joint Labor-Management Initiative that was led by a seven-member team of district and union leaders. With ongoing facilitation from the Rennie Center, the team spent the first eighteen months cultivating collaborative relations and defining the characteristics of a successful school. They conducted a comprehensive districtwide survey about the changes needed to create successful schools. In 2007, the team released a report that provided a vision of successful schools and a set of objectives for stakeholders that included administrators, teachers, parents, and students.

By 2012, the district's culture had been transformed. Signs of collaboration were everywhere, and it was having a positive effect on student learning. "Union and district leaders present together to teachers, principals, and the school committee, and support each other on potentially controversial issues," the Rennie Center reported. "The district-union collaboration is building community and business partnerships, expanding family engagement programming, and supporting school-based instructional leadership and shared decision-making."

The impact on student achievement indicated that the partnership was working. "[S]ince 2008," the Rennie Center revealed, "the percentage of Springfield students proficient or above on the English language arts state test was up seven points; math increased by two points. In high school, the percentage of tenth grade students proficient or above in math and English language arts increased four and fourteen points, respectively, during the same period."[17] The dramatic cultural change was years in the making, and it continues to require constant attention.

Strategy 4: Build Trust Through Better Relationships

None of us likes working with people we can't trust. It saps our energy, makes us cynical, and prevents us from reaching our goals. Many people flee from these situations, while others learn to cope and dismiss the possibility of change because they assume that others won't change.

Without trust, though, collaboration is impossible, according to organizational researchers Ken Blanchard, Cynthia Olmstead, and Martha Lawrence. Without trust, they wrote, "people bail on relationships and leave organizations, cynicism reigns, progress grinds to a halt, and self-interest trumps the common good. For organizations to thrive, trust is not a nice-to-have; it's a must-have."[18]

Many collaborative districts choose collaboration only after bitter and protracted conflicts. But leaders on all sides can choose collaboration *before* they hit rock bottom by mustering the courage to pursue an alternative path that calls for trust. I served as a facilitator and witnessed dramatic turnarounds in relationships in which trust was missing. Here's the story of one of them.

Several years ago, my colleagues at WestEd and I were hired to help turn around several struggling schools in California's Central Valley, which runs from north of Sacramento to south of Fresno. Over 90 percent of students at these schools were minority, over 85 percent were from poor families, and over a quarter were English language learners. Administrators and teachers were pressed to improve student performance or face the risk that their schools would close or that a new set of administrators and teachers would replace them. Staff turnover was high, relations between principals and union representatives were tense, and trust among the various relevant parties, including parents, was virtually nonexistent. Anyone could sense the frustration, the anxiety, and the loss of hope by walking around the school or spending time in the teachers' lounge. Only a fifth of staff agreed that "our school is a supportive and inviting place to work," based on surveys.

Teachers and administrators agreed on almost nothing except this: they hated the situation. While some enjoyed working with children in the confines of their classroom, life in the schools was barely tolerable. Due to their intense dissatisfaction, teachers and administrators volunteered to meet with WestEd after school, on their own time, to explore solutions. Teachers and administrators knew that they couldn't improve student learning until they established a foundation of trust with one another. They allowed WestEd to facilitate these conversations because, after several months, the partner agency had built trusting relationships with them—by learning about their schools and offering help to those who sought it.

WestEd began the after-school sessions by asking teachers and administrators to reflect on the reasons they entered the teaching profession. These responses were typical:

"Because I wanted to pass on my love for learning to my students."
"Because I wanted to make a difference in my community."
"Because I thought I could reach children and wanted to make sure they realized their potential."

Sadly, almost none of the teachers and administrators thought they were achieving their goals. "So, what are you accomplishing?" WestEd asked. "Have your goals changed?" One teacher replied, "I don't know that I have any goals anymore other than getting through the day and keeping my sanity."

WestEd then shifted the focus to the future and asked the educators to identify the values they thought should guide their work as colleagues. Frequently, they said honesty, integrity, transparency, humor, forgiveness, and mutual support. The value that they mentioned most often, however, was *trust*.

WestEd then guided the educators on hand to make two lists: one with actions that *support* their values and the second with actions that *harm* them. Supportive actions typically included listening without judgment, fulfilling commitments, addressing problems early and optimistically, sharing skills and knowledge, assuming positive intent from others, seeking assistance, and speaking truthfully. Actions that harm collaboration typically included speaking disparagingly about colleagues, parents, or children; gossiping; withholding important information; complaining without offering to find solutions; and ignoring interpersonal or professional problems.

After a discussion about how these actions manifested themselves, each participant was asked whether he or she would make a good-faith effort to uphold the group's collective values—to pursue the supportive actions on the lists and to avoid the harmful ones. Virtually every teacher and every administrator in each school offered a public commitment to do so.

In all of the educational settings in which WestEd has used this approach, participants have come together this way. That shows how energized people can become, whether in California's Central Valley or anywhere else, by the prospect of better professional relationships.

Strategy 5: Pursue Sound Education Policy

A key obstacle to collaboration is federal, state, and district-level education policy that's overly prescriptive, misguided, or poorly implemented. Administrators and unions should create wise policy at the district level, and they should encourage federal and state policy makers to do the same.

What would wise education policy look like? For starters, it would focus more on capacity building and less on accountability. For the past several decades, US education policy has largely revolved around accountability, driven by a belief that carrots and sticks are the best levers of reform. But, as educational change theorist Michael Fullan observed, "no system in the world has ever achieved whole system reform by leading with accountability." An international study of twenty improving educational systems, which Fullan cited, found that capacity building, not accountability measures, has been the primary driver of improved student outcomes. "Whole system success," he continued, "requires the commitment that comes from intrinsic motivation and improved technical competencies of groups of educators working together purposefully and relentlessly."[19]

Specifically, countries such as Finland and Singapore have produced dramatic improvements in their education systems by

- investing heavily in preparing beginning teachers and providing ongoing professional development for veterans;
- attracting and retaining accomplished educators by offering competitive salaries and ensuring high-quality teaching conditions—for example, well-maintained facilities, reasonable class sizes, time to

plan and collaborate, and access to learning materials and technology; and

- designing educator evaluation systems to help all teachers improve, not just to remove the struggling ones.

Accountability remains an important part of reform, Fullan said, but "[s]trange as it sounds, leading with accountability is not the best way to get accountability, let alone whole system reform."[20] In other words, school systems will likely benefit more by giving educators what they need to succeed. Unions, in particular, are likelier to participate in the accountability conversation if they're not spending most of their time fighting for adequate teaching conditions.

One way schools and districts can prioritize capacity building while retaining accountability is through peer assistance and review programs. They build capacity through the intensive support that struggling teachers receive from accomplished colleagues. Many teachers who enroll in PAR programs get better. But when they don't get better—whether they're beginning teachers or veterans with tenure—they're held accountable.[21] Many leave their positions voluntarily, whereas others are let go, often without costly proceedings. PAR programs are an excellent way to boost teacher quality, ensure teacher accountability, and avoid contentious and distracting debates over tenure.

PAR programs have other potential benefits. "PAR can introduce and promote a new set of norms and responsibilities among all teachers, gradually changing and strengthening the professional culture of teaching in the schools and district," Harvard researcher Susan Moore Johnson and her colleagues observed. "Thus, PAR is not simply about assisting and assessing individuals, but also about building a more effective organization in which professional learning is valued and supported.

"The process of jointly developing PAR," they continued, "also can lead the way to a more collaborative labor management relationship. Increasingly, districts find that adversarial confrontations over rights and resources undermine the work of teachers, the experience of students, and the success of the schools. Jointly planning and implementing PAR can help union leaders and administrators bridge the traditional labor-management divide."[22]

Districts cannot implement successful PAR programs on the cheap, however. Most importantly, they will need to select, develop, and pay for the consulting teachers who set aside their normal teaching assignments to help their colleagues.

When it comes to federal and state education policy, teachers and their unions should seek a seat at the table, and policy makers would be wise to give them one. Too often, officials who set education policy have little expertise in education, and they work in settings that are far from the schools where educators must implement it. To be sure, policy makers and teachers may not always reach consensus about policy. Nevertheless, the chance that such policy will achieve its goal will rise significantly if educators have the chance to shape it.

Once again, those who are skeptical about giving teachers and unions a greater role in shaping education policy, who believe that teachers and unions will only protect their own interests rather than consider the broader goals of education policy, should consider the counterevidence—the growing number of highly collaborative partnerships in districts around the country (and in other countries like Finland and Singapore) where unions have been at the leading edge of successful change efforts. To date, education policy makers and administrators have done little to promote labor-management collaboration. Were they to trust teachers and unions more, were they to invite them to the policy-making table, the payoffs could be substantial.

Teachers and unions can play important roles in ensuring that districts and schools implement education policy effectively. They can help ensure that, when policy makers and administrators develop education policy, they don't underestimate what it really takes to turn good ideas at the policy table into effective practices in schools. They can help ensure that districts and schools pick the right people for key jobs, budget adequately by way of time and money, and sufficiently monitor progress and make necessary adjustments. The alternative is to shut out teachers and unions, raising the chance that new policies will fail on the ground, causing more distrust among the parties and serving students poorly.

Strategy 6: Bargain Better

Collective bargaining lies at the heart of the labor-management relationship. Except in the few states that have banned or restricted it, labor and management use this formal process to determine teachers' wages, fringe benefits, and working conditions.[23] Before collective bargaining for teachers grew popular in the 1960s, unions met with management over the terms and conditions of employment, but management had the final say, with no obligation to reach agreement with teachers. Collective bargaining was a boon for teachers and the profession because it led to standardized work rules, prevented management from making arbitrary employment decisions, and forced administrators to enter into enforceable contracts with teachers.

The bargaining process can be harmful, though, when it becomes overly contentious, when each side stakes out firm positions—usually extreme ones at the beginning—and fights to get all it can. When labor and management bargain this way, they frequently withhold information, make misleading statements, and discredit the other side in hopes of gaining a negotiating advantage. That behavior, in turn, can diminish trust, undermine collaboration, distract from issues affecting teaching and learning, and inflict wounds that don't quickly heal.

Collective bargaining, however, need not work this way. An alternative approach, interest-based bargaining (IBB), relies on trust and collaboration and often produces fair agreements that are good for students. With IBB, representatives from each side come to the bargaining table prepared to discuss a broad range of problems that they will solve together. Rather than stake out positions, parties share their interests and seek to understand each other's perspectives. The goal of negotiations is no longer about winning or securing concessions but, instead, finding common ground and solving problems of mutual concern.

The impact can be substantial. IBB reduces the number of conflicts that require outside mediators to intervene and raises public hopes that negotiations between labor and management can serve the interests of all stakeholders including, most importantly, students. It also enables management and labor to better innovate and solve problems with one another and improves communication, trust, and morale, according to researchers who have studied the practice.[24]

Due to its positive effects on professional relationships, IBB has been the impetus for a number of labor-management partnerships in which collaboration has extended well beyond the bargaining table. In the San Juan Unified School District of Sacramento, efforts to promote collaboration faltered until management and labor leaders received IBB training from the Harvard Negotiation Project. "This training was extremely successful, stuck with the district, and became the foundation for all future collaboration," according to the union's executive director, Tom Alves.[25]

In Nevada's Clark County School District, district leaders decided to replace their dysfunctional bargaining practices, which had produced particularly divisive contract negotiations in the late 1990s, with IBB in 2003. "Through the IBB process," researchers found later, "[management] and [the union] were able to address a range of key issues during negotiations, including working conditions in all schools, incentives for teachers in at-risk schools, incentives to bring special education teachers back from regular education positions, support for new teachers, and increased salaries for all teachers.

"The local administrators' association and [the district]," the researchers wrote, "went on to use IBB in contract negotiations to change the administrative salary schedule and attract strong, effective principals to the most challenging schools. IBB has also been widely accepted by the Board of School Trustees. It has made it possible for the Trustees to focus on creating a vision and implementing policies to support that vision instead of being embroiled in labor disputes. As the IBB process is implemented, the collaborative atmosphere makes it difficult for an observer to identify to which team—[the district or the teachers union]—each participant belongs."[26]

For many districts, IBB has spurred innovation, solved critical problems, and helped to create a culture that embraces collaboration. But IBB is no panacea for turning conflict into collaboration, and it requires ongoing investments of time for leaders to learn how it works. Thus, while districts should tap its potential, I also recommend two other approaches for districts to build on IBB and deepen labor-management collaboration: pursuing living contracts and expanding the scope of bargaining.

Living Contracts

Collective bargaining, even when IBB is used, has a fundamental limitation. Labor and management tap it only when contracts come up for renewal, which might be every two to three years, if not longer. In between contract renewals, labor and management can make no further contract changes unless they both agree to reopen negotiations or they make separate (or "sidebar") agreements. Districts rarely take that step, however. Until a contract expires, management and labor are stuck with what they've got even if it doesn't serve their interests.

In cities that include Rochester, New York; Toledo, Ohio; and Eugene, Oregon, however, districts have overcome this IBB limitation by employing "living contracts," which Linda Kaboolian describes as "comprehensive, district-wide collective-bargaining contracts that contain provisions to allow continual renegotiation and modification during the course of their stated term. More radical than waivers or override language, living contracts make provisions for continual negotiations and make the assumption that fundamental changes are possible through the work of a standing committee that negotiates new terms. Living contracts allow the parties to operate outside of the boundaries of negotiated contract language, in accordance with a process designed to protect the rights of the parties."[27]

In the Rochester City Schools, a committee of labor and management officials is authorized "to discuss any issue of mutual interest or concern and to reach tentative agreements on issues in a timely manner without delaying action until the expiration and re-negotiation of the collective bargaining Agreement."[28]

In 2004, Rochester's union and district leaders took the concept of living contracts a step further by establishing School-Level Living Contract Committees (SLLCCs). The idea behind them—giving more autonomy to administrators and teachers in individual schools—was originally proposed by Charles Taylor Kerchner, Julia A. Koppich, and Joseph G. Weeres, who wrote, "The real power . . . lies in allowing the heart of the educational enterprise to be shaped by the people who must make it work—the ones at each school site. Rather than ironing out the details once for everyone, as the current system does, we picture a new kind of document, an educational compact that each school would prepare and administer."[29]

Rochester's SLLCCs can negotiate their own contract provisions, and they take effect if the school administration and 80 percent of teachers agree to the changes. In establishing these school-level committees, Rochester's education leaders recognized that programs and policies that work in one setting don't necessarily work in another. The school-level autonomy paid off when the district sought ways to expand learning time for students. In some schools, administrators and teachers agreed that some teachers would start the day earlier, while others would work later. Teachers didn't work longer hours, but the staggered schedule significantly boosted student learning time. Eventually, nearly a third of district schools adopted this new schedule through their SLLCCs. Around the country, other districts have struggled to expand learning time (or support innovation in general) because schools lack the autonomy to innovate and one-size-fits-all solutions often don't work.

Giving schools the flexibility to bargain their own contract provisions is a sensible way to promote innovation, but it will undoubtedly make some district and union leaders nervous; they'll have to cede some decision-making power to practitioners on the ground. Other schools might want to follow suit, further diluting district and union power. That's hardly attractive for leaders who like exerting control. But that's how innovation works, how schools become learning organizations and continuously improve the educational experiences of their students. Education leaders at every level must be advocates for innovation and change.

Beyond Collective Bargaining

With effective collaboration, management and unions work together on everything that affects teaching and learning. After all, they won't have much opportunity to innovate or solve problems if they focus narrowly on wages, hours, and working conditions. In highly collaborative settings, administrators and teachers talk almost daily about problems that demand immediate attention as well as longer-term efforts to improve teaching and learning. When they craft solutions to important professional challenges, they often write them into the contract, even though bargaining rules may not require them to do so.

Collective bargaining rules vary from state to state, but no state prohibits districts and unions from creating such additional agreements as nonbinding compacts, memoranda of understanding, or "trust agreements." That's what leaders of the public schools in Providence, Rhode Island, did in 2010 after the US Department of Education forced them to select one of several reform options for several of their underperforming schools. Management and the union formed a partnership that would be guided by a short document, separate from their collective bargaining agreement, that they called the United Providence (or UP!) Compact. The compact was designed, in its own words, "to lead the charge for reform by eliminating previous barriers and constraints imposed by contractual agreements, past practices, and bureaucratic procedures." It set expectations for management and the union under the guiding principle of "reciprocal obligations," which "recognizes the mutual responsibility and commitment between labor and management in public education to ensure student and school success. It also embodies the shared belief that student and school success will either be enhanced or diminished based on a cooperative or contentious labor-management relationship, respectively."[30]

The compact is young, and we may not know for years whether it's made a difference for students. As for its impact and long-term viability, Peter McWalters, former Rhode Island Education Commissioner and a strong advocate for labor-management partnerships, said the question is simple: "Will [Superintendent Tom Brady and former union President Steve Smith] have the courage to keep it up when they want to kill each other? . . . One thing I have learned is that change gets complicated when it gets real . . . Something will happen that's out of line, something will go wrong. It always does, and that's the test."[31]

More Lessons from California

California's successful implementation of the Common Core State Standards was due, in large part, to a high degree of collaboration among state policy makers and education leaders. They agreed to delay high-stakes testing of student progress until educators were ready to incorporate the new standards into the classroom. The state also invested significant funding for technology, materials, and training to make this happen.

Until recently, labor-management collaboration at the local level was the rare exception rather than the rule in California. In 2015, the state's management and labor leaders launched the California Labor Management Initiative (LMI) and invited representatives from all of the state's districts to attend a symposium to learn more about this approach. The demand for the event was so great that over half of the district teams were told they would have to wait for future symposia.

These two events were no coincidence. The successful collaboration that paved the way for a successful launch of Common Core in California created a context that spurred the California LMI, which is spawning new collaborative partnerships across the state. The lessons from this dramatic shift have important implications for other states interested in jump-starting labor-management partnerships.

What lessons does California teach? One is that state leaders had to go slow before they could go fast. Four years passed between the time they first considered the idea of greater collaboration and the time they launched the formal initiative. During that period, leaders had many opportunities to engage in dialogue, build better relationships, and experience, firsthand, the benefits of collaboration. Indeed, they had codeveloped two policy reports (the *Blueprint for Great Schools* and *Greatness by Design*) with recommendations on a wide range of complex issues, and they had agreed on a way to implement Common Core. In 2015, California's education leaders convened again over several months and produced an updated version of its *Blueprint for Great Schools*, which provided new recommendations on Common Core and ways to promote educator effectiveness and student success. The report also highlighted the emergence of "The California Way," which its authors said, "builds on a collaborative team approach to positive education change and . . . rests on the belief that educators want to excel, trusts them to improve when given the proper supports, and provides local schools and districts with the leeway and flexibility to deploy resources so they can improve.[32]

After the initial policy reports were released, leaders from the state's labor and management organizations also needed time to fully consider the implications of a public endorsement of labor-management partnerships. The meetings they attended together over a two-year period allowed them to discuss the benefits as well as the pitfalls. They asked local educators from districts like ABC Unified, San Juan Unified, and Poway Unified to join the group and help move the process forward by describing the positive impact on district culture, reform efforts, and student outcomes. They also dispelled common myths about collaboration that some leaders worried about—that it might lead to collusion or that it would be impractical because each side would be expected to reach consensus on every decision. The local leaders assured them that they could avoid collusion (even the appearance of it) if leaders were fully transparent with their respective constituents and included them in the collaborative process. Local leaders also acknowledged that while collaboration does not put an end to disagreements, professional relationships built on trust create a context in which disagreements have a better chance of getting solved.

Time will tell whether the rapidly growing interest in collaboration will take firmer hold in California and ultimately have the same positive impact it has had in districts such as the Montgomery County Public Schools, Maryland; and the Cincinnati Public Schools. That will depend on whether state leaders remain committed to collaboration and whether all of the districts that have shown interest in this approach can obtain the assistance needed to cultivate effective partnerships. If this does happen, the prospects for change are unmistakably bright in a state where many students have struggled in recent decades. And that will set an example for other states to follow.

We now know the strategies to pursue if we want to cultivate collaboration. We know that we need to develop new mindsets and build new capacity, to start slow and build trust, to implement sound education policy and bargain better. But while strategies are important to provide an overall approach to the challenge at hand, they'll take us only so far. To bring collaboration to life, educators will need specific tactics. So, let's get practical.

CHAPTER 5

Cultivating Collaboration, Part II: Tactics

T O CULTIVATE COLLABORATION, I recommend six specific tactics that flow from the six strategies described in the preceding chapter. This chapter outlines these tactics and also describes an additional set of tactics that apply to particular groups of educators—school board members, superintendents, union leaders, teachers, community leaders, parents, and state organizations.

To be clear, I'm not offering a recipe for change. In the end, local districts have to build their own strategic plans that account for the unique dynamics among leaders in a district, the particular educational challenges they face, and other local factors. Having said that, I developed these tactics from years of experience in the trenches of education reform—witnessing successes and failures from New York to California, Wisconsin to Arizona—and from successful programs like Keys to Excellence for Your Schools (KEYS), a collaborative, research-based approach to continuous school improvement that the NEA developed.[1] Field tested by hundreds of schools, KEYS describes activities that are particularly useful in fostering a collaborative school culture that's focused on better outcomes for students. I also drew from another valuable source—a series of online courses that the NEA Foundation developed to cultivate educators' collaborative skills.

District leaders can learn important lessons about cultivating labor-management collaboration from the strategies and tactics that have proven successful around the country.

With that in mind, here are six tactics for all educators, each of which is discussed in detail:

- *Tactic 1*: Start with yourself.
- *Tactic 2*: Pitch it first.
- *Tactic 3*: Commit publicly to collaborative norms and monitor progress.
- *Tactic 4*: Strengthen collaboration through safe, anger-free dialogue.
- *Tactic 5*: Find personal spaces to promote reflection and dialogue.
- *Tactic 6*: Seek solutions to solvable problems.

Later, I outline additional tactics that apply only to particular groups of educators.

Tactic 1: Start with Yourself

Because education leaders who say they want to embrace collaboration must be willing to view themselves and others in a new light, they need a way to get started.

Richard DuFour, an expert on professional learning communities, urged educators to look first in the mirror, rather than out the window. "The . . . strategy, which I call the 'if only' approach, bases hopes for school improvement on others: 'if only the school board would reduce class sizes, if only the parents were more supportive, if only the students were better prepared and more motivated.'" In the context of union-management relations, this "if only" approach might lead a superintendent to think, "If only the union were really willing to focus on students," or a union president to think, "If only the superintendent wasn't such an autocrat." The alternative, according to DuFour, is to focus first on things over which one has control.[2]

Leaders can begin by asking themselves a series of questions that will make clear just what it will take for them to truly pursue collaboration. The questions include the following:

- Am I really willing to listen and to try to understand someone else's perspective?
- Am I really willing to entertain other people's ideas, or do I think that I just need others to help me implement mine?
- Do I really believe that our success depends on working together, or is it about getting others to do what I ask?
- Am I willing to ask others how they would answer these questions about me?
- If I answer "no" to any of these questions, am I ready to adopt a different mindset?

What's true of a single administrator and single union leader is true of the groups they represent. That is, both management and labor have perceptions about themselves when it comes to collaboration, and each often assumes that the obstacles to collaboration reside with the other side, not within its own ranks. To help each group assess its own interactive patterns, groups might ask themselves these questions:

- How well do we collaborate with each other?
- Are we respectful toward, and transparent with, each other?
- Have we established a foundation of trust?
- Do we resolve our own conflicts effectively?
- How do others perceive the way we collaborate?

I urge leaders to ask these questions because doing so will help enable them to collaborate with one another within their own group before they collaborate with the other side. In fact, leaders need to pay as much attention to their own group as to those with whom they'll partner.

Leaders of the Springfield Public Schools in Massachusetts did just that when they used NEA's KEYS survey to assess teachers' and administrators' perceptions of school conditions, including their ability to collaborate effectively. A team of union and management leaders who analyzed the survey results initially pointed fingers at one another for the problems that surfaced in the results, according to a case study conducted by the Rennie Center.[3] Eventually, however, the team worked through its differences, moved past the "if only" mindset, and agreed to work together on three problem areas that surfaced from the survey.

Tactic 2: Pitch It First

If educators should "go slow to go fast," then the tactical way to do so is to foster consensus about collaboration by pitching the idea to colleagues and building support for it.

Skeptics of collaboration will fear it for the very reasons that former skeptics once did, and they will ask themselves the same questions: What does it mean to collaborate? Will it lead to collusion? Will we be pressured to accept things that violate our values or sacrifice our interests?

Proponents should create opportunities to explain what effective collaboration really means, and for skeptics to come to understand its impact on relationships, motivations, teaching conditions, and student learning. The skeptics will appreciate their role in the exploration process, and they'll be more enthusiastic about collaboration if the larger group decides to pursue it.

Here are some ways to have the conversation:

- Introduce the concept of collaboration in small groups—even one-on-one—where people feel safe to share their concerns. For example, the union president can discuss the concept with fellow officers, and academic leaders can discuss it with school principals.

- Broaden the conversation later by expanding the size of the discussion groups, enabling leaders from management and unions to discuss the approach with one another.
- Invite management and union leaders from collaborative districts to share their experiences and respond to questions.[4]
- Send a team on a site visit to see how a collaborative district works. "Role-alike meetings," in which educators meet with their counterparts in other districts (union president with union president, principal with principal), are especially useful.
- Send a team to a regularly held conference by a regional chapter of the Teacher Union Reform Network (TURN), the Consortium for Educational Change (CEC), and the Massachusetts Education Partnership (MEP).[5] As with site visits, these events provide opportunities for district teams to interact with those who have established collaborative partnerships.

Interactions between skeptics and those from collaborative districts could prove particularly important. Experienced practitioners are often the most credible sources of knowledge, and management and labor leaders often remain skeptical of collaboration until they understand what it really looks like elsewhere.

When the leaders of Culver City Unified decided they wanted to establish a districtwide culture of collaboration after attending a labor-management institute hosted by ABC Unified, they didn't simply tell their district colleagues that this was the district's new direction. Instead, the team of management and union leaders that had attended the institute visited each of the district's schools to share what they had learned about the potential benefits of collaboration.

"I remember the first school we went to," local union president Dave Mielke said. "The principal automatically turned to superintendent LaRose assuming he was going to kick things off. But Dave [LaRose] turned to me and asked me to get things started. Well that said a lot to me, and it also said a lot to teachers that the superintendent, there with a school board member, asked me to lead the discussion."[6] LaRose and Mielke said later that after teachers and administrators had a chance to ask questions about collaboration and learned that it would mean frequent interactions between site-level union representatives and school principals on educational matters, all but one of the district's nine schools expressed support for the proposed shift toward collaboration. Because principals and union site representatives now meet frequently at most schools, they're solving many problems at those schools that teachers used to take to Mielke, the union president.

Culver City's transformation to collaboration has caught the attention of its local media. "We . . . have been very intentional," Superintendent Dave LaRose told a Culver City reporter, "in our efforts to collaborate, build trust, define common goals, communicate as partners, share and review information together and model our belief that 'success for all takes us all.'"[7]

Tactic 3: Commit Publicly to Collaborative Norms and Monitor Progress

In collaborative organizations, leaders establish explicit norms to guide their work. They commit to them publicly, often put them in writing, and share them with other stakeholders. Of critical importance, leaders monitor progress to ensure that, through their collaborative efforts, they are tangibly changing the culture of their workplace.

That's what the board of education, superintendent, and union did in Montgomery County, Maryland, in 2010. They created a document, R.E.S.P.E.C.T., that defined how they would interact, and they followed up periodically with one another to identify problems they needed to address.[8] The document delineated their commitment to collaboration; the processes and initiatives they'd pursue to support it; the behaviors they'd foster; and the positive work environment they'd create.[9]

As collaborative districts create their own norms, they should consider the following ones that other districts have adopted:

- Assume positive intent;
- Follow through on commitments;
- Hold one another accountable;
- Listen to dissenting views and ensure no retribution;
- Recognize contributions of all employees;
- Act civilly in all interactions;
- Do not let each other fail;
- Talk with colleagues when norms are broken;
- Maintain high expectations for all leaders, staff, and students;
- Work as teams, not as individuals;
- Support positions with data;
- Do not speak disparagingly about the other side;
- Refrain from any tactic that breaks trust;
- During negotiations, collaborate as long as possible to avoid going to impasse;
- Use the collective bargaining process to enhance a collaborative culture;
- Be fiscally responsible; and
- For meetings—begin and end on time; stick to an agenda unless group agrees to modify it; avoid inappropriate use of technology (e.g., using cell phones, texting, reading/sending emails, browsing); encourage participation from all participants; leave meeting with an action plan when possible (i.e., who does what by when); and debrief meeting norms before adjourning.

The process of creating norms may seem superfluous, but it's vital. When leaders make their commitments public, they have the means to hold themselves accountable. They can ask themselves, in focus groups or with surveys (or "pulse checks" as one district calls them), whether they're adhering to the norms. They can set aside time to talk about trouble spots, why they exist, and how to address them.

Even in the most collaborative settings, people eventually violate norms. The real question is what happens next. If leaders ignore these breaches or handle them poorly, their progress on other issues will stall. The next tactic gives leaders a way to respond when violations occur.

Tactic 4: Strengthen Collaboration Through Safe, Anger-Free Dialogue

"Twenty years of research involving more than 100,000 people reveals that the key skill of effective leaders, teammates, and loved ones is the capacity to skillfully address emotionally and politically risky issues," Kerry Patterson and his colleagues wrote in *Crucial Conversations*.[10]

You'd be hard-pressed to find more emotionally and politically risky issues than the ones that union and management leaders face. Unfortunately, many of these leaders lack the will or capacity to respond effectively when conflicts arise. Remaining silent, ignoring the problem, and hoping it will somehow vanish seldom works, but people often follow this approach anyway, assuming that speaking up won't do any good or fearing that it might make things even worse. ("He'll be livid," a person may think, "if I tell him what's bothering me.") Some people do, in fact, make things worse by getting angry and saying things that put others on the defensive. In either case—when conflicts remain unaddressed or when people address them poorly—trust is compromised, communication suffers, and problems go unresolved.

Effective leaders pursue a third course of action. They address conflicts head-on with colleagues through safe, anger-free dialogue. The skills required for anger-free dialogue may come naturally only to some, but they can be learned by all. The company VitalSmarts offers frequent training programs throughout the country on *Crucial Conversations* and *Crucial Accountability*, and they publish books by the same name.[11] Another company, Fierce, Inc., offers books, webinars, and training on a similar approach, called *Fierce Conversations*.[12] Creating a more trusting, collaborative, and accountable culture requires different kinds of conversations. If they're not occurring now, or if the conversations that *are* occurring are counterproductive, leaders on all sides might consider taking the time to learn how to converse in ways that preserve relationships and generate meaningful change.

Remember the discussion in the preceding chapter about the struggling schools in California's Central Valley, for which I led a team of WestEd facilitators to improve relations and build trust between administrators and teachers? After a year, relationships had improved dramatically in most of them. The percentage of staff who agreed that "our school is a supportive and inviting place to work" rose, on average, from 20 percent to 80 percent. Teachers and administrators say they now spend considerably more time collaborating with each other on educational matters. Relations between the union's site representatives and school principals also improved.

Most importantly, academic achievement rose at those schools more than at almost any others in the district by the end of the 2013 academic year. Four of the district's fifty-five schools with the greatest growth on California's Academic Performance Index had worked with WestEd to strengthen trust and collaboration. Six out of the seven of WestEd's partner schools met or exceeded the state's schoolwide academic growth targets. All seven exceeded the average academic growth by schools in the district and the state. We can't prove a causal link between greater trust and higher academic achievement, but we and the parties involved believe that better relationships led to a greater focus on teaching, and that played a large role in boosting academic achievement.

Through our work, my colleagues and I have learned a few lessons about building trust, some of which are reflected in the preceding discussion. Most educators want to work on trust when they consider what their professional lives are like without it. The parties involved must clearly define their underlying values and necessary actions because commitments to vague notions of trust won't work. Trust building requires investments in time and skills because years of mistrust are not quickly reversed, no matter how inspiring the call for change might be. A trusted and experienced third-party facilitator is often essential to success. The parties must monitor their progress closely and learn lessons from their successes and setbacks. The parties must address broken promises swiftly and effectively; otherwise, their colleagues will lose hope and abandon their efforts. Finally, leaders should begin to work together even before they've cultivated high levels of trust because collaboration on shared initiatives (e.g., the school calendar or targeted support for at-risk students) will strengthen trust.

Tactic 5: Find Personal Spaces to Promote Reflection and Dialogue

For one superintendent, the most valuable part of a labor-management conference that he attended with the district's union president was the car ride they shared to and from the conference. That's where they got to know each other and where trust between them first emerged.

The spaces in which we interact matter—a lot. Familiar physical cues reinforce the status quo, so the parties that want to change their culture and the relationships between them find it hard to do so when their interactions continue to occur solely in their usual settings.

Like all leaders, educators like to hold off-site retreats because they usually can find pleasant places for them, away from the usual cues that prompt people to expect the same attitudes and behaviors from others. Retreats cultivate a more personal interaction among participants. Colleagues who know little about one another have time for genuine conversation. They eat together, take walks, and tell stories—the kinds of things they may never do on the job.

Unfortunately, retreats can be expensive and time consuming, so some districts never have them. For those that do, the glow, energy, and good will that people experience during a retreat often fade as they return to their familiar settings and plunge back into their familiar routines. That's why leaders in high-trust environments create new structures and practices that cultivate collaboration without the need for expensive retreats.

In Massachusetts' Chelsea public schools, the deputy superintendent and union president say their informal, off-site meetings played a critical role in their collaborative journey. "Eating breakfast and dinner together further solidified trust among stakeholders in the district," said Mary Ferriter, the union president. The interactions, she said, "made us all human."[13] In California's San Juan Unified School District, administrators and union leaders begin budget meetings and negotiation sessions with a "check-in" to cultivate personal relations. "The check-in," according to Tom Alves, the local union's executive director, "can be personal or professional and is designed to humanize the relationships as we jump into the challenging work ahead. When convening joint committees, the check-in is intended to connect committee members with their task. At the beginning of the meeting, participants might be asked to share their reasons for joining the committee. They might be asked to respond to the question, 'What are two to three wishes you have for your school?'"[14]

"Spending time together," Dave LaRose, the Culver City superintendent, reflected, "having the meals together, going to conferences together with Dave Mielke [the union president], we're now at this point where we talk about our kids and our golf game. When I am at his high school, I make a point of dropping into his classroom. I really appreciate the opportunity to see him work with kids. More importantly, the time in his classroom affirms that we are partners and that we share the same vision and purposes."[15] It also means a lot to Dave Mielke and to the productive relationship that has developed.

"[O]nce people rediscover the art of talking together," Peter Senge wrote in the foreword to *Dialogue: The Art of Thinking Together*, "they do not go back. This discovery seems to awaken something deep within us, some recognition of what we have lost as our societies have drifted away from the core practices that can make them healthy. Once awakened, people do not go back to sleep. . . . [T]hey continue to get together with the pure goal of simply talking, and thinking, together."[16]

Tactic 6: Seek Solutions to Solvable Problems

The aphorism "success breeds success" doesn't always apply in the real world. Fortunately, however, sometimes it *does*—such as when it comes to cultivating labor-management collaboration.

Nothing instills greater confidence in a new approach, such as collaboration, than positive results. That's why when union leaders and administrators begin to work more closely together, they often start small, with manageable challenges that raise the odds of success. If they can secure a success and proudly say "look what we did together," they naturally seek new opportunities to work together in the hopes of achieving more successes. If, however, they work together and fail, they avoid new endeavors with one another.

How might they start small? They might create an orientation program for new students and their families or launch a joint labor-management newsletter to communicate with staff. They might investigate the causes of serious student disciplinary problems and implement policies to reduce student suspensions. Or they might ensure that staff have access to well-maintained technology, reduce litter and graffiti and enhance the look of public spaces, and establish a mentor program for at-risk students.

Once they've achieved successes of that magnitude, leaders on both sides can explore longer-term, more consequential projects on which to work together. That's what districts participating in the Massachusetts Education Partnership's District Capacity Project do after they create their initial collaborative structures. These are some projects on which they've worked during the first year of their partnerships, according to the Rennie Center:

- Brockton's district team is working to accelerate student achievement and respond to community needs by designing a new international dual-language immersion school.
- Berkshire Hills and Fall River are researching and developing Professional Learning Communities to support focused educator learning that can accelerate student growth.

- Leominster has created a new set of Teacher Leader positions, offering career advancement to veteran teachers, support for newer teachers, and increased system capacity.
- Malden has pursued intensive leadership development training, with a focus on building a culture of dialogue across the school system.
- Springfield uses skillful engagement in difficult conversations and effective teaming to support implementation of its districtwide educator development and evaluation system.[17]

Over one hundred other districts have attended one or more of MEP's annual conferences to explore expanded learning time, innovation schools, peer assistance and review (PAR) programs, implementation of Common Core Standards, and new teacher evaluation systems.

In other collaborative efforts around the country, district teams have focused on serious challenges such as implementing Common Core State Standards and creating Linked Learning and multiple pathway programs that expose high school students to real-world career opportunities. They have also worked on establishing comprehensive educator evaluation systems; expanding learning time for students and collaboration time for teachers; creating professional learning programs for teachers and administrators; providing wrap-around health and social support services for families; and setting up peer assistance and review, as well as career lattice programs for teachers.

As new district teams prepare to begin their work, the following practical approaches might prove useful:

- Choose a problem that's solvable in a few weeks or months. "Quick wins" show what labor and management leaders can accomplish as partners.
- Build an organizational commitment to addressing the problem; in other words, per Tactic 2, *pitch it first.*
- Identify all potential obstacles to success, and develop contingency plans to address each one.

- Identify implementation teams and ensure that their members have the interest, skills, and time to complete their projects effectively.
- If needed, give implementation teams the guidance and training to plan and complete their tasks.
- Ask implementation teams to create action plans and timelines that describe who is doing what and by when.
- Ensure that the teams have adequate administrative supports, including funding, time, and space.
- Assess and report progress regularly, and be prepared to adjust plans and provide additional support, as needed.
- Recognize the efforts of implementation teams to reinforce the impact of collaboration.

Tactics for Particular Educators

Superintendents, school board members, and union presidents are obviously critical players in collaborative partnerships. But other stakeholders play important roles as well. They include teachers, because they elect union leaders and strongly influence how their unions represent them; community leaders and parents, because they elect school boards that hire superintendents and set a tone for the way the district addresses its problems; and state-level unions and management organizations, because they can provide critical support to the local unions and administrators they are supposed to serve. This section offers a number of targeted recommendations for each of these important sets of players.

School board members. School boards can make or break collaboration, depending on the superintendents they hire to lead their districts. If they select tough-minded superintendents who think they can succeed without union support, they will give collaboration virtually no chance to emerge. If they hire superintendents who say they are committed to collaboration (and most will say so) but lack the capacity to do it well, collaboration will flounder—not just with the union, but with the board and every other stakeholder group. So the board should recruit candidates who have a proven track record with collaboration, who can describe what effective collaboration looks like, and who can point to accomplishments that were generated by their own collaborative efforts.

In addition, school boards set an important tone for how districts conduct school business. When board meetings are acrimonious and rancorous, when members do not act in a civil manner themselves or do not demand such behavior of those who attend their meetings, they send a powerful message that they do not value collaboration, trust, and respectful interactions. Board members need not agree on all issues (after all, rigorous debate lies at the heart of democratic institutions), but as public trustees they have an obligation to their communities, their employees, and especially their students to show how to properly accommodate differences of opinions. Boards may want to invest in their own ability to conduct themselves in a civil manner if civil discourse and collaboration among their members are frequently absent.

Superintendents. Superintendents should recognize that acting collaboratively—listening respectfully, acting civilly, suspending judgment, sharing power—is not a sign of weakness. If anything, it's a sign of strength, a reflection of a leader who is confident enough to see all sides of an issue and to work closely with those who represent different interests and constituencies. Those who proudly battle unions to promote their reform agendas may get high marks from the media, but they'll likely get low marks when they're judged on whether they created high-functioning school systems that improved student learning.

Superintendents will need to explore the concept of collaboration with their district's union leader. These conversations will be more fruitful if superintendents hold them in neutral places, perhaps over meals and away from the office. They should invest the time to build the relationship, because trust does not develop overnight.

Once union leaders have bought in, superintendents should then discuss their plans for collaboration with school board members and other district leaders. They'll likely face resistance from those who fear that overly friendly ties to unions amount to collusion. Superintendents need patience, because others may need time to confront their fears and to evaluate the risks and benefits of a different approach. During that period, superintendents may want to share research findings that show the positive impact of collaboration, and they should arrange for skeptics to speak with their counterparts in other districts. Superintendents may also want to ask skeptics to accompany them to a labor-management conference so they can hear the stories of change firsthand.

In addition, superintendents who set an example by creating a collaborative working environment at their district offices will send a strong signal to their future partners that they don't only "talk the talk" but also "walk the walk," laying a strong foundation for change. Superintendents should, for instance, hire administrators, or promote those from within, who know how to collaborate. Collaboration will be significantly harder if the leaders who surround superintendents can't or won't follow their collaborative lead.

Local union presidents. Just as superintendents will meet resistance from skeptical school board members and fellow administrators, so, too, will local union presidents undoubtedly face opposition from colleagues who don't want their union cozying up to untrustworthy managers. The local presidents will need to convince them that collaboration is the best way to secure fair agreements for teachers, to give voice to teachers on educational issues, and to achieve better outcomes for students. They might suggest that the skeptics read case studies, and they can arrange for the skeptics to speak directly to union leaders in districts that have formed successful partnerships.

When the time is right, local presidents and their executive teams should consider holding exploratory meetings with superintendents and other district leaders—ideally, away from district or union offices and with third-party facilitators leading the discussions. Once the superintendent is on board, a union president can bring teachers into the conversation. If history is any guide, some teachers will embrace prospects of a civil, open relationship with management and the union's chance to participate in discussions about education matters. Others, however, will worry that by collaborating, the union president will no longer be fighting for teachers' rights.

If union presidents don't address these concerns, they'll risk losing the confidence of their members and, in turn, find themselves bounced from their union posts. To avoid that fate, local presidents should develop plans to ensure that *all* teachers understand the proposition at hand. If teachers support it, enabling the president to form a partnership, the local president should then provide frequent, ongoing communication with teachers about the collaborative activities under way. Without such communication, some teachers will invariably suspect that unions are making decisions behind their backs. The call for collaboration is not just a call for transparent communication, more trust, and honest dialogue *between* management and union. It's also a call for all of those positive features *within* the ranks of unions and management.

Unions take a strong interest in school board elections. I suggest that they follow the example set by the union in Plattsburgh, New York. "The union vets board candidates for a disposition towards collaboration and is highly involved in school board elections," according to researcher Jonathan Eckert and several associates. "[Board Vice President Tracy] Rotz said, 'The nice thing is they are up front about the endorsement—it is about continuity and trust.' According to [Superintendent Jake] Short, 'The union is looking for education-minded people, not union-loving people.' Subsequently, board members who understand the Plattsburgh collaborative culture look for superintendents with demonstrated skill managing collaborative labor-management relationships."[18]

Principals and union site representatives. One feature of effective collaboration is that it occurs at all levels of the education system, including school sites. Recalling the Rubenstein and McCarthy study of ABC Unified, the greatest improvements in student learning occurred in schools where partnerships between principals and building-level union representatives were the strongest. To build strong partnerships, principals and union leaders should meet regularly to address *any* issue that affects teaching and learning. These conversations can serve not only to remove impediments to teaching and learning; they can explore new and better ways to educate children—for instance, creating professional learning communities, improving communications with parents, or constructing high-quality professional development activities for teachers.

Principals are often considered their schools' instructional leaders. They are, in terms of creating a *system* that supports effective instruction. But the most powerful instructional leadership occurs when principals share it with teachers, as in Cincinnati through their instructional leadership teams.

To be sure, union site representatives have an obligation to represent teachers' interests on contractual matters. But in schools that embrace collaboration, they also ensure that teachers have a voice in all other professional matters, whether it's through instructional leadership teams, school committees, or other mechanisms.

Teachers. When discussing the obstacles to collaboration, I cited a 2012 Education Sector report showing that the percentage of teachers that thought unions should "stick to traditional issues" had dropped from 52 percent to 42, and the percentage that thought unions should focus more on teacher quality and student achievement jumped from 32 percent to 43.[19] Those trends indicate that many more teachers would be open to collaboration because, presumably, it would give teachers a greater voice in educational issues.

Teachers who support labor-management collaboration have an important role to play in promoting it. Even teachers who aren't active union members, or union members at all, have a vested interest in the leaders who represent them. If they want leaders who embrace a collaborative approach, then they should encourage such people to run for union office and vote them in. In fact, teachers who support a new collaborative approach with management should consider whether to pursue it by seeking office as union leaders themselves.

To teachers who remain skeptical about collaboration, fearing that it will dilute union efforts to secure decent wages, good working conditions, and reasonable employment protections, I would simply note that collaborative unions remain strong advocates for teachers and they often succeed in negotiating better contracts for their teachers than do unions with adversarial relationships with management. Sometimes that's precisely because management appreciates their accomplishments and good will. At other times, the reason is that collaborative unions do not hesitate to fight to secure fair contracts. But when they do fight, they base their case on good data and cogent arguments and fight in a way that maintains trust and allows other collaborative work to continue.

As teachers should keep in mind, collaborative unions can do more than win fair contracts. They also can secure a prominent seat for themselves at the tables where education policies are made, innovative programs are developed, and problems are solved. In these districts, students get a better education because the collective wisdom of teachers is taken seriously.

Community leaders and parents. Community leaders and parents have powerful voices to influence the way a district's management and union work with each other. They help elect school board members, and those board members, in turn, hire superintendents, negotiate employment contracts, and set the educational direction for the district. Community leaders and parents who support labor-management collaboration should support like-minded school board candidates—not those with clear biases toward unions or management. I suggest that they do what, as noted earlier, Plattsburgh's union leaders do.

Because many board members are not educators themselves, the concept of labor-management partnerships will be new to many of them. I believe that most board members would welcome the idea. Very few like their roles in the middle of bitter and protracted labor disputes, and most understand at least intuitively that districts can accomplish more if people work together. Thus, community leaders and parents should educate boards about labor-management partnerships and the impact they can have on student learning. They also should suggest that board members visit collaborative districts and speak with their counterparts who participate in successful partnerships.

State union and management organizations. State union and management organizations—for example, the Delaware State Education Association, a statewide teacher union; and the Wyoming Association of School Administrators, a statewide superintendents group—can be important sources of information and guidance about collaboration. Thus, they should take the time to learn more about what labor-management collaboration can offer and how to make it an effective tool in districts and schools.

State organizations can begin by taking stock, such as through a survey, of what their colleagues know and think about this approach. To strengthen the knowledge of their staffers, state organizations can invite labor-management teams from collaborative districts to share their experiences with them. Many of those teams are well prepared to do so because they've already made presentations at regional and national conferences. In addition, state organizations should consider meeting with their counterparts in states such as Massachusetts, Illinois, and California, whose state organizations have promoted collaborative partnerships.

State organizations that represent teachers, administrators, and school boards also should explore the idea of creating a state labor-management initiative. Massachusetts launched such an initiative in 2003 and, in 2011, it helped produce the highly acclaimed Massachusetts Education Partnership, which "seeks to improve student achievement and success in school districts across the Commonwealth through the application of effective models of labor-management collaboration, interest-based bargaining, and district capacity."[20] In Illinois, the Consortium for Educational Change, a long-time leader in state-level collaboration with nearly twenty partners and affiliates, has made significant contributions to educational policy in over eighty districts in its region. These contributions include the Burnham Plan, which created a comprehensive reform agenda for the state, and the Performance Evaluation Reform Act (PERA), which requires all districts in the state to implement multiple-measure teacher evaluation systems.[21]

California, a state with a history of bitter labor-management relations in education, launched a labor-management initiative in 2014 and conducted a statewide labor-management symposium a year later for California-based district leadership teams. All of that came after the state's two unions and other key stakeholder groups codeveloped a *Blueprint for Great Schools* and, later, a comprehensive plan, *Greatness by Design*, to improve educator effectiveness in the state.[22] The positive experience of education leaders in cocreating a new educational vision catalyzed the labor-management initiative that followed.[23]

For labor-management collaboration to flourish more broadly in education, each side needs to bring a fresh perspective not only to one another but also to itself.

CHAPTER 6

Needed Reforms for Management and Unions

T HE PREVIOUS DISCUSSIONS about the nature and benefits of labor-management collaboration have outlined what each side needs to do to build new partnerships with the other. They have also delineated the specific strategies that educators of all stripes—school boards, superintendents, principals, union leaders, teachers, and so on—should pursue and the tactics they should employ. This chapter takes a deeper look at what management and labor should do, within their own spheres, to cultivate real collaboration by addressing some key issues that continue to place barriers between them, sowing distrust and ill will.

The preceding chapters laid the predicate for this additional look beneath the covers of both management and labor. They discussed the need for management and labor to adopt new mindsets and to develop more capacity, for educators to start with themselves and build support for collaboration among their colleagues. Here, though, the argument goes further by recommending a set of specific internal reforms for management and then another set for labor that will enable each side to more fully leverage the power of collaboration for years to come.

On the management side, administrators should create the environment and supply the tools that will enable teachers to succeed, and they also should provide the tangible feedback and professional development that teachers can use to continually improve their skills. On the labor side, unions should seek alternatives to controversial policies related to tenure, seniority, and compensation, and they also should reform their own structures to provide more autonomy to local unions and a greater voice for individual teachers.

By building their internal capacities and addressing contentious issues, management and unions that make these changes will pave the way for better management-labor partnerships and strengthen both sides' capacity to fulfill their obligations to students, to communities, and to each other. They'll also help to quiet the education wars that pit management against unions, vilify teachers, and divert attention from creating better schools for children.

Let's take a closer look at, first, what management should do and, second, at the same for labor.

How Management Should View Unions

For starters, management should accept unions as equal partners in providing a quality education to students. Management can't engage in real collaboration with unions if they don't view them this way.

Collaborative management does not try to co-opt unions to accept its preset agenda; instead, managers reach out to union leaders so the two can create an agenda for change together. Collaborative managers open the district's books and craft district and school budgets *with* their unions. They share power not as a concession, but because they believe that sound educational decision making can come only from the full participation of the teachers that unions represent.

"There is complete transparency," Bonnie Cullison, president of the teacher union in Montgomery County from 2003 to 2009, said of relations in that highly successful collaborative district. "The unions sit down at the table with the district leaders to craft the budget." That's because Jerry Weast, the then-superintendent who spearheaded management's collaborative efforts years ago, was committed to the idea that "power is something to be shared, not hoarded."[1]

Collaborative management builds the capacity of teachers and embraces the concept of "reciprocal accountability," as promoted by Harvard education professor Richard Elmore. "For every increment of performance I demand from you," Elmore wrote in describing the concept, "I have an equal responsibility to provide you with the capacity to meet that expectation. Likewise, for every investment you make in my skill and knowledge, I have a reciprocal responsibility to demonstrate some new increment in performance."[2]

Management that's truly collaborative builds the capacity of teachers, for instance, by

- providing meaningful opportunities for teacher input and discussion before they make important decisions;
- creating a clean and safe teaching and learning environment;
- exerting respectful and responsive leadership;
- ensuring teacher access to supplies, books, technology, and support personnel;
- enabling teachers to exercise professional judgment in the classroom;
- carving out time for teachers to plan, collaborate, and analyze student work;
- providing teachers with meaningful evaluations; and
- offering meaningful professional development for both teachers and administrators.

Unfortunately, in too many places, managers do not provide teachers with these essential supports. As an abundance of evidence shows,[3] the teacher turnover that's especially high in schools serving significant numbers of poor students and students of color is largely attributable to poor teaching conditions that hinder teachers' abilities to promote student learning.[4]

Of the preceding list of essential supports, the last two items—meaningful evaluations and meaningful professional development—are largely under management's control to make happen. Consequently, let's take a closer look at why each one is so important for teachers.

Providing Meaningful Teacher Evaluation

"The typical teacher evaluation in public education consists of a single, fleeting classroom visit by a principal or other building administrator untrained in evaluation who wields a checklist of classroom conditions and teacher behaviors that often don't focus directly on the quality of instruction," according to Thomas Toch, former codirector of the Washington, DC, think tank Education Sector.[5]

Research bears out Toch's observation. For instance, a 2009 study of teacher evaluation in twelve districts found that three of every four teachers who participated in a formal evaluation received no recommendations from their administrators on how to improve their teaching.[6] Only 43 percent of novice teachers said they received feedback that identified areas for them to develop further. Teachers also were unlikely to receive help from administrators outside of the formal evaluation process. As the survey found, "47 percent of teachers report not having participated in a single informal conversation with their administrator over the last year about improving aspects of their instructional performance."[7]

In another survey of 1,010 public school teachers, Education Sector researchers found that nearly a third viewed their formal evaluations as "not particularly helpful." Asked about the process of granting tenure, 69 percent of teachers characterized the evaluation process as "just a formality—that it has very little to do with whether a teacher is good or not."[8]

Perhaps administrators provide so little feedback and support to teachers because virtually all of them seem pleased with their teachers' performances. A 2012 MetLife survey of five hundred US principals found that 98 percent of them gave positive ratings to their teachers (rating 63 percent of them "excellent" and 35 percent "pretty good").[9] Beyond their apparent satisfaction with their own teachers, administrators typically offer two reasons why they conduct teacher evaluations so poorly—neither of which holds up under close scrutiny.

First, they say that with all of their other responsibilities—paperwork, meetings, parent conferences, and so on—principals lack the time to conduct thorough evaluations. I recognize the enormous demands that principals face, but districts that view evaluation as a vital part of instructional leadership create systems that enable principals to perform this function well. Linda Darling-Hammond described some of these districts, like San Mateo Union High School District and Long Beach Unified in California, in her book, *Getting Teacher Evaluation Right*.[10] If some administrators can do it, others can as well.

Montgomery County's Professional Growth System, which management and the union implemented systemwide in 2000 after several years of development, recognizes that teacher evaluations are not the sole purview of principals. Instead, teacher evaluations are conducted by any number of "qualified observers" who include assistant principals, student support specialists, resource teachers, consulting teachers, and retired administrators. To become qualified, these observers must complete district professional development programs that prepare them to observe and evaluate teacher performances.[11]

Effective evaluation systems such as that one—which ensure that teachers (and, just as importantly, administrators) are evaluated thoroughly and reliably—have existed for some time. However, far too many districts ignore them and continue to say they lack the capacity to conduct quality evaluations.

Second, administrators say that teacher evaluations are pointless because tenure laws make it virtually impossible to fire incompetent teachers. That type of thinking, however, misses the point about teacher evaluations.

Their primary purpose is not to pinpoint teachers to fire; it's to provide meaningful feedback and pinpoint areas of needed development to enable *all* teachers to improve. Even if a school could more easily fire its under-performing teachers (and replace them with high-quality ones), far more students would benefit if meaningful evaluations enabled the rest of the school's teachers to continuously enhance their teaching skills.

Moreover, if tenure laws explain why administrators weren't evaluating teachers appropriately, one would expect administrators to fire large numbers of underperforming teachers *before* they received tenure. Harvard researcher Matthew M. Chingos, however, found that's not the case. After studying teacher employment patterns in North Carolina, where beginning teachers can't get tenure for four years, he found that "there is no evidence that principals use the four-year decision point to cull the pool of teachers." He posited several explanations for the relatively modest dismissal rates for young teachers: "a limited supply of effective teachers (it's rational to keep a mediocre teacher if the likely replacement will be no better), a lack of administrator ability to discern teacher quality (their observations are less predictive of value-added than those of outside observers), or a simple unwillingness to make the unpleasant decision of firing someone."[12]

Chingos's explanations make sense. One could understand why, for instance, a principal would be reluctant to fire an untenured teacher if he or she didn't have a better replacement. Teacher shortages do, in fact, exist, particularly in high-poverty schools. A 2004 study by Kacey Guin of employment patterns in urban schools found the average number of applicants for every teaching position in high-poverty schools was five or fewer—compared to, typically, more than 150 in other schools.[13] To be sure, some principals may be responsible for making their schools less attractive to applicants. The paucity of applicants in some schools, however, could very well be a symptom of management decisions at the district level, such as not ensuring adequate teaching conditions.

In the end, administrators have an obligation to conduct robust and effective teacher evaluations, and Montgomery County and other districts with similar programs show that it's doable. Administrators (and accomplished teachers who also can play a role in the evaluation process) should be able to discern teacher quality, and they also should be able to have a difficult conversation with a struggling teacher who either needs support or must be let go.

Whatever their reasons for granting tenure to teachers they haven't thoroughly evaluated, administrators who do that and also complain that it's too hard to fire bad teachers are being more than a little hypocritical.

Building Teacher Capacity

The "professional development 'system' for teachers is, by all accounts, broken," said Harvard Professor Heather C. Hill.[14] Poor-quality, incoherent, nontransferable training, often delivered by trainers who lack the necessary capacity, often does more harm than good, Hill found.

Teaching is exceedingly challenging, particularly for those working in schools in which most students are poor, perform well below grade-level expectations, and have limited proficiency with English. Numerous studies attest to the impact of well-executed professional development (i.e., development that's intensive, connected to the practice of teaching, and focused on student learning) on teacher quality, including a 2007 report by the Institute for Education Sciences, which found that such development raised student academic achievement by an average of 21 percentile points.[15] Nevertheless, many schools don't provide the meaningful professional development that's critical to teacher (and administrator) success.

Collaborative managers hold themselves accountable for ensuring that teachers and administrators have ample opportunity to engage in high-quality professional development. They lead with capacity and follow with accountability, which is what all successful school systems outside the United States do, according to Michael Fullan.[16]

More specifically, collaborative managers replace the traditional one-size-fits-all approach to professional learning with a targeted and multifaceted system that serves educators' unique needs. That creates the time and space for such activities as professional learning communities, common planning time, peer observation, instructional coaching, and professional development from external and internal providers. Managers closely monitor the quality of professional development activities, and they ensure that educators can apply what they learn to their own assignments.

That's how, working together, leaders in the Springfield Public Schools (SPS) of Massachusetts strengthened their system of professional support: "The district and union . . . collaborated on a new professional development (PD) system aligned with its new, less experienced teacher workforce," a Rennie Center case study reported. "Prior to 2008, the PD offered was a relic from when a majority of SPS teachers had more than ten years of experience. [NEA Uniserve director Nancy] deProsse explained the new reality, 'Two-thirds of teachers were new, but PD kept on going like that wasn't the case.'

"To revise the district's PD offerings," the report said, "the [Springfield Education Association's] Professional Development Committee met regularly with SPS staff members from the Professional Development Office. Together, they shifted PD from a centralized weeklong process to a school-based one where school leadership teams decided how to use PD funds. New teacher orientation was also revamped with union input."[17]

Embracing Teacher Advocacy

Broadly speaking, collaborative managers don't begrudge unions when they fight for decent compensation, sensible employment protections, and supportive teaching conditions.

These managers understand that adult and student interests are not mutually exclusive. When managers lack the resources to provide fair compensation or to support capacity building for teachers, they work *with* unions and other stakeholders to get them. In Plattsburgh, New York, for instance, management and unions have done this quite successfully for many years by approaching the local community together in hopes of finding ways to augment school funds.

"Over the years," Saul A. Rubinstein and John E. McCarthy wrote in a 2010 case study of the district, "the board [in Plattsburgh] became composed of members who considered the union a valuable partner in shared decision making. . . . The community strongly supports the school district, and has never defeated a school budget or rejected a bond vote or referendum."[18]

That burden of change, however, does not fall solely on management. Unions, too, need to change.

Moving Beyond Industrial-Style Unionizing

"As the industrial model of schooling begins to crumble," Adam Urbanski wrote more than a decade ago, "so too must industrial-style unionizing. Teacher unions must lead the education-reform movement, not simply react to it. Whatever is to become of the 'new unionism,' however, must be built on the essential commitments of what teacher unions have always stood for: democratic dynamics, fairness and due process, self-determination, unity without unanimity, social justice, and the dignity of all work and workers."[19]

The need for union reform is just as important today. Unions should start by putting the interests of students first, recognizing that teachers will do well only when students do well. To do that, they should expand the scope of collective bargaining so that teachers can help shape education programs and policies.

As many advocates for progressive unionism have argued, unions also need to articulate more clearly what they're for, not just what they're against. Former Massachusetts Teachers Association President Paul Toner headlined an article he wrote on union reform this way: "We Can't Just Say 'No': Teachers Unions Must Lead Change."[20] When education officials enact misguided reform policy, unions not only should speak out in opposition, but also should offer thoughtful alternatives. Take, for example, the federal Race to the Top (RTTT) program, which teachers, unions, and many researchers have justifiably criticized because of the way states were driven to use test scores as part of teacher evaluations. Most educators admit that current teacher evaluation systems are generally meaningless and unhelpful, which is why unions and management should work together to build or adopt robust, multiple-measure alternatives.[21] Hoping to spur change, Toner and the MTA worked closely with multiple stakeholders on the state's RTTT application, a new teacher evaluation system, and new teacher layoff procedures.

Unfortunately, too many of today's teacher unions are defining their missions too narrowly on bread-and-butter issues, rather than on improving systems, giving voice to teachers, and building educator capacity. They still view managers as adversaries rather than potential partners. And they still devote more time to submitting grievances on behalf of a small number of teachers and reacting to management's actions, rather than advancing viable alternatives and systemic solutions that would reduce the need for grievances in the first place. The defensive stance worked in the past when management often viewed teachers as mere "hired hands"—and it still may be necessary today if management is unwilling to view teachers as equal partners—but it behooves unions to advocate for collaboration and to call on management to do the same. In the end, this approach will build a stronger profession, and it will be better for students.

Fixing Teacher Tenure Laws

Collaborative unions don't sidestep controversial issues, and they're open to sensible reforms of policies that protect teachers, such as tenure. Critics complain that tenure virtually guarantees teachers a job for life, causing students to suffer because administrators can't fire incompetent ones. In reality, tenure merely guarantees due process, not permanent employment. Districts can fire incompetent teachers, but only if management can document that they're incompetent.

States first enacted tenure laws nearly a century ago, before teacher unions existed, to protect teachers from arbitrary dismissals (for getting married, for instance, or getting pregnant). Today, other laws protect teachers (and most employees) from losing their jobs for these reasons, but without tenure, administrators could fire teachers for a number of other reasons—to save money by hiring cheaper replacements, to oust teachers who question their policies, or for no reason at all since administrators wouldn't have to justify their decision. The due process that tenure provides is a vital protection that allows teachers to work without fear of retribution, and it avoids arbitrary and capricious dismissals.

So why should unions discuss tenure? Because the process of adjudicating cases of alleged incompetence is "usually adversarial, cumbersome, and costly," according to a 2009 report by the Center for American Progress. "Dismissal of tenured teachers tends to be more about procedure than about substance—not surprising given the fact that hearing officers are frequently not educators and can more easily make judgments about process than about teaching practice. In fact," the report continues, "because reasons are often nebulous, bureaucratic procedures are complex, and administrators are inept at following the rules. The process can take months—if not years—involve the school administration as well as the courts, and be very costly to all concerned—including unions and the administration."[22]

I was an expert witness for the defense in *Vergara v. California,* in which the Los Angeles Superior Court threw out California's teacher tenure laws. If the decision holds up under appeal, it will be much easier for administrators in California to fire teachers. After the decision, I wrote in the *Los Angeles Times,* "It should not take years and hundreds of thousands of dollars to fire an ineffective teacher if he or she has been given a reasonable chance to improve, has been carefully evaluated and hasn't done better."[23]

The solution is not to abolish tenure, but to fix it—by ensuring that the process remains fair *and* efficient. In my *Times* piece, I recommended that stakeholders come together around a "grand bargain" that would address problems with the state's teacher protections as well as conditions that prevent teachers from being as effective as they can be.

In 2011, upon a request by the American Federation of Teachers (AFT), well-known attorney Ken Feinberg issued a report recommending ways to expedite cases of alleged teacher misconduct.[24] The AFT welcomed these recommendations, but they applied only to misconduct cases and not to incompetence—and state and local unions aren't required to follow them. Unions, management, and policy makers should develop fair and efficient ways to address all cases in which administrators believe a teacher is unfit to teach.[25] Most teachers agree. "More than six in 10 (63 percent) teachers in the overall sample," according to a 2008 Education Sector teacher survey, "say they would support the union or association in their district taking the lead on ways to simplify the process for removing teachers who are past the probationary period and who are clearly ineffective and shouldn't be in the classroom. Just 16 percent would oppose it."[26]

In fact, some districts have solved the problem. The peer assistance and review (PAR) programs that I've discussed have existed since the mid-1980s, and they've helped many struggling teachers improve enough to avoid dismissal proceedings. Moreover, most teachers who don't improve leave voluntarily and the rest are fired, often without costly proceedings. Across the country, many districts have successfully used PAR programs, but the number remains small—partly because some union leaders and some managers oppose the idea of teachers evaluating their peers.

PAR programs tend to be most controversial in places where they don't exist. Given the successful record of well-run PAR programs, unions and management should study them and work with local education officials to adopt robust ones of their own.[27] To be sure, well-run PAR programs aren't cheap. Thus, if state and district education officials sincerely want to improve teacher quality, they'll have to pay for it.

Fixing Seniority Regulations

Unions also should not shy away from the controversial topic of seniority protections for teachers.

Critics of seniority regulations say that administrators should make personnel decisions based on ability, not years of service. That is, administrators should not automatically fire the least-senior teachers first when districts must lay off teachers. Further, they should not necessarily first honor the requests of the most-senior teachers when teachers seek transfers 'from one school to another.

In fact, however, administrators do not make personnel decisions in the way that critics suggest. For one thing, transfer rules are typically established through collective bargaining. Unions and management often agree that the most-senior teachers should have priority when opportunities to transfer become available. For another thing, some districts address seniority differently. For the past twenty-five years in the Rochester City Schools, school-based committees that consist mostly of teachers have decided which teachers transfer into their schools when vacancies occur. The committees base their decisions on a variety of factors, including a teacher's qualifications, experience, and fit for the position at hand.

The situation in which budget cuts or declining student enrollments force districts to fire teachers is more challenging. Proponents of seniority policies argue that these policies encourage teachers to stay in the classroom due to the added job security. That's an important consideration in districts striving to retain more of their accomplished teachers. Research also shows that seniority tends to go hand-in-hand with teacher experience and effectiveness.[28]

When districts lay off teachers, often with little notice, they argue that students *generally* are better off when the least experienced teachers go first. But that approach risks losing younger teachers who may be more effective than the experienced ones who remain. The solution, again, is not to abolish seniority protections but to fix them.

Without seniority, someone has to decide who goes and who stays. If we had highly reliable evaluation systems that could accurately rank teachers from least effective to most effective, then administrators could lay off teachers based on merit. We don't, however, and that's why we shouldn't simply leave the high-stakes dismissal decisions up to principals. They're the ones charged with evaluating teachers, and, in some cases, they could well make decisions arbitrarily on whether to fire or retain teachers. In addition, some principals who are looking for ways to cut salary expenses may give weaker evaluations to more expensive veteran teachers, making it easier to let them go if they must institute layoffs.

Fourteen states now forbid districts from using any factor *other than* length of service to make layoff decisions, and lawmakers in several other states have proposed similar legislation.[29] On the other hand, California's *Vergara* decision struck down the state's laws on seniority and, unless a higher court overturns it, the state will have to find another way to impose layoffs. Either way, negative public sentiments toward unions will only intensify unless unions, working with management and policy makers, develop sensible alternatives that allow administrators to weigh seniority as one, but only one, consideration when imposing layoffs.

Montgomery County, Maryland, provides an interesting alternative. It "offers protection to tenured teachers who have more than six years of experience—but less, experienced teachers, even though they earn tenure after two years, are to be laid off first in order of licensure category (starting with those who do not have full-fledged provisional licenses and continuing through fully licensed and tenured teachers)," according to a 2010 National Center on Teacher Quality report.

"Within each type, however," the report continues, "performance is given equal weight with years of experience up until the six-year mark. For teachers at that point in their careers, experience is weighed more heavily, and absent a serious performance problem, a six-year, tenured teacher would not likely face a layoff."[30]

Fixing Compensation Systems

In addition, forward-looking unions are open to alternative compensation systems to the traditional single-salary schedules, in which beginning teachers start at the bottom of the salary schedule and receive pay increases for each additional year of service (or "step").

Union critics have long complained about single-salary systems (sometimes called "step-and-lane" systems), which have existed for decades and which the vast majority of America's school districts still use. Critics say they treat all teachers alike, giving them no incentive to improve their skills. Nevertheless, many districts with such systems also allow teachers to receive relatively small raises for additional professional development (which are the "lanes").

Critics might be surprised to learn that unions didn't invent single-salary compensation systems. They're a vestige of civil service programs dating to the 1920s that were designed to ensure that government employees were treated fairly. Until recently, unions supported them strongly for that reason. In 2013, however, National Education Association (NEA) President Dennis Van Roekel said that educators should replace these systems with one that differentiates pay more sensibly.[31] More than a decade earlier, the AFT had passed a resolution recommending improvements to the single-salary schedule.

"As typically implemented," the AFT resolution stated, "the traditional salary schedule does not reward additional skills and knowledge that benefit children (e.g., licensure in multiple fields), exemplary practice (e.g., attainment of National Board Certification) or extraordinary circumstances (e.g., teaching in hard-to-staff schools). It does not respond to market forces (e.g., shortages in particular teaching fields such as science, math and special education), nor does it provide incentives for teachers to assume differentiated roles (e.g., mentor, lead teacher, curriculum developer). Finally, it fails to provide incentives for teachers to acquire skills and knowledge needed to deliver standards-based instruction."[32]

The teacher compensation issue became so contentious in recent years that even President Obama weighed in. "It's time," he said in a 2009 speech, "to start rewarding good teachers, [and] stop making excuses for bad ones."[33] Reflecting Obama's exhortation, the $4.3 billion Race to the

Top Program that US Secretary of Education Arne Duncan announced a few months later required states receiving grants from this program to offer merit pay systems that would reward teachers who boost their students' achievement scores.

Although unions generally oppose merit pay systems based on test scores, some state unions agreed to adopt them in order to win Race to the Top funds and, in some cases, because they thought those systems might produce better outcomes. As it turns out, however, merit pay is no magic bullet to what ails our education system. A year after Duncan unveiled Race to the Top, the first scientific analysis of merit pay for teachers found that it does not raise test scores.[34] Also in 2010, a study of merit pay for New York City teachers came to the same conclusion but went even further, saying, "If anything, teacher incentives may decrease student achievement, especially in larger schools."[35] That study helped to end the program.[36]

Moreover, merit pay also has some undesirable side effects. For instance, the competition for limited resources diminishes collaboration among teachers. For another, some educators game the system by "teaching to the test," for instance, or by outright cheating.[37]

Beyond merit pay, however, educators have other alternatives to traditional single-salary schedules from which to choose. Many of the collaborative districts highlighted here have adopted such alternatives. Montgomery County has a career lattice program that allows teachers to apply for lead teacher status. As lead teachers, they can earn additional pay for such roles as a PAR consulting teacher, a mentor to beginning teachers, and a staff development teacher.

In Portland, Maine, the union and management developed the Professional Learning Based Salary System (PLBSS) whose goals included, "improving instructional practice through professional learning; compensating teachers for the acquisition of new skills and knowledge; reducing the number of years to reach maximum salary; improving career earnings; and rewarding teachers who take on leadership roles." NEA researchers reported the following benefits:

- Teachers have embraced quality professional development opportunities targeted at improving their students' learning.
- [Union] members view the system as strengthening the professional culture.
- The system has fostered collaborative relationships between teachers and administration.
- The new system has increased [the local union's] capacity and enhanced [its] positive image in the community.
- Although the system boasts high support, some teachers expressed frustration concerning what they viewed as inequities.[38]

The last finding is worth noting. Despite the many benefits of Portland's alternative compensation system, one teacher said, "I still find that some experienced teachers resent the teachers with less experience making the same kind of money that they had to wait many years to get to."[39] That reflects the kind of resistance union leaders can face when they propose something new.

Notwithstanding the coming resistance, however, the benefits of alternative compensation systems are clear. That's why state and local unions should work diligently with management and policy makers to develop new systems of their own. As Mark Simon, former president of the Montgomery County Education Association, said, "There is a sufficient degree of openness on the details that teacher unions and other organizations that represent teachers need to jump in with ideas and pilot projects. This is the moment for educators to not just be part of the conversation, but to drive the conversation. Shame on us if we don't."[40]

Empowering Teachers

While addressing such tough issues as tenure, seniority, and compensation, unions can do even more.

As Adam Urbanski has often recommended, unions should serve as the voice *of* teachers, but they should also give voice *to* teachers. That is, union leaders should create structures for teachers to express their views (for example, through member surveys, teacher forums, and listening tours) and then accurately promote those views at the bargaining table. That's particularly important as the scope of bargaining and informal problem solving expands to matters related to teaching and learning. Without regularly soliciting teachers' views, union leaders can't know what they want on a multitude of complex issues.

National and state unions also should give local chapters the autonomy to make their own decisions. Bob Peterson, former president of the Milwaukee Teachers' Education Association, said his local union's challenge is to become a member-driven organization, not one driven by staff from its national parent, the NEA. That's necessary, he said, to give voice to district teachers on issues related to teaching and learning. But the shift to local control has not been easy, Peterson said, because the NEA often adheres to a decades-old philosophy that the NEA director assigned to a local district "was the one who should be the public spokesperson, develop agendas for elected executive boards, and direct most of the union's affairs."[41]

The AFT doesn't operate this way, nor do some NEA locals that have ironed out alternative arrangements with the national affiliate. Now that the NEA has publicly pledged support for labor-management partnerships and for teachers who become more involved in educational issues, the organization's leaders should rethink the way it supports its local unions.

Finally, union leaders at all levels have to recognize that the policies and programs that work for some teachers don't work for others. That's why unions in districts like Rochester, New York; Toledo, Ohio; and Eugene, Oregon, have promoted "living contracts" that encourage teachers to negotiate their own contract provisions. Some union leaders, however, still believe that different approaches will weaken their position. But that one-size-fits-all thinking is a vestige of industrial unionism. By restricting healthy innovation, such union leaders disempower their unions, feed suspicions that unions are impediments to reform, and erode hard-won protections.

Today, unions should remain united on core principles such as due process, fair wages, and adequate school funding, but they also should become increasingly nimble, creative, and open to diverse perspectives.

Thus, management and unions both have changes to make. Management should invite unions to serve as equal partners in reform and hold themselves accountable for providing all of the supports—including well-administered evaluations and high-quality professional development—that teachers need to succeed. Unions should expand their traditional role by helping to cultivate the capacity of teachers, helping to build better systems of education, and expanding on innovative alternatives to increasingly controversial policies like tenure and seniority.

The epilogue takes a final look at the lessons we can learn about labor-management collaboration, the system changes required to bring it about, and the single most important commodity for fueling change.

The Future We Choose

"FOR DEMOCRACY TO SURVIVE, let alone thrive," political scientist Wendy Brown once said, "the people must be able to know and analyze the powers organizing our lives. The people must be able to reflect on the perils and possibilities of our time and develop considered views about how to navigate them. The people must be able to analyze written and oral arguments, journalistic accounts, images and sound bites . . . distinguishing the reasonable from the sensational, the serious from the simplistic, the well founded from the fatuous. If such capacities have always been important to democratic citizenship, our increasingly complex world demands them all the more, and quality public education is the keystone to their acquisition. Without quality public education in our future, there is no future for democracy."[1]

If so, we should be concerned. Once a high performer among industrialized nations, the United States now ranks near the middle in reading, math, and science.[2] The No Child Left Behind Act, which President George W. Bush signed in early 2002, was designed to boost academic outcomes and close a widening achievement gap between poor minority students and their wealthier nonminority counterparts. But in 2013, just 26 percent of all twelfth graders were proficient in math, and the proficiency gap between Asians and whites (who were at 47 percent and 33 percent, respectively) and Hispanics and African Americans (at 12 percent and 7 percent) was striking. The same pattern held for reading, where overall proficiency was 38 percent, while it was 47 percent for Asians and whites and 23 and 16 percent for Hispanics and African Americans, respectively.[3]

Today, many policy makers agree that the primary federal education law—the Elementary and Secondary Education Act—is flawed, but they don't agree on how to change it. Some want the federal government to continue striving to improve outcomes through testing and accountability measures and, thus, that policy makers should just tweak the law. Others, like Tennessee's Republican Senator Lamar Alexander, chairman of the Senate Health, Education, Labor, and Pensions Committee, want drastic changes—arguing that states, not Washington, should evaluate school performance and determine what to do when schools struggle.

Debates over the future of education, however, are underway far beyond Washington. States are wrestling with the academic standards they want for their schools, which tests will best measure progress, how to allocate resources, how to evaluate teachers, and what job protections teachers should enjoy. Meanwhile, local districts spend lots of time complying with federal and state education policies. However they view these policies, they would pay a steep price in funding losses and other sanctions if they didn't comply with them.

Local education stakeholders also face critical questions about how best to educate students. How will they recruit and retain the best teachers and administrators? How will they ensure that educators have the professional support they need to succeed? How will they apply information about student learning to improve instruction? How will they allocate human and fiscal resources to ensure that every student has a chance to learn? How will they empower students, families, and community members to help shape the reform agenda?

As they debate which reform paths to pursue, federal, state, and local education leaders should heed the lessons from Montgomery County, Cincinnati, ABC Unified in Los Angeles, and other districts where management and union leaders are producing better outcomes for students by addressing problems together rather than fighting with one another. Policy makers should consider how their policies support or hinder labor-management efforts to work as partners. Too often, ill-conceived policies pit one side against the other, set unreasonable performance targets, and provide inadequate support to achieve them, impeding collaboration and ultimately hampering student learning.

But, while labor-management collaboration is necessary for educational improvement, it's no silver bullet. Effective partnerships are hard to create and hard to sustain. Even successful ones do not always generate better outcomes for students. As partners, management and labor still must adopt a sensible reform agenda and implement it well. Moreover, they face problems beyond their control—for example, students who are hungry, in poor health, and in unstable living arrangements, and communities that lack the resources to invest in their schools. Consequently, many districts have crowded classes and poorly maintained facilities, and they don't have enough books and learning materials.

Thus, while establishing effective labor-management partnerships, educators must craft comprehensive, systemwide solutions to the challenges before them. They must invest more in education, provide more support for teachers, take the right approach to pursuing and measuring educational progress, and find the best way to hold educators accountable for results.

In fact, educators must seek answers not just in successful districts across America but in education systems far from our borders—in Finland, for instance. Though vastly different than America in size, ethnic makeup, and other key characteristics, Finland struggled with some of the very issues that confront the United States. As a result, its success provides important lessons about how we can initiate and implement systemwide educational reform.

Lessons from Abroad

Decades ago, Finland's schools lagged behind those of countries like Sweden, the United Kingdom, the United States, and Germany. In 1970, most of Finland's students received just a "basic education," and only 14 percent completed high school. Not surprisingly, this system fueled an achievement gap that mirrored the country's deep socioeconomic divide.

The transformation to a more egalitarian system did not come easily. "My challenge," recalled Jukka Sarjala, a top official with the Ministry of Education at the time, "was to develop a plan that guaranteed that this reform would ultimately be implemented in every Finnish community. There were lots of municipalities that were not eager to reform their system, which is why it was important to have a legal mandate. This was a very big reform, very big and complicated for teachers accustomed to the old system."[4]

While convincing communities and teachers to accept a dramatically different, more ambitious approach to education, the government invested heavily to enhance the capacity of its educators. The reforms and investments paid off and, in recent years, Finland's schools have performed extraordinarily well. The nation has consistently ranked near the top in reading, math, and science when compared with twenty-nine other countries in the Organisation for Economic Co-operation and Development (OECD).[5] Today, over 90 percent of Finland's students graduate high school.[6]

Unlike America, Finland avoided the temptation of high-stakes standardized testing. Instead, Finns accepted the apparent paradox that Finnish educator Pasi Sahlberg described as "test less, learn more." "While nations around the world introduced heavy standardized testing regimes in the 1990s," education scholar Samuel E. Abrams wrote in 2011, "the Finnish National Board of Education concluded that such tests would consume too much instructional time, cost too much to construct, proctor, and grade, and generate undue stress."[7]

The Finns believe their sharp focus on teaching, their authentic assessment of student learning, and their avoidance of external pressure explain their consistently high results on international exams. (A small number of randomly selected students in Finland take internationally normed exams to determine how well their schools are doing.) "Instead of test-based accountability, the Finnish system relies on the expertise and professional accountability of teachers who are knowledgeable and committed," Sahlberg said.[8]

Teaching is a well-regarded profession in Finland, and teaching jobs are highly competitive; only 15 percent of those who apply to teacher education programs get in. In addition, Finland invests heavily in its new teaching prospects. Unlike US preparation programs that typically take twelve to eighteen months to complete, teachers in Finland spend two to three years in preparation, and the government pays all tuition and living expenses.[9]

Once teachers are hired in Finland, they're far likelier to remain teachers than their US counterparts—largely because they receive ongoing support for professional learning, opportunities to participate in local decision making, and supportive teaching conditions. Only 10 to 15 percent of Finnish teachers leave the profession before their careers end. In the United States, by contrast, close to half of new teachers in urban schools leave the profession in the first five years.

US educators can learn important lessons from Finland. For one thing, its experience shows that systemic change does not come quickly. Reflecting my recommendation that education reformers go slow to go fast, Sahlberg said, "While [the Finnish] lessons hold great promise, they call for patience. In this age of immediate results, education requires a different mindset. Reforming schools is a complex and slow process. To rush this process is to ruin it."[10]

In addition, Finland shows, reforms to bring quality education to all students require significant and strategic investments. Finland ensures that all schools receive the support they need to succeed, rather than opting for market-based competition (e.g., vouchers and charter schools) that characterizes so much of US reform efforts. Finland also assures that prospective teachers are well prepared before they're hired by subsidizing the tuition and living costs associated with teacher preparation.

Moreover, Finland proves Michael Fullan's dictum that "leading with accountability is not the best way to get accountability, let alone whole system reform."[11] Finland stresses capacity building (e.g., by investing in teacher quality) over accountability (e.g., by avoiding high-stakes standardized tests). Finally, through its highly collaborative and trusting relationships between administrators and the teacher union, Finland shows that unions can and should be essential partners in the quest for better schools and higher student achievement.

For America, the question is whether we can apply not just the lessons of Montgomery County and other successful US districts but also those of Finland to fulfill the promise of a quality education for every student in America.

A Call for Courageous Leadership

Less than a century ago, women in America could not vote. Until the nineteenth amendment to the Constitution was ratified in 1920, most Americans thought they never would—and many fought hard to make sure they didn't. Just a half-century ago, many African Americans could not vote, prompting President Lyndon B. Johnson and Congress to enact the Voting Rights Act of 1965. That effort, too, was strongly resisted in some quarters.

Both of these monumental achievements reflected America's continuing desire, in the words of our Constitution, "to form a more perfect union"—in these cases, to extend the reach of justice and equality. But if Americans of all sexes and colors can now vote, all too many still can't get a quality education. What do we need to create a world-class, equitable education system?

We need the same thing that brought voting rights to women and African Americans: *courageous leadership*. We need education leaders with the courage to reject quick fixes, to abandon programs that don't work, and to take a long and comprehensive view of reform. We need policy makers and school managers with the courage to promote labor-management collaboration because they surely will be criticized for peddling soft solutions to hard problems, for not confronting their "adversaries" on the other side, for capitulating from the start.

We also need union leaders with the courage to promote collaboration because unionists who are still wedded to industrial-unionism will accuse them of selling out. But, as former Massachusetts Teachers Association President Paul Toner put it, "The only way we can bring about lasting and meaningful change in our schools for the benefit of our students is to provide teachers with meaningful voice in the decisions affecting their day-to-day work life and developing strong labor-management collaboration at all levels—national, state and local."[12]

In this era of educational warfare, with administrators fighting with unions, school boards encouraging superintendents to stand firm, and teachers pushing unions to confront district management, we need educators in all positions with the courage to *wage peace*. We need educators who refuse to see their fellow educators as adversaries, who do everything they can to maintain civil and productive relationships, and who think children have a right to expect adults to work together on their behalf—that is, who do the very thing that we teach our children to do.

Fortunately, we have many courageous education leaders in America, some of whom I've named in this book. We just need more of them. We also need civic leaders who will echo their calls for collaboration. We can address an education system that's failing our children, particularly our poor and minority children, only when educators quiet the education wars—and when unions, management, and other stakeholders work together toward a better future for *all* of our children.

A Guide to Resources on Labor-Management Collaboration in Education

Organizations

Teacher Union Reform Network (TURN)

www.turnweb.org

Founded in 1995, TURN was one of the first national organizations to promote labor-management collaboration and progressive unionism. Its website says, "Teacher Union Reform Network is a union-led effort to strengthen the nation's teachers unions by promoting progressive reforms that will ultimately lead to better learning for all students. Because teachers are closest to students, to the learning process, and because of their link to parents and the larger communities, we are in a unique position to stimulate the necessary changes that will lead to sustaining more equitable and effective schools for all students."

Regional TURN affiliates:
California (www.turnweb.org/california)
Great Lakes (www.turnweb.org/great-lakes)
Mid-Atlantic Southeast (www.turnweb.org/mid-atlantic-southeast)
Northeast (www.turnweb.org/northeast)
Northwest (www.turnweb.org/northwest)
Southwest (www.turnweb.org/southwest)

Consortium for Educational Change (CEC)
www.cecillinois.org

Located in Lombard, Illinois, the CEC has been promoting organizational change and labor-management partnerships since 1987. Its website says, "The Consortium for Educational Change (CEC) builds collaborative structures, processes and cultures with and among key educational stake-holders, including labor and management, to transform educational systems to continuously improve learning and achievement for all students."

The CEC focuses on three areas of labor-management collaboration:

- Interest-based strategies (IBS)
- Relationship and skill building
- New structures and processes

The Tom Mooney Institute for Teacher and Union Leadership
www.mooneyinstitute.org

The Institute's mission, according to its website states: "[The Tom Mooney Institute for Teacher & Union Leadership] provides leadership and organizational development services to teacher union locals by engaging in a multi-year consulting relationship with the locals and providing a cohort experience for a group of 'critical friend' locals. MITUL contracts with interested teacher union locals to engage in a process of self-analysis, leadership development and capacity building. We ask for a commitment to the consultation and cohort process from a defined leadership team in the local.

"MITUL also engages in broad communication, education and advocacy around the role of teacher unions in defining and leading public education reform. We seek to continually build and deepen a progressive vision and analysis for teacher unions, opinion leaders, policy-makers and advocacy organizations. We engage with our colleagues at the NEA, the AFT, TURN, and with public education advocates nationally."

Rennie Center for Educational Research and Policy
www.renniecenter.org

According to its website, the mission of the Rennie Center "is to improve public education through well-informed decision-making based on deep knowledge and evidence of effective policymaking and practice. As Massachusetts' preeminent voice in public education reform, we create open spaces for educators and policymakers to consider evidence, discuss cutting-edge issues, and develop new approaches to advance student learning and achievement."

Massachusetts Education Partnership (MEP)
www.renniecenter.org/programs/MEP.html

The MEP was created in 2012 and is managed by the Rennie Center for Educational Research and Policy. According to its website, "[t]he MEP works in close partnership with local teams of superintendents, union leaders, school committee members, administrators, and teachers to strengthen labor-management relations and school-site operations and develop the collaborative practices necessary to achieve effective and sustainable reform."

The MEP oversees two initiatives: the Interest-Based Bargaining Institute (IBBI) and the District Capacity Project (DCP).

"The Interest-Based Bargaining Institute (IBBI) offers training and facilitation to school districts and locals wishing to transform the way they engage in collective bargaining. The Institute's IBB program was developed to provide an alternative to traditional collective bargaining, which takes a more adversarial approach."

"The District Capacity Project (DCP) enables collaborative labor-management teams to identify common education interests and design and pursue innovative projects to advance student learning."

The California Labor Management Initiative (CA LMI)

www.cdefoundation.org/lmi

The CA LMI, cosponsored by the state's labor and management organizations and the California Department of Education, was launched in 2015. Its goals are to

- build the collective knowledge base for supporting local labor-management collaborations in California
- build capacity and resources at the state, regional, and local levels to support local labor-management collaborations
- facilitate learning and sharing of promising labor-management practices among local labor-management teams
- improve a wide range of educational outcomes

The National Education Association (NEA)

www.nea.org

With over three million members, the NEA is the largest professional employee union in the country. In 2011, the NEA signed a pledge with other national education organizations to support labor-management partnerships. Among the initiatives the NEA has developed in support of collaboration is the KEYS 2.0 Online Action Guide, a comprehensive training resource to help local stakeholders improve teaching and learning through collaboration. The guide is available at http://keys3.obiki.org/guide/index.htm.

The American Federation of Teachers (AFT)

www.aft.org

The AFT represents 1.6 million members and has been a strong advocate for labor-management collaboration. Like its counterpart, the NEA, the

AFT signed a pledge with other national education organizations to support labor-management collaboration. The AFT's Innovation Fund, which provides financial support for "solution-driven" projects, is one of several ways the organization promotes labor-management partnerships.

The NEA Foundation

www.neafoundation.org

According to its website, "The NEA Foundation is a public charity supported by contributions from educators' dues, corporate sponsors, foundations, and others who support public education initiatives."

Among several initiatives the NEA supports is a series of online courses designed to assist district leaders develop their capacity to collaborate effectively. "The courses promote union-district collaboration as a tool for systems change and were developed by field experts, using a rich selection of resources," according to the foundation's website at www.neafoundation. org/pages/courses/.

Dialogos

www.dialogos.com

Dialogos has provided support to a wide range of organizations, including San Juan Unified School District in Sacramento, that seek to strengthen their collaborative practices. The Dialogos website states, "We help clients create inspired futures, awaken shared purpose and activate collective intelligence to produce committed and aligned performance. In partnership with us, leaders discover new ways of working together that generate profound transformations in their organizations—and in themselves."

VitalSmarts

www.vitalsmarts.com

VitalSmarts is the publisher of several books, including *Crucial Conversations* and *Crucial Accountability*, both of which provide useful strategies for resolving conflict and improving communication. VitalSmarts also conducts training courses on these strategies.

Fierce, Inc.

www.fierceinc.com

Fierce, Inc., offers training and other resources to organizations, including specialized training for educators. "Fierce in the Schools (FITS) provides teachers, administrators and students with practical easy-to-learn skills to make daily conversations more effective, build trust, improve learning, and prepare for the future—academically, professionally, and personally." ABC Unified, one of the districts featured in this book, uses resources from Fierce, Inc., to develop its leaders.

Federal Mediation and Conciliation Service (FMCS)

www.fmcs.gov

According to its website, "For over 50 years, FMCS has promoted sound and stable labor-management relations by providing mediation assistance in contract negotiation disputes between employers and their unionized employees."

FMCS offers training on numerous subjects including interest-based bargaining, interpersonal communications, and labor-management roles and responsibilities.

Books

United Mind Workers: Unions and Teaching in the Knowledge Society

Authors: Kerchner, Charles, T., Koppich, Julia E., & Weeres, Joseph G.
Publication Year: 1997
Publisher: Jossey-Bass

From the back cover:

> "How teacher's unions can serve as advocates of innovative school reform. In this groundbreaking work, the authors make a compelling case for transforming teacher unions to become champions of quality schooling. This new model of teacher unions would be organized around issues of quality teaching and professional development, as well as, economic fairness. The authors propose strategies for expanding the influence of

unions by involving them in the setting of educational standards, evaluating teacher performance, and promoting career security, portable pensions, and employment services for teachers. The book maps out new contracting strategies and labor law reforms that would allow unions to be more flexible and responsive to change."

Win-Win Labor-Management Collaboration in Education: Breakthrough Practices to Benefit Students, Teachers, and Administrators
Author: Kaboolian, Linda
Publication Year: 2005
Publisher: The Rennie Center for Education Research and Policy

The book's introduction states, "This 'best practices' handbook provides a catalogue of innovative labor-management practices in public education for educational practitioners who are engaged in labor-management relations and collective bargaining."

Collaborating: Finding Common Ground for Multiparty Problems
Author: Gray, Barbara
Publication Year: 1989
Publisher: Jossey-Bass

In this analysis of collaboration for a broad range of organizations, Gray describes the features of collaboration and the benefits that accrue for the organizations that collaborate effectively.

Leading for Equity: The Pursuit of Excellence in Montgomery County Public Schools
Authors: Childress, Stacey M., Doyle, Denis P., & Thomas, David A.
Publication Year: 2009
Publisher: Harvard Education Press

This book tells the story of labor-management collaboration and dramatic student improvement in Montgomery County Public Schools.

Getting Teacher Evaluation Right
Author: Darling-Hammond, Linda
Publication Year: 2013
Publisher: Teachers College Press

Darling-Hammond addresses one of the most contentious issues in education today: how to evaluate the performance of teachers. She describes a number of evidenced-based models that are helping teachers improve their practice and that are widely supported by labor and management.

The Teacher Wars: A History of America's Most Embattled Profession
Author: Goldstein, Dana
Publication Year: 2014
Publisher: Doubleday

In her historical account of teaching in America, Goldstein focuses on the increasingly contentious battles that are playing out between teachers' supporters and critics. The best way to quiet the teacher wars and to improve schools, she argues, is to learn from and support teachers who are producing positive outcomes from their students.

Beyond the Education Wars: Evidence That Collaboration Builds Effective Schools
Author: Anrig, Greg
Publication Year: 2013
Publisher: The Century Foundation Press

Drawing upon case study research of several highly collaborative school districts, Anrig makes the case that labor-management partnerships provide the best chance for organizational change and improved student outcomes. Anrig argues, "student outcomes are much more likely to improve when educational stakeholders strive to pivot away from counterproductive arguments over unproven reforms and instead emulate the team-based approaches implemented in many effective schools."

Trust in Schools
Authors: Bryk, Anthony S., & Schneider, Barbara L.
Publication Year: 2002
Publisher: Russell Sage Foundation

Bryk and Schneider provide evidence that increased trust and strong relationships among educators is a strong predictor of positive student outcomes. They also show how educators build and sustain trust and avoid
the forces that often hinder it.

Radical Collaboration: Five Essential Skills to Overcome Defensiveness and
    Build Successful Relationships
Authors: Tamm, James W., & Luyet, Ronald J.
Publication Year: 2005
Publisher: HarperCollins

The book's back cover says, "*Radical Collaboration* is a how-to-manual
for anyone that wants to create trusting, collaborative environments, and
transform groups into motivated and empowered teams."

Finnish Lessons
Author: Sahlberg, Pasi
Publication Year: 2010
Publisher: Teachers College Press

Sahlberg explains how Finland created a world-class education system by
reducing poverty, building the capacity of its educators, and collaborating
with its teacher unions.

The Human Side of School Change
Author: Evans, Robert
Publication Year: 1996
Publisher: Jossey-Bass

The book's inside cover reads, "In this insightful look at the human side of school reform, Robert Evans examines the difficult hurdles to implementing innovation and explains how the best-intended efforts can be stalled by the resistance of educators who too often feel burdened and conflicted by the change process."

Reports and Articles

Labor Management Community Collaboration: Resources for Educators and Community Partners

Author(s): Massachusetts Education Partnership

Publication Year: 2015

Publisher: Massachusetts Education Partnership

URL: www.renniecenter.org/research/LMC_Toolkit.pdf

Toward a New Grand Bargain: Collaborative Approaches to Labor-Management Reform in Massachusetts

Author(s): Bluestone, Barry, & Kochan, Thomas A.

Publication Year: 2011

Publisher: The Boston Foundation

URL: http://50.87.169.168/Documents/EPRN/Collaborative-Approaches-to-Labor-Management-Reform-in-Massachusetts.pdf

"From Picket Line to Partnership: A Union, a District, and Their Thriving Schools"

Author: Dubin, Jennifer

Publication Year: 2009

Publisher: American Educator

URL: www.aft.org/periodical/american-educator/spring-2009/picket-line-partnership

Partnerships in Education: How Labor-Management Collaboration Is Transforming Public Schools

Author: Paris, Abigail
Publication Year: 2011
Publisher: American Rights at Work Education Fund
URL: www.jwj.org/wp-content/uploads/2013/12/110531partnershipsin
education_final.pdf

"Moving Meriden"
Author: Dubin, Jennifer
Publication Year: 2013–2014
Publisher: American Educator
URL: www.aft.org/periodical/american-educator/winter-2013-2014/
moving-meriden

Local Labor Management Relationships as a Vehicle to Advance Reform:
Findings from the U.S. Department of Education's Labor Management
Conference
Author: Eckert, Jonathan
Publication Year: 2011
Publisher: U.S. Department of Education
URL: www.ed.gov/sites/default/files/labor-management-collaboration-
district-case-studies_o.pdf

"Cultivating Collaboration"
Author: Anrig, Greg
Publication Year: 2013–2014
Publisher: American Educator
URL: www.aft.org/sites/default/files/periodicals/Anrig.pdf

Forward, Together: Better Schools Through Labor-Management Collaboration
Authors: Futernick, Ken, McClellan, Sara, & Vince, Scott
Publication Year: 2012
Publisher: WestEd

URL: www.wested.org/wp-content/files_mf/1371767244forwardtogether1.
pdf

"Reform or Be Reformed"
Author: Urbanski, Adam
Publication Year: 2001
Publisher: EducationNext
URL: http://educationnext.org/reform-or-be-reformed/

"We Can't Just Say 'No': Teachers Unions Must Lead Change"
Author: Toner, Paul
Publication Year: 2014
Publisher: Real Clear Education
URL: www.realcleareducation.com/articles/2014/03/12/we_cant_just_
say_no_teachers_unions_must_lead_change_897.html

*Trending Toward Reform: Teachers Speak on Unions and the Future of the
Profession*
Authors: Rosenberg, Sarah, & Silva, Elena
Publication Year: 2012
Publisher: Education Sector
URL: http://studentsmatter.org/wp-content/uploads/2012/09/SM_
Trending-Toward-Reform-Ed-Sector-Survey_07.10.12.pdf

*Teachers Unions and Management Partnerships: How Working Together
Improves Student Achievement*
Authors: Rubinstein, Saul, & McCarthy, John
Publication Year: 2014
Publisher: Center for American Progress
URL: www.americanprogress.org/wp-content/uploads/2014/03/
Rubinstein-EduReform-report.pdf

"Improving Relationships Within the Schoolhouse"
Author: Barth, Roland
Publication Year: 2006
Publisher: Educational Leadership
URL: www.ascd.org/publications/educational-leadership/mar06/vol63/
num06/Improving-Relationships-Within-the-Schoolhouse.aspx

**"Successful School Turnarounds Through Labor-Management Partner-
ships: The Role in State Education Agencies," in** *The State Role in
School Turnaround: Emerging Best Practices*
Authors: Futernick, Ken, & Urbanski, Adam
Publication Year: 2013
Publisher: WestEd
URL: http://centeronschoolturnaround.org/wp-content/uploads/2013/
09/CST_State_Role_Labor_Management.pdf

Case Study: Labor-Management-Community Collaboration in Springfield
Authors: Rennie Center for Educational Research and Policy
Publication Year: 2012
Publisher: Rennie Center for Educational Research and Policy
URL: www.renniecenter.org/research/LaborMgmtCommunityCollab.
pdf

*Reducing the Achievement Gap Through District/Union Collaboration:
The Tale of Two School Districts*
Authors: The National Commission on Teaching and America's Future
Publication Year: 2007
Publisher: The National Commission on Teaching and America's Future
URL: http://nctaf.org/wp-content/uploads/2012/01/Reducingthe
AchievementGapThroughDistrictUnionCollaborationfull.pdf

Human Capital: Unions and School Districts Collaborating to Close
Achievement Gaps
Author: The NEA Foundation
Publication Year: 2010
Publisher: The NEA Foundation
URL: www.neafoundation.org/downloads/HumanCapital.pdf

Interest-Based Bargaining in Education
Author: Klingel, Sally
Publication Year: 2003
Publisher: Cornell University ILR School
URL: http://digitalcommons.ilr.cornell.edu/cgi/viewcontent.cgi?article=
1015&context=reports

"Improving Student Achievement Through Labor-Management
Collaboration in Urban School Districts."
Author: Urbanski, Adam
Publication Year: 2003
Publisher: *Educational Policy*, 17(4), 503–518.
URL: http://epx.sagepub.com/content/17/4/503.full.pdf

Shared Responsibility: A U.S. Department of Education White Paper
Author: U.S. Department of Education
Publication Year: 2012
Publisher: U.S. Department of Education
URL: www2.ed.gov/documents/labor-management-collaboration/white-
paper-labor-management-collaboration.pdf

"The As-Yet-Unfulfilled Promise of Reform Bargaining," in *Collective*
Bargaining in Education.
Author: Koppich, Julia

Editors: Hannaway, Jane & Rotherham, Andrew J.
Publication Year: 2006
Publisher: Harvard Education Press
URL: http://hepg.org/HEPG/Media/Documents/collective-bargaining_
introduction.pdf

Notes

PREFACE

1. The compact between the district and its three labor unions is titled R.E.S.P.E.C.T. and is available at https://www.montgomeryschoolsmd.org/staff/respect/.
2. Geoff Marietta, *The Unions of Montgomery County*, Harvard Education Press, 19, http://hepg.org/hep-home/case/the-unions-in-montgomery-county-public-schools_85.
3. Joe Nathan, "Cincinnati Shows How to Close the Achievement Gap," Center for School Change, June 1, 2011, http://centerforschoolchange.org/2011/06/cincinnati-shows-how-to-close-the-achievement-gap/.
4. Ken Futernick et al., *Forward, Together: Better Schools Through Labor-Management Collaboration* (San Francisco, CA: WestEd, 2012).
5. Ken Futernick et al., *Labor-Management Collaboration in Education: The Process, the Impact, and the Prospects for Change* (Unpublished report, San Francisco, CA: WestEd, 2013).

INTRODUCTION

1. Stacey M. Childress, Denis P. Doyle, and David A. Thomas, *Leading for Equity: The Pursuit of Excellence in Montgomery County Public Schools* (Cambridge: Harvard Education Press, 2009).
2. Carin Dessauer, "The Last Lessons of Jerry Weast: A Question and Answer Session with the Retiring Superintendent of Montgomery County Public School," Bethesda Magazine, March/April 2011, http://www.bethesdamagazine.com/Bethesda-Magazine/March-April-2011/The-Last-Lessons-of-Jerry-Weast/index.php?cparticle=1&siarticle=0#artanc.
3. Michael Winerip, "Helping Teachers Help Themselves," *New York Times*, June 5, 2011.
4. Joel Klein and Michelle Rhee, "How to Fix Our Schools: A Manifesto by Joel Klein, Michelle Rhee and Other Education Leaders," *Washington Post*, October 10, 2010, http://www.washingtonpost.com/wp-dyn/content/article/2010/10/07/AR2010100705078.html.
5. Joel Klein, "The Failure of American Schools," *The Atlantic*, June 2011.

6. Bill Turque, "D.C. Has Long History of Troubled Education Reform," *Washington Post*, October 31, 2009, http://www.washingtonpost.com/wp-dyn/content/article/2009/10/31/AR2009103102357.html

7. Statement by Jonathan Alter, *Newsweek* commentator, in *Waiting for Superman*, directed by Davis Guggenheim (2010; Beverly Hills, CA: Participant Media), Film.

8. John Heilemann, "Schools: The Disaster Movie," *New York Magazine*, September 6, 2010.

9. Frederick Hess and Martin R. West, "Strike Phobia," *Education Next* 6, no. 3 (Summer 2006), http://educationnext.org/strikephobia/.

10. See, for instance, David C. Berliner and Gene V. Glass, *50 Myths and Lies That Threaten America's Public Schools—The Real Crisis in Education* (New York: Teachers College Press, 2014), which provides a detailed analysis of data upon which the alleged gains in student achievement and a closing of the achievement gap were based. In *Reign of Error* (New York: Alfred A. Knopf, 2013), Diane Ravitch also points to data showing that the achievement gap among Washington, DC's black and white students did not change during Chancellor's Rhee's tenure.

11. Sharon Otterman and Robert Gebeloff, "Triumph Fades on Racial Gap in City Schools," *New York Times*, August 15, 2010, http://www.nytimes.com/2010/08/16/nyregion/16gap.html.

12. Berliner and Glass, *50 Myths and Lies*, 52.

13. Alan Ginsburg, "The Rhee DC Record: Math and Reading Gains No Better Than Her Predecessors Vance and Janey," January 2011, http://therheedcrecord.wikispaces.com/file/view/The+Rhee+DC+Math+And+Reading+Record+.pdf.

14. Richard L. Colvin, *Tilting at Windmills* (Cambridge: Harvard Education Press, 2013), Kindle edition.

15. Daphna Bassok and Margaret E. Raymond, "Performance Trends and the Blueprint for Student Success," in *Urban School Reform*, ed. Frederick M. Hess (Cambridge: Harvard Education Press, 2005), 305–308.

16. Heather E. Quick et al., "Evaluation of the Blueprint for Student Success in a Standards Based-System, Year 2 Interim Report," American Institutes of Research, July 31, 2003, xii.

17. Diane Ravitch, *The Death and Life of the Great American School System: How Testing and Choice Are Undermining Education* (New York: Basic Books, 2010), 65.

18. Colvin, *Tilting at Windmills*, Kindle edition.

19. Alan D. Bersin, "Notes from my conversation with Tony. Issues re: discussion of staff developer" (memo), Bersin personal papers, undated, quoted in Colvin, *Tilting at Windmills*, Kindle edition.

20. The full mission statement of StudentsFirst is located at https://www.studentsfirst.org/OurMission.

21. Anna M. Phillips, "Group Aims to Counter Influence of Teachers' Union in New York," *New York Times*, April 3, 2012.

22. Ibid.

23. Linda Kaboolian, *Win-Win Labor-Management Collaboration in Education: Breakthrough Practices to Benefit Students, Teachers, and Administrators* (Cambridge: The Rennie Center for Educational Research and Policy, 2005), 5.

24. Carl A. Cohn, "Empowering Those at the Bottom Beats Punishing Them from the Top," *Education Week* 26, issue 34 (April 25, 2007): 32–33.

25. Daniel C. Humphrey et al., "Peer Review—Getting Serious About Teacher Support and Evaluation," SRI International and J. Koppich and Associates, 2011, 30, http://www.sri.com/work/publications/peer-review-getting-serious-about-teacher-support-and-evaluation.

26. Adam Urbanski, "TURNing Unions Around," *Contemporary Education* 69, no. 4 (Summer 1998), 186–190.

27. Charles T. Kerchner, Julia E. Koppich, and Joseph G. Weeres, *United Mind Workers: Unions and Teaching in the Knowledge Society* (San Francisco: Jossey-Bass Publishers, 1997), 7.

28. Ibid., 11.

29. Kaboolian, *Win-Win Labor-Management Collaboration in Education*, 60–65.

30. See, for instance, Humphrey et al., "Peer Review," http://www.sri.com/work/publications/peer-review-getting-serious-about-teacher-support-and-evaluation; and Susan M. Johnson et al., *Teacher to Teacher: Realizing the Potential of Peer Assistance and Review*, Center for American Progress, May 2010, https://cdn.americanprogress.org/wp-content/uploads/issues/2010/05/pdf/par.pdf.

31. Information about these conferences is available at http://www.ed.gov/labor-management-collaboration.

32. See, for instance, Stephanie Simon, "The Fall of Teachers Unions," *Politico*, June 13, 2014, http://www.politico.com/story/2014/06/teachers-union-california-court-decision-107816.html.

33. Michael B. Henderson and Paul E. Peterson, "The 2013 Education Next Survey," *EducationNext* 14, no. 1 (Winter 2014), http://educationnext.org/the-2013-education-next-survey/.

34. Membership has also declined because of state ballot initiatives and legislation, which have rolled back collective bargaining and agency fee laws.

35. Paul Toner, "We Can't Just Say 'No': Teachers Unions Must Lead Change," Real Clear Education, March 12, 2014, http://www.realcleareducation.com/articles/2014/03/12/we_cant_just_say_no_teachers_unions_must_lead_change_897.html.

36. The signed, shared vision statement is available at http://www.ed.gov/documents/labor-management-collaboration/vision-statement-sigs.pdf.

37. Sarah Rosenberg and Elena Silva, *Trending Toward Reform: Teachers Speak on Unions and the Future of the Profession*, Education Sector, 2012, http://studentsmatter.org/wp-content/uploads/2012/09/SM_Trending-Toward-Reform-Ed-Sector-Survey_07.10.12.pdf.

38. Nicholas D. Kristof, "The New Haven experiment," *New York Times*, February 15, 2002, http://www.nytimes.com/2012/02/16/opinion/kristof-the-new-haven-experiment.html.

39. Researchers try to control for other variables to determine the impact of a single strategy, but this is exceedingly difficult to do well when studying complex systems.

40. See, for instance, David C. Berliner, *Poverty and Potential: Out-of-School Factors and School Success*, Education and the Public Interest Center & Education Policy Research Unit, Arizona State University and University of Colorado, March 2009, http://files.eric.ed.gov/fulltext/ED507359.pdf; Richard Rothstein, *Class and Schools: Using Social, Economic, and Educational Reform to Close the Black-White Achievement Gap* (New York: Teachers College Press, 2004); Ravitch, *Reign of Error*; and Helen F. Ladd, "Education

and Poverty: Confronting the Evidence," *Journal of Policy Analysis and Management* 31, no. 2 (2012): 203–227.

41. Berliner and Glass, *50 Myths and Lies*, 15.

CHAPTER 1

1. Julie E. Koppich, *Labor-Management Collaboration: Still Necessary, Not Sufficient* (San Francisco: Koppich and Associates, 2014).

2. "Agreement Between the Montgomery County Education Association and Board of Education of Montgomery County, Rockville, Maryland for the School Years 2011–2014," http://www.montgomeryschoolsmd.org/uploadedFiles/departments/association relations/teachers/MCEA_Contract.pdf.

3. Barbara Gray, *Collaborating: Finding Common Ground for Multiparty Problems* (San Francisco: Jossey-Bass Publishers, 1989).

4. Richard DuFour, "The Key to Improved Teaching and Learning," *The AdvancED Source* (Fall 2009): 2.

5. Jennifer Dubin, "From Picket Line to Partnership: A Union, a District, and Their Thriving Schools," *American Educator* (Spring 2009), www.aft.org/periodical/american-educator/spring-2009/picket-line-partnership.

6. David LaRose (superintendent of Culver City Unified School District) and David Mielke (president of the Culver City Federation of Teachers), in discussion with author, January 5, 2015.

7. Ibid.

8. Gray, *Collaborating*, 11.

9. Koppich, *Labor-Management Collaboration*.

10. Tom Alves (executive director of the San Juan Teachers Association), in discussion with author, February 18, 2015.

11. David LaRose (superintendent of Culver City Unified School District) and David Mielke (president of the Culver City Federation of Teachers), in discussion with author, January 5, 2015.

12. Gray, *Collaborating*, 13–14.

13. Abigail Paris, *Partnerships in Education: How Labor-Management Collaboration Is Transforming Public Schools,* American Rights at Work Education Fund, May 2011, www.jwj.org/wp-content/uploads/2013/12/110531partnershipsineducation_final.pdf.

14. Jennifer Dubin, "Moving Meriden," *American Educator* (Winter 2013–2014): 35.

15. Ibid., 35.

16. Jonathan Eckert et al., *Local Labor Management Relationships as a Vehicle to Advance Reform: Findings from the U.S. Department of Education's Labor Management Conference* (Washington, DC: US Department of Education, 2011), 38.

17. Ibid.

18. Candy Smiley, e-mail message to author, February 10, 2015.

19. Greg Anrig, "Cultivating Collaboration," *American Educator* (Winter 2013–2014): 10, http://www.aft.org/pdfs/americaneducator/winter1314/Anrig.pdf.

20. Eckert et al., *Local Labor Management Relationships*, 26.

21. Claire Handley and Robert A. Kronley, "Lessons Learned: A Report on the Benwood Initiative," Public Education Foundation (n.d.), http://www.pefchattanooga.org/wp-content/uploads/2012/08/Lessons-Learned.pdf.

22. WestEd, "Materials Overview: Extended Time for Student Learning and Teacher Collaboration," WestEd, 2011, http://www.wested.org/lmc.

23. Paris, *Partnerships in Education: How Labor-Management Collaboration Is Transforming Public Schools.* Note: At the time this report was published, only nine Community Learning Centers existed.

24. The central purpose of evaluation systems should be to help educators improve. Incompetent teachers who have been given an adequate chance to improve should be removed, and well-designed evaluation and peer assistance and review programs do that. The real tragedy with most of today's teacher evaluation systems is not that they don't get rid of bad teachers, but that they do nothing to boost the skills of the rest— those who are willing and able to improve.

25. See, for instance, Richard Rothstein et al., *Problems with the Use of Student Test Scores to Evaluate Teachers* (Washington, DC: Economic Policy Institute, 2010), http://www. epi.org/ publication/bp278; Daniel F. McCaffrey et al., *Evaluating Value-Added Models for Teacher Accountability* (Santa Monica, CA, RAND Corporation, 2005); American Statistical Association, "ASA Statement on Using Value-Added Models for Educational Assessment," American Statistical Association, April 8, 2014, http://www.scribd.com/doc/217916454/ASA-VAM-Statement-1.

26. See, for instance, Rennie Center for Educational Research and Policy, *Case Study: Labor-Management-Community Collaboration in Springfield*, Spring 2012, www.renniecenter. org/research/LaborMgmtCommunityCollab.pdf; Saul A. Rubinstein and John E. McCarthy, *Teachers Unions and Management Partnerships: How Working Together Improves Student Achievement*, Center for American Progress, March 2014, https://www. americanprogress.org/wp-content/uploads/2014/03/Rubinstein-EduReform-report. pdf; and Eckert et al., *Local Labor Management Relationships.*

27. Information about the national labor-management conferences and a link to the shared vision statement are available at http://www.ed.gov/labor-management-collaboration.

28. Tom L. Macaluso, "Principals May Take Vote of No Confidence Against Vargas," *Rochester City Newspaper*, January 15, 2014.

29. Jason A. Grisson and Stephanie Anderson, "Why Superintendents Turn Over," *American Educational Research Journal* 49, no. 6 (2012): 1146–1180.

30. Marcia Davis, "Teacher Union Infighting Intensifies," *D.C. Wire*, July 21, 2008.

31. Nina Bascia, "What Teachers Want from Their Unions—What We Know from the Research," in *The Global Assault on Teaching, Teachers, and Their Unions*, eds. Mary Compton and Lois Weiner (New York: Palgrave Macmillan, 2008), 103.

32. Nina Bascia and Pamela Osmond, "Teacher Unions and Educational Reform: A Research Review," National Education Association Center for Great Public Schools Research Department (2012), 18.

33. Tim Fitzgerald (labor-management facilitator with the Rennie Center), in conversation with the author, December 18, 2014.

34. Michael Fullan, *Change Forces—The Sequel*, (Philadelphia: Falmer Press, 1999), 43.

35. Susan M. Johnson and Susan M. Kardos, "Reform Bargaining and Its Promise for School Bargaining," in *Conflicting Missions? Teachers Unions and Educational Reform*, ed. Tom Loveless (Washington, DC: Brookings Institution Press, 2000), 26.

36. Tim Fitzgerald (labor-management facilitator with the Rennie Center), in conversation with the author, December 18, 2014.

37. See US Department of Education, "Data Tools," https://title2.ed.gov/Public/DataTools/Tables.aspx.

38. See, for instance, "Improving Teacher Retention with Supportive Workplace Conditions," The Center for Comprehensive School Reform and Improvement, June 2007; Barnett Berry, Mark Smylie, and Ed Fuller, "Understanding Teacher Working Conditions: A Review and Look to the Future," Center for Teaching Quality, November 2008, http://www.teachingquality.org/sites/default/files/Understanding%20Teacher%20Working%20Conditions-%20A%20Review%20and%20Look%20to%20the%20Future.pdf.; Liz Riggs, "Why Do Teachers Quit. And Why Do They Stay?" *The Atlantic*, October 18, 2013; Ken Futernick, *A Possible Dream: Retaining California Teachers So All Students Learn* (Sacramento: California State University, 2007).

39. Mary Ronan (superintendent of the Cincinnati Public Schools) and Julie Sellers (president of the Cincinnati Federation of Teachers), in conversation with the author, December 10, 2014.

40. Eckert et al., *Local Labor Management Relationships*, 28.

41. Ibid., 28.

CHAPTER 2

1. Diane Ravitch, *The Death and Life of the Great American School System: How Testing and Choice Are Undermining Education* (New York: Basic Books, 2010), 66.

2. See, for instance, Wayne Au, *Unequal by Design: High-Stakes Testing and the Standardization of Inequality* (New York: Routledge, 2009); Ravitch, *The Death and Life of the Great American School System*; Sharon L. Nichols and David C. Berliner, *Collateral Damage: How High-Stakes Testing Corrupts America's Schools* (Cambridge: Harvard Education Press, 2007).

3. Saul A. Rubinstein and John E. McCarthy, *Teachers Unions and Management Partnerships: How Working Together Improves Student Achievement*, Center for American Progress, March 2014, 1, www.americanprogress.org/wp-content/uploads/2014/03/Rubinstein-EduReform-report.pdf.

4. Carrie R. Leana, "The Missing Link in School Reform," *Stanford Social Innovation Review* (Fall 2011), 34.

5. Anthony S. Bryk and Barbara L. Schneider, *Trust in Schools* (New York: Russell Sage Foundation, 2002), 33.

6. Ibid., 33.

7. Ibid., 33.

8. Ken Futernick et al., *Labor-Management Collaboration in Education: The Process, the Impact, and the Prospects for Change* (Unpublished report, San Francisco, CA: WestEd, 2013), 17.

9. Christine Porath and Christine Pearson, "The Price of Incivility," *Harvard Business Review* (January–February 2013), https://hbr.org/2013/01/the-price-of-incivility/ar/1.

10. Christine Porath, "No Time to be Nice at Work," *New York Times*, June 19, 2015.

11. James W. Tamm and Ronald J. Luyet, *Radical Collaboration: Five Essential Skills to Overcome Defensiveness and Build Successful Relationships* (New York: HarperCollins, 2005), 5.

12. Roland Barth, "Improving Relationships Within the Schoolhouse," *Educational Leadership* 63, no. 6 (2006): 8–13.

13. Dan Beyers, "Montgomery Teachers Union to Focus on Classroom Issues," *Washington Post*, July 20, 1997.

14. Jonathan Eckert et al., *Local Labor Management Relationships as a Vehicle to Advance Reform: Findings from the U.S. Department of Education's Labor Management Conference* (Washington, DC: US Department of Education, 2011).

15. Education World, "Making Teacher Evaluations Work," 2010, http://www.education-world.com/a_admin/admin/admin224.shtml.

16. Montgomery County Public Schools' Professional Growth System Handbook is available at http://mceanea.org/publications/teachers-guide-to-par/.

17. Montgomery County Education Association, "MCEA National Board Certification Support Program," http://mceanea.org/teaching-and-learning/national-board-program/.

18. Montgomery County Education Association, "Career Lattice," http://mceanea.org/teaching-and-learning/career-lattice/.

19. Montgomery County Education Association, "Leadership Team Institute," http://mceanea.org/teaching-and-learning/leadership-team-institute/.

20. Scott Thompson, ed., "Breaking the Links Between Race, Poverty, & Achievement," *Strategies for School System Leaders on District Level Change* 13, no. 1, (December 2007): 9–10.

21. Education World, "Making Teacher Evaluations Work."

22. Annenberg Institute for School Reform, "Profiles in Transformation: Montgomery County (MD) Public Schools Professional Growth System," http://annenberginstitute.org/profiles-transformation-montgomery-county-md-public-schools-professional-growth-system.

23. Carin Dessauer, "The Last Lessons of Jerry Weast: A Question and Answer Session with the Retiring Superintendent of Montgomery County Public School," *Bethesda Magazine*, March/April 2011, http://www.bethesdamagazine.com/Bethesda-Magazine/March-April-2011/The-Last-Lessons-of-Jerry-Weast/index.php?cparticle=1&siarticle=0#artanc.

24. See, for instance, Mariana Haynes, "On the Path to Equity: Improving the Effectiveness of Beginning Teachers," Alliance for Excellent Education, July 2014, http://all4ed.org/reports-factsheets/path-to-equity/; Matthew Ronfeldt et al., "How Teacher Turnover Harms Student Achievement," National Bureau of Economic Research, 2011, http://www.nber.org/papers/w17176; Ken Futernick, *A Possible Dream: Retaining California Teachers So All Students Learn* (Sacramento: California State University, 2007); Richard Ingersoll et al., "What Are the Effects of Teacher Education and Preparation on Beginning Teacher Attrition?" Consortium for Policy Research in Education, July 2014, http://www.cpre.org/prep-effects.

25. "2014 Maryland Report Card," http://www.mdreportcard.org/CohortGradRate.aspx?PV=160:12:15:AAAA:1:N:0:13:1:1:0:1:1:1:3.

26. In 2008, MCPS exceeded the expected graduation rate by 10 percentage points, according to the Editorial Projects in Education (EPE) Research Center, http://www.edweek.org/ew/articles/2011/06/09/34analysis.h30.html. In 2010, MCPS margin was 4 percentage points, http://www.edweek.org/media/dc-large-school-exceeds-expectations-p14-c1.pdf.

27. "2013 Maryland Report Card," http://www.mdreportcard.org/DocumentedDecisions.aspx?PV=38:12:15:AAAA:1:N:0:13:1:2:1:1:1:1:3.

28. Eckert et al., *Local Labor Management Relationships.*

29. "Diplomas Count 2012: Trailing Behind, Moving Forward," *Education Week*, June 7, 2012, http://www.edweek.org/go/dc12.

30. Geoff Marietta, *The Unions of Montgomery County*, Harvard Education Press, Exhibit 1, http://hepg.org/hep-home/case/the-unions-in-montgomery-county-public-schools_85.
31. Thomas Riley died of leukemia in 1998 and was replaced by Ron Barnes, who entered into a formal partnership agreement with the local union in 1999.
32. Jennifer Dubin, "From Picket Line to Partnership: A Union, a District, and Their Thriving Schools," *American Educator* (Spring 2009), www.aft.org/periodical/american-educator/spring-2009/picket-line-partnership; and "The ABC's of Partnership: Creating a Labor-Management Partnership Focused on Student Achievement," American Federation of Teachers, http://www.abcusd.k12.ca.us/pages/ABC_Unified_School_District/About_ABC/ABC_Labor_Management_Partnersh.
33. "The ABC's of Partnership," American Federation of Teachers, 5.
34. Ibid, 5.
35. Dubin, "From Picket Line to Partnership," 11.
36. Ibid., 12.
37. Mary Sieu (superintendent of ABC Unified School District) and Ray Gaer (president of the ABC Federation of Teachers), in discussion with the author, August 20, 2014.
38. Ibid.
39. Ibid.
40. Rubinstein and McCarthy, "Teachers Unions and Management Partnerships," 13.
41. Information about the Community Learning Centers in Cincinnati is available at http://www.cps-k12.org/community/clc.
42. "Cincinnati Public Schools Community Learning Centers Evaluation Report, 2012–13," Innovations in Community Research and Program Evaluation, http://www.cincinnaticlc.org/sites/www.cincinnaticlc.org/files/pdfs/CCHMC-Independent_Evaluation-2012-13.pdf.
43. Mary Ronan (superintendent of the Cincinnati Public Schools) and Julie Sellers (president of the Cincinnati Federation of Teachers), in conversation with the author, December 10, 2014.
44. Joe Nathan, "Cincinnati Shows How to Close the Achievement Gap," Center for School Change, June 1, 2011, http://centerforschoolchange.org/2011/06/cincinnati-shows-how-to-close-the-achievement-gap/.
45. Greg Anrig, "Cultivating Collaboration," *American Educator* (Winter 2013–2014): 11, http://www.aft.org/pdfs/americaneducator/winter1314/Anrig.pdf.
46. Ibid., 10.
47. NEA Press Release, "NEA Partners to Develop Standards for Measuring 21st Century Skills," February 23, 2009, http://www.nea.org/home/30696.htm.
48. Randi Weingarten, "Statement by Randi Weingarten, President, American Federation of Teachers, On Common Core Standards," June 3, 2010, http://www.aft.org. newspubs/press/2010/060310.cfm.
49. "NEA President: We Need a Course Correction on Common Core," *NEAToday*, February 19, 2014, http://neatoday.org/2014/02/19/nea-president-we-need-a-course-correction-on-common-core/.
50. See, for instance, Rebecca Mead, "Louis CK Against the Common Core," *The New Yorker*, April 30, 2014, http://www.newyorker.com/news/daily-comment/louis-c-k-against-the-common-core; and Javier C. Hernandez, "Common Core, in Nine-Year Old Eyes," *New York Times*, June 14, 2014.

51. Nolan Feeny, "Gates Foundation Calls for Delay in 'Common Core'–Based Teacher Evaluations," *Time*, June 10, 2014, http://time.com/2854644/gates-foundation-common-core-delay/.

52. According to *USA Today*, "As of May 15, lawmakers introduced over 340 bills in 46 states—every state that had had a regular legislative session this year— that addressed college- and career-readiness education standards, including the Common Core. Of those, 30 would slow down or delay college- and career-readiness standards and 35 would halt or revoke implementation altogether." Adrienne Lu, "State Lawmakers Push Common Core agenda with 340 bills," *USA Today*, June 13, 2014, http://www.usatoday.com/story/news/nation/2014/06/13/stateline-lawmakers-common-core/10415269/.

53. Arne Duncan, "A Back-to-School Conversation with Teachers and School Leaders," Homeroom–The Official Blog of the U.S. Department of Education, August 2014, http://www.ed.gov/blog/2014/08/a-back-to-school-conversation-with-teachers-and-school-leaders/.

54. Tom Torlakson, *A Blueprint for Great Schools* (Sacramento: California Department of Education, 2011).

55. Task Force on Educator Excellence, *Greatness by Design—Supporting Outstanding Teaching to Sustain a Golden State*, California Department of Education, 2012, http://www.cde.ca.gov/eo/in/documents/greatnessfinal.pdf.

56. Ibid.

57. Ken Futernick and Adam Urbanski, "Successful School Turnarounds Through Labor–Management Partnerships: The Role in State Education Agencies," in *The State Role in School Turnaround: Emerging Best Practices*, ed. Lauren M. Rhim and Sam Redding (San Francisco, CA: WestEd), 65–80, http://centeronschoolturnaround.org/wp-content/uploads/2013/12/Labor_Management_Partnerships1.pdf.

58. See Californians Dedicated to Education Foundation, "Common Core," http://cdefoundation.org/what-we-do/common-core/.

59. Linda Darling-Hammond and Randi Weingarten, "It's Time for a New Accountability in American Education," Huffington Post, May 19, 2014; updated July 19, 2014, http://www.huffingtonpost.com/linda-darlinghammond/its-time-for-a-new-accoun_b_5351475.html.

60. Andrew Ujifusa and Stephen Sawchuk, "Common-Core Tensions Cause Union Heartburn," *Education Week*, February 19, 2014.

CHAPTER 3

1. This number is based on attendance by district teams at recent state and national conferences on labor-management collaboration and on research literature that has focused on district partnerships.

2. The Stuart Foundation and the Bechtel Foundation provided the initial financial support for the California Labor Management Initiative.

3. See http://cdefoundation.org/lmi/.

4. Half of the districts were turned away because of lack of conference space. Additional symposia have been conducted to accommodate them.

5. Robert Evans, *The Human Side of School Change* (San Francisco: Jossey-Bass, 1996), 25.

6. Ibid., 45.

7. Ibid., 47.

8. Chris Argyris, *Organizational Traps: Leadership, Culture, Organizational Design* (Oxford: Oxford University Press, 2010), 17.

9. Mary Ronan (superintendent of the Cincinnati Public Schools) and Julie Sellers (president of the Cincinnati Federation of Teachers), in conversation with the author, December 10, 2014.

10. Christine Porath, "No Time to Be Nice at Work," *New York Times*, June 19, 2015.

11. Margaret Heffernan, *Willful Blindness: Why We Ignore the Obvious at Our Peril* (New York: Walker and Company, 2011), 91.

12. Jonathan Eckert et al., *Local Labor Management Relationships as a Vehicle to Advance Reform: Findings from the U.S. Department of Education's Labor Management Conference* (Washington, DC: US Department of Education, 2011), 25.

13. Bill Turque, "D.C. Has Long History of Troubled Education Reform," *Washington Post*, October 31, 2009, http://www.washingtonpost.com/wp-dyn/content/article/2009/10/31/AR2009103102357.html.

14. Joel Klein, "The Failure of American Schools," *The Atlantic*, June 2011.

15. Diane Ravitch, *The Death and Life of the Great American School System: How Testing and Choice Are Undermining Education* (New York: Basic Books, 2010), 65.

16. Michael Fullan, *Change Forces, The Sequel* (Philadelphia: Falmer Press, 1999), 36–37.

17. Ibid., 38.

18. Ibid., 37.

19. Mary Ronan (superintendent of the Cincinnati Public Schools) and Julie Sellers (president of the Cincinnati Federation of Teachers), in conversation with the author, December 10, 2014.

20. Rachel Gottlieb, "Hartford Teachers' Vote Draws National Attention," *Hartford Courant*, May 6, 2002, A-1.

21. Frederick Hess and Martin R. West, "Strike Phobia," *Education Next* 6, no. 3 (Summer 2006), http://educationnext.org/strikephobia/.

22. Ibid.

23. *Unlikely Allies: The Next Chapter*, Education Sector, July 23, 2012, http://www.education sector.org/publications/unlikely-allies-next-chapter.

24. Rennie Center for Educational Research and Policy, *Case Study: Labor-Management-Community Collaboration in Springfield*, Spring 2012, 9, http://www.renniecenter.org/research/LaborMgmtCommunityCollab.pdf.

25. Ibid., 9.

26. Charles T. Kerchner, "Deindustrialization," *Education Next* 1, no. 3, (Fall 2001), 46–50, http://educationnext.org/deindustrialization/.

27. Ibid.

28. Sarah Rosenberg and Elena Silva, *Trending Toward Reform: Teachers Speak on Unions and the Future of the Profession*, Education Sector, 2012, http://studentsmatter.org/wp-content/uploads/2012/09/SM_Trending-Toward-Reform-Ed-Sector-Survey_07.10.12.pdf.

29. Kerchner, "Deindustrialization," 46.

30. Emily K. Qazilbash et al., "Peer Assistance and Review: A Cross-Site Study of Labor-Management Collaboration Required for Program Success" (Paper presented at American Educational Research Association, San Diego, April 13–17, 2009), http://isites.harvard.edu/fs/docs/icb.topic1239491.files/Teachersleadingteachers_SEF_AERA_2009.pdf.

31. Rosenberg and Silva, *Trending Toward Reform*.

32. Dana Goldstein, *The Teacher Wars: A History of America's Most Embattled Profession* (New York: Doubleday, 2014), 231.

33. Nina Bascia and Pamela Osmond, "Teacher Unions and Educational Reform: A Research Review," National Educational Association Center for Great Public Schools Research Department (2012), 13.

34. Arne Duncan, "Winning the Future with Education: Responsibility, Reform and Results," Oral testimony to Congress, March 9, 2011, http://www.ed.gov/news/speeches/winning-future-education-responsibility-reform-andresults.

35. Carl A. Cohn, "Empowering Those at the Bottom Beats Punishing Them from the Top," *Education Week* 26, issue 34 (April 25, 2007): 32–33.

36. Linda Darling-Hammond, *Getting Teacher Evaluation Right* (New York: Teachers College Press, 2013), 70.

37. Goldstein, *The Teacher Wars*, 228.

CHAPTER 4

1. Christine Porath and Christine Pearson, "The Price of Incivility," *Harvard Business Review* (January–February, 2013), https://hbr.org/2013/01/the-price-of-incivility/ar/1.

2. Carol S. Dweck, *Mindset* (New York: Ballantine Books, 2006).

3. Chris Argyris, *Organizational Traps: Leadership, Culture, Organizational Design* (Oxford: Oxford University Press, 2010), 107.

4. Evaluation results from the 2011 Labor-Management Collaboration Conference are available at http://www.ed.gov/conference-evaluation-results.

5. James W. Tamm and Ronald J. Luyet, *Radical Collaboration: Five Essential Skills to Overcome Defensiveness and Build Successful Relationships* (New York: HarperCollins, 2005), 4.

6. The website for Dialogos is located at http://dialogos.com/.

7. Information about TURN and its regional affiliates is available at http://turnweb.org.

8. Founded in 1987, the Consortium for Educational Change assists policy makers and districts that want to advance reform through labor-management partnerships. Information about CEC can be found at http://cecillinois.org/.

9. For more information, see http://www.neafoundation.org/pages/institute-for-innovation-in-teaching-learning/.

10. Information about the Rennie Center and the DCP can be found at http://www.rennie-center.org/; information about the Massachusetts Education Partnership can be found at http://www.renniecenter.org/programs/MEP.html.

11. After the first year, 88 percent of the district leaders participating in DCP indicated that it had improved their communication and problem-solving efforts. Ninety-six percent reported a positive impact on their vision for improving student achievement.

12. The appendix provides a guide to resources on labor-management collaboration, including organizations that support national, state, and local collaboration efforts and a list of related books, research reports, and articles.

13. Christopher Emigholz, "A Greater Sense of Urgency in Education Reform," New Jersey Business and Industry Association, March 2010, 12, http://www.njbia.org/docs/default-source/pdf-files/aii003.pdf?sfvrsn=0.

14. Jocelyn R. Davis and Tom Atkinson, "Need Speed? Slow Down," *Harvard Business Review*, May 2010, 1.

15. Tamm and Luyet, *Radical Collaboration*, 5.

16. Ibid., 8.

17. Rennie Center for Educational Research and Policy, *Case Study: Labor-Management-Community Collaboration in Springfield*, Spring 2012, 2, http://www.renniecenter.org/research/LaborMgmtCommunityCollab.pdf.

18. Ken Blanchard, Cynthia Olmstead, and Martha Lawrence, *Trust Works! Four Keys to Building Lasting Relationships* (New York: HarperCollins, 2013), 102.

19. Michael Fullan, *Choosing the Wrong Drivers for Whole System Reform*, Centre for Strategic Education, 2011, 9, http://www.michaelfullan.ca/media/13396088160.pdf.

20. Ibid., 8.

21. Susan M. Johnson et al., *Teacher to Teacher: Realizing the Potential of Peer Assistance and Review*, Center for American Progress, May 2010, https://cdn.americanprogress.org/wp-content/uploads/issues/2010/05/pdf/par.pdf.

22. Ibid., 21.

23. Collective bargaining for teachers is illegal in Georgia, North Carolina, South Carolina, Texas, and Virginia. Policy makers in Wisconsin, Idaho, and Tennessee have recently narrowed the scope of bargaining, and other states are considering similar restrictions. For more information about state-by-state collective bargaining policies, see Milla Sanes and John Schmitt, "Regulation of Public Sector Collective Bargaining in the States," Center for Economic Policy Research, March 2014, http://www.cepr.net/documents/state-public-cb-2014-03.pdf.

24. See, for instance, Sally Klingel, *Interest-Based Bargaining in Education*, Cornell University ILR School, 2003, http://digitalcommons.ilr.cornell.edu/cgi/viewcontent.cgi?article=1015&context=reports ; Renaud Paquet, Isabelle Gaétan, and Jean-Guy Bergeron, "Does Interest-Based Bargaining (IBB) Really Make a Difference in Collective Bargaining Outcomes?" *Negotiation Journal* (July 2000), 281–296; Linda Kaboolian, *Win-Win Labor-Management Collaboration in Education* (Cambridge: The Rennie Center for Education Research and Policy, 2005).

25. WestEd, *Labor/Management Collaboration: A Conference for California Educators*, 2011, 30, http://www.wested.org/lmc.

26. The National Commission on Teaching and America's Future, *Reducing the Achievement Gap Through District/Union Collaboration: The Tale of Two School Districts*, 2007, http://nctaf.org/wp-content/uploads/2012/01/ReducingtheAchievementGapThroughDistrictUnionCollaborationfull.pdf.

27. Kaboolian, *Win-Win Labor-Management Collaboration*, 35.

28. "The Contractual Bargaining Agreement between the City School District and the Rochester Teachers Association," July 1, 2013, 82, http://www.rochesterteachers.com/Rochester_Teachers_Association/Home_files/Teacher%20Contract.pdf.

29. Charles T. Kerchner, Julia E. Koppich, and Joseph G. Weeres, *United Mind Workers: Unions and Teaching in the Knowledge Society* (San Francisco: Jossey-Bass Publishers, 1997), 128.

30. Center for Teaching Quality, "United Providence UP! Compact," May 23, 2014, http://www.teachingquality.org/content/united-providence-compact.

31. Elena Silva and Susan Headden, *Unlikely Allies: Unions and Districts in the Battle for School Reform*, Education Sector, 2011, 11, http://www.educationsector.org/sites/default/files/publications/Unlikely_Allies_RELEASE.pdf.

32. See California Department of Education, "A Blueprint for Great Schools 2.0," July 28, 2015, http://www.cde.ca.gov/eo/in/bp/bp2contents.asp.

CHAPTER 5

1. See http://keys3.obiki.org/.
2. Richard DuFour, "Leading Edge: Are You Looking Out the Window or in a Mirror?" *Journal of Staff Development* 5, no. 3 (Summer 2004): 63–64.
3. Rennie Center for Educational Research and Policy, *Case Study: Labor-Management-Community Collaboration in Springfield*, Spring 2012, http://www.renniecenter.org/research/LaborMgmtCommunityCollab.pdf.
4. Collaborative districts can be found at the US Department of Education's website, www.ed.gov/labor-management-collaboration.
5. Information about regional chapters of TURN, including conference dates and agenda, is available at www.turnweb.org; information about CEC is available at www.cecillinois.org; information about MEP is available at http://renniecenter.org/programs/MEP.html.
6. David LaRose (superintendent of Culver City Unified School District) and David Mielke (president of the Culver City Federation of Teachers), in discussion with author, January 5, 2015.
7. Gary Walker, "CC School Leaders Hailed for Alliance with Union, Management," *Culver City News*, October 31, 2014, http://www.culvercitynews.org/latest-news/cc-school-leaders-hailed-for-allaince-with-union-management_1414789808/.
8. R.E.S.P.E.C.T. stands for "Resolving differences; Enhancing collaboration; Supporting our coworkers; Promoting civility; Encouraging creativity; Communicating openly; and Team building through trust."
9. Geoff Marietta, *The Unions of Montgomery County*, Harvard Education Press, http://hepg.org/hep-home/case/the-unions-in-montgomery-county-public-schools_85.
10. Kerry Patterson et al., *Crucial Conversations: Tools for Talking When Stakes Are High*, Second Edition (New York: McGraw-Hill, 2012), 2.
11. See www.vitalsmarts.com.
12. See www.fierceinc.com.
13. WestEd, "Materials Overview: Extended Time for Student Learning and Teacher Collaboration 2011 Report," 2011, 12, http://www.wested.org/wp-content/uploads/extended-complete-tab.pdf.
14. Tom Alves (executive director of the San Juan Teachers Association), in discussion with author, February 18, 2015.
15. David LaRose (superintendent of Culver City Unified School District) and David Mielke (president of the Culver City Federation of Teachers), in discussion with author, January 5, 2015.
16. Peter Senge, "Foreword," in *Dialogue and the Art of Thinking Together*, William Isaacs (New York: Doubleday, 1999), Kindle edition.
17. The Rennie Center for Educational Research and Policy, *The District Capacity Project: A Report on Year One*, 2013, www.renniecenter.org/research/district_capacity_project_year_one.pdf.
18. Jonathan Eckert et al., *Local Labor Management Relationships as a Vehicle to Advance Reform: Findings from the U.S. Department of Education's Labor Management Conference* (Washington, DC: US Department of Education, 2011), 40.
19. Sarah Rosenberg and Elena Silva, *Trending Toward Reform: Teachers Speak on Unions and the Future of the Profession*, Education Sector, 2012, http://studentsmatter.org/wp-content/uploads/2012/09/SM_Trending-Toward-Reform-Ed-Sector-Survey_07.10.12.pdf.

20. Information about the Labor Management Initiative in Massachusetts is available at www.renniecenter.org/labor_management.html. Information about the MEP is available at http://renniecenter.org/programs/MEP.html.

21. Information about the CEC is available at http://cecillinois.org.

22. *A Blueprint for Great Schools* and *Greatness by Design* are available at the California Department of Education's website, www.cde.ca.gov.

23. Information about California's Labor Management Initiative is available at http://cdefoundation.org/lmi/.

CHAPTER 6

1. Panasonic Foundation, "Breaking the Links Between Race, Poverty, & Achievement," *Strategies for School System Leaders on District-level Change* 13, no. 1 (December 2007): 15.

2. Richard F. Elmore, "Accountability in Local School Districts: Learning to Do the Right Things," in *Improving Educational Performance: Local and Systemic Reforms*, eds. Paul W. Thurston and James G. Ward (Greenwich, CT: JAI Press, Inc., 1997), 59–82.

3. See, for instance, Richard M. Ingersoll, Lisa Merrill, and Daniel Stucky, "Seven Trends: The Transformation of the Teaching Force," The Consortium for Policy Research in Education, (2014), http://repository.upenn.edu/cgi/viewcontent.cgi?article=1261&context=gse_pubs; Richard M. Ingersoll, "Teacher Turnover and Teacher Shortages: An Organizational Analysis," *American Educational Research Journal* 38, no. 3, (2011): 499–534; Susan M. Johnson et al., *Who Stays in Teaching and Why? A Review of the Literature on Teacher Retention* (Washington, DC: National Retired Teachers Association, 2005).

4. See, for instance, Elaine Allensworth, Stephen Ponisciak, and Christopher Mazzeo, *The Schools Teachers Leave: Teacher Mobility in Chicago Public Schools* (Chicago: Consortium on Chicago School Research, University of Chicago, 2009); Susan M. Johnson, Mathew A. Kraft, and John P. Papay, "How Context Matters in High-Need Schools: The Effects of Teachers' Working Conditions on Their Professional Satisfaction and Their Students' Achievement," *Teachers College Record* 114, no. 10 (2010): 1–39.

5. Thomas Toch, "Fixing Teacher Evaluation," *Educational Leadership* 66, no. 2 (October 2008): 32–37.

6. Daniel Weisberg et al., *The Widget Effect: Our National Failure to Acknowledge and Act on Differences in Teacher Effectiveness* (Brooklyn, NY: The New Teacher Project, 2009).

7. Ibid., 14.

8. Ann Duffet et al., *Waiting to Be Won Over: Teachers Speak on the Profession, Unions, and Reform* (Washington, DC: Education Sector, 2008).

9. MetLife Foundation, "The MetLife Survey of the American Teacher: Challenges of School Leadership," MetLife, Inc., February 2013, https://www.metlife.com/assets/cao/foundation/MetLife-Teacher-Survey-2012.pdf.

10. Linda Darling-Hammond, *Getting Teacher Evaluation Right* (New York: Teachers College Press, 2013).

11. Montgomery County's Professional Growth System is described at http://www.montgomeryschoolsmd.org/departments/professionalgrowth/.

12. Matthew M. Chingos, "Ending Teacher Tenure Would Have Little Impact on Its Own," The Brown Center Chalkboard, September 18, 2014, http://www.brookings.edu/research/papers/2014/09/18-teacher-tenure-chingos.

13. Kacey Guin, "Chronic Teacher Turnover in Urban Elementary Schools," *Education Policy Analysis Archives* 12, no. 42, (August 16, 2004), http://epaa.asu.edu/ojs/article/download/197/323.

14. Heather C. Hill, "Fixing Teacher Professional Development," *Phi Delta Kappan* 90, no. 7, (March 2009): 470–477.

15. Kwan Suk Yoon et al., "Reviewing the Evidence on How Teacher Professional Development Affects Student Achievement" (Issues & Answers Report, REL 2007–No. 033). Washington, DC: US Department of Education, Institute of Education Sciences, National Center for Education Evaluation and Regional Assistance, Regional Educational Laboratory Southwest, http://ies.ed.gov/ncee/edlabs.

16. Michael Fullan, *Choosing the Wrong Drivers for Whole System Reform*, Centre for Strategic Education, 2011, 9, http://www.michaelfullan.ca/media/13396088160.pdf.

17. Rennie Center for Educational Research and Policy, *Case Study: Labor-Management-Community Collaboration in Springfield*, Spring 2012, http://www.renniecenter.org/research/LaborMgmtCommunityCollab.pdf.

18. Saul A. Rubinstein and John E. McCarthy, *Collaborating on School Reform: Creating Union-Management Partnerships to Improve Public School Systems* (New Brunswick, NJ: Rutgers School of Management and Labor Relations, 2010).

19. Adam Urbanski, "Reform or Be Reformed," *EducationNext* 1, no. 3 (Fall 2001), http://educationnext.org/reform-or-be-reformed/.

20. Paul Toner, "We Can't Just Say 'No': Teachers Unions Must Lead Change," Real Clear Education, March 12, 2014, http://www.realcleareducation.com/articles/2014/03/12/we_cant_just_say_no_teachers_unions_must_lead_change_897.html.

21. See, for instance, Darling-Hammond, *Getting Teacher Evaluation Right.*

22. Joan Baratz-Snowden, *Fixing Tenure: A Proposal for Assuring Teacher Effectiveness and Due Process*, Center for American Progress, June, 2009, 9–10, http://cdn.americanprogress.org/wp-content/uploads/issues/2009/06/pdf/teacher_tenure.pdf.

23. Ken Futernick, "State Needs a 'Grand Bargain' on Teachers' Effectiveness, Obstacles," *Los Angeles Times*, September 20, 2014,

24. Ken Feinberg's statement is available at http://www.aft.org/sites/default/files/news/FinalFeinbergSummary.pdf.

25. For recommendations on ways to improve tenure regulations, see Patrick McGuinn, *Ringing the Bell for K–12 Teacher Tenure Reform*, Center for American Progress, 2010, http://cdn.americanprogress.org/wp-content/uploads/issues/2010/02/pdf/teacher_tenure.pdf.

26. Duffet et al., *Waiting to Be Won Over.*

27. See, for instance, Daniel C. Humphrey et al., "Peer Review: Getting Serious About Teacher Support and Evaluation," SRI International and J. Koppich and Associates (2011), http://www.sri.com/sites/default/files/publications/par-report-2011-final-sept6.pdf; Emily K. Qazilbash et al., "Peer Assistance and Review: A Cross-Site Study of Labor-Management Collaboration Required for Program Success" (paper presented at the Annual Meeting of the American Educational Research Association, San Diego, April 2009); and "A User's Guide to Peer Assistance and Review," Harvard Graduate School of Education, http://www.gse.harvard.edu/~ngt/par/.

28. See, for instance, Steven G. Rivkin, Eric A. Hanushek, and John F. Kain, "Teachers Schools, and Academic Achievement," *Econometrica* 73, no. 2 (March, 2005), 417–458; Donald Boyd et al., "The Narrowing Gap in New York City Teacher Qualifications and

Its Implications for Student Achievement in High-Poverty Schools," *Journal of Policy Analysis and Management* 27, no. 4 (2008), 793–818; Dan Goldhaber and Michael Hansen, "Assessing the Potential of Using Value Added-Estimates of Teacher Job Performance for Making Tenure Decisions," National Center for Analysis of Longitudinal Data in Educational Research, November 2008, http://www.urban.org/Uploaded PDF/1001265_Teacher_Job_Performance.pdf.

29. The New Teacher Project, "The Case Against Quality-Blind Teacher Layoffs," February 2011, http://tntp.org/files/TNTP_Case_Against_Quality_Blind_Layoffs_Feb2011.pdf.

30. "Teacher Layoffs: Rethinking 'Last-Hired, First-Fired' Policies," National Council on Teacher Quality, 2010, http://www.nctq.org/p/docs/nctq_dc_layoffs.pdf.

31. Kaitlin Pennington, *The Nation's Largest Teachers Union Calls for Revamp of Teacher-Pay System*, Center for American Progress, October 25, 2013, https://www.americanprogress.org/issues/education/news/2013/10/25/77986/the-nations-largest-teachers-union-calls-for-revamp-of-teacher-pay-system/.

32. AFT Resolution, "Professional Compensation for Teachers," 2002, http://www.aft.org/resolution/professional-compensation-teachers.

33. Kenneth R. Bazinet, "President Obama Education Plan Calls for Performance-Based Pay, Firing Poor Performing Teachers," *New York Daily News*, March 11, 2009, http://www.nydailynews.com/news/politics/president-obama-education-plan-calls-performance-based-pay-firing-poorly-performing-teachers-article-1.367353.

34. Mathew G. Springer et al., *Teacher Pay for Performance: Experimental Evidence from the Project on Incentives in Teaching* (Nashville, TN: National Center on Performance Incentives at Vanderbilt University, 2010).

35. Roland G. Fryer, "Teacher Incentives and Student Achievement: Evidence from the New York City Public Schools," National Bureau of Economic Research, 2010, http://www.nber.org/papers/w16850.

36. Sarah D. Sparks, "Study Leads to End of New York City Merit-Pay Program," *Education Week*, July 20, 2011, http://blogs.edweek.org/edweek/inside-school-research/2011/07/a_new_study_by_the.html.

37. David C. Berliner and Gene V. Glass, *50 Myths and Lies That Threaten America's Public Schools—The Real Crisis in Education* (New York: Teachers College Press, 2014).

38. Linda Davin and Sarah Ferguson, (n.d.) *Alternative Compensation Models and Our Members*, National Education Association Teacher Quality Department, http://www.eiaonline.com/NEAAlternativeCompensationModels.pdf.

39. Ibid.

40. Barbara Miner, "The Debate Over Differentiated Pay: The Devil Is in the Details," *Rethinking Schools* (n.d.), http://www.rethinkingschools.org/special_reports/quality_teachers/24_01_pay.shtml.

41. Bob Peterson, "A Revitalized Teacher Union Movement," *Rethinking Schools* 29, no. 2 (Winter 2014–2015), http://www.rethinkingschools.org/archive/29_02/29-2_peterson.shtml.

EPILOGUE

1. Wendy Brown, "Without Quality Public Education, There Is No Future for Public Education," Public Affairs, UC Berkeley, March 5, 2010, http://newscenter.berkeley.edu/2010/03/05/wendybrown/.

2. Programme for International Assessment, "PISA 2012 Results in Focus: What 15-Year-Olds Know and What They Can Do with What They Know," Organisation for Economic Co-operation and Development, 2012, http://www.oecd.org/pisa/keyfindings/pisa-2012-results-overview.pdf.

3. The National Assessment of Educational Progress, "2013 Mathematics and Reading: Grade 12 Assessments," 2013, http://www.nationsreportcard.gov/reading_math_g12_2013/#/The Nation's Report Card.

4. OECD, *Lessons from PISA for the United States, Strong Performers and Successful Reformers in Education*, OECD Publishing, 2011, 120, http://dx.doi.org/10.1787/9789264096660-en.

5. OECD, "PISA 2012 Results in Focus," Programme for International Student Assessment, 2012. http://www.oecd.org/pisa/keyfindings/pisa-2012-results-overview.pdf

6. OECD, *Education at a Glance 2012: Highlights*, OECD Publishing, 2012, http://dx.doi.org/10.1787/eag_highlights-2012-en.

7. Samuel E. Abrams, "The Children Must Play," *New Republic*, January 28, 2011.

8. Pasi Sahlberg, "Lessons from Finland," *American Educator* (Summer 2011), 35.

9. L. Darling-Hammond, *The Flat World and Education* (New York: Teachers College Press, 2010).

10. Sahlberg, *Finnish Lessons*, 35.

11. Michael Fullan, *Choosing the Wrong Drivers for Whole System Reform*, Centre for Strategic Education, 2011, 8, http://www.michaelfullan.ca/media/13396088160.pdf.

12. Paul Toner, "We Can't Just Say 'No': Teachers Unions Must Lead Change," Real Clear Education, March 12, 2014, http://www.realcleareducation.com/articles/2014/03/12/we_cant_just_say_no_teachers_unions_must_lead_change_897.html.

Acknowledgments

Few things of any significance are accomplished alone. That goes not just for running a school but also for writing a book. This book is the product of collaboration with many wise people—teachers, administrators, policy makers, researchers, and writers.

No education leader has done more to advance the idea of labor-management partnerships and progressive unionism than Adam Urbanski. Since the mid-1990s, when he founded the Teacher Union Reform Network (TURN), Adam has argued persuasively that the only way to achieve excellence and equity in education is to give teachers a strong voice on education policy and practice. The labor-management partnerships that have spurred innovation, strengthened trust, increased graduation rates, and closed achievement gaps are traceable to Adam and other courageous education leaders who have promoted collaboration over confrontation. Adam helped me understand the complex political dynamics surrounding this topic and devoted countless hours discussing (and sometimes debating) relevant issues with me. I was flattered when he urged me to write this book, and I'm deeply grateful for his encouragement and support.

I am grateful as well to those who sat for interviews and provided invaluable ground-level insights into the challenges of labor-management partnerships: Mary Sieu, superintendent of ABC Unified School District; Ray Gaer, president of the ABC Federation of Teachers; Tom Alves, executive director of the San Juan Teachers Association and codirector of TURN; Mary Ronan, superintendent of the Cincinnati Public Schools; Julie Sellers, president of the Cincinnati Federation of Teachers; David LaRose, superintendent of the Culver City Unified School District; David Mielke, president of the Culver City Federation of Teachers; Candy Smiley, president of the Poway Federation of Teachers and codirector of CalTURN; Tim Fitzgerald, codirector of the District Capacity Project for the Massachusetts Education Partnership; and Alan Bersin, former superintendent of the San Diego Unified School District.

I thank those who provided critical feedback on the manuscript, including Paul Toner, former president of the Massachusetts Teachers Association and current president of New Voice Strategies; Chad d'Entremont, executive director of the Rennie Center; Emily Murphy, director of programs at the Rennie Center; Andrew Bundy, codirector of the District Capacity Project for the Massachusetts Education Partnership; Mark Simon, former president of the Montgomery County Teachers Association; Ellen Swartz, associate professor at Nazareth College; Thomas Gillett, regional staff director of the New York State United Teachers; Peter McWalters, former superintendent of the Rochester City Schools and former commissioner of elementary and secondary education for Rhode Island; Bob Pearlman, senior consultant for UNITE-LA; and Paul Hetland, treasurer of the Rochester Teachers Association.

I have profited enormously from others who shaped my thinking about labor-management partnerships and the role of unions in education. They include Charles Kerchner, Julie Koppich, and Joseph Weeres, authors of the groundbreaking book *United Mind Workers* and many other important works on the subject; Greg Anrig, researcher and vice president of policy and programs at The Century Foundation; Linda Darling-Hammond, professor of education at Stanford University; Susan Moore Johnson, professor of education at Harvard University; Michael Fullan, former dean of the Ontario Institute for Studies in Education; Diane Ravitch, former US Assistant Secretary of Education and research professor at New York University; Tom Alves, codirector of TURN and executive director of the San Juan Teachers Association; Ellen Bernstein, codirector of TURN; Saul Rubenstein and John McCarthy, researchers from Rutgers University; Shannan Brown, president of the San Juan Teachers Association; Ed Burgess, high school director of the San Juan Teachers Association; John Collins, superintendent of Poway Unified School District; Arielle Zurzolo, executive director of Strategic Partnerships at Teacher Plus; Kate McKenna, codirector of CalTURN; Pat Dolan, Jo Anderson, and Mary McDonald, leaders at the Consortium for Educational Change; David Rattray, president of UNITE-LA; Mary Sieu, superintendent of ABC Unified School District; Joe Boyd, president of Advocacy Research Group; Ray Gaer, president of the ABC Federation of Teachers; Chris Steinhauser, superintendent of Long Beach Unified; Aaron Price, president of the Glen Price Group; Shelly Masur, chief executive officer, CDE Foundation; Glen Price, chief deputy superintendent, California Department of Education; Fred Frelow, senior program officer at the Ford Foundation; Dean Vogel, former president of the California Teachers Association; Eric Heins, president of the California Teachers Association; and Josh Pechthalt, president of the California Federation of Teachers.

I am grateful to those who collaborated with me on research we conducted together on labor-management collaboration. They include Sara McClellan, Scott Vince, Jan Agee, and Scott Sargent from WestEd in California and Dennis Shirley from Boston College in Massachusetts.

I thank the Ford Foundation for support that enabled me to conduct research for this book and to assist many educators along the way. I thank, in particular, Ford's Fred Frelow and Jeannie Oakes for advocating for labor-management collaboration and supporting my work.

In this book, I sought to blend research with examples to make a clear and compelling case for labor-management partnerships. If I succeeded, it's due to the extraordinary assistance I received from my editors. I am especially grateful to Lawrence Haas, a gifted writer who offered helpful revisions on virtually every page of this book. Nancy Walser at Harvard Education Press provided critical guidance with the organization of the book and urged me to address questions that readers would want answered.

Lastly, I thank my family. Jennifer Futernick, my sister-in-law and masterful editor and writer, offered valuable guidance and inspiration during the early stages of the project. My brother, Bob, a wise thinker, a highly accomplished organizational leader, and a great friend, helped me think through countless problems that I faced while writing the book. More than anything, I'm indebted to my wife, Joy, one of the most thoughtful and dedicated educators I know, for her feedback on the manuscript but, most importantly, for her boundless love, encouragement, and support.

About the Author

KEN FUTERNICK is an educational consultant to schools, school districts, and policy makers across the United States. He's a member of a team supporting the California Labor-Management Initiative, which provides technical assistance to state and local school leaders who are pursuing labor-management collaboration.

Futernick began his career as an elementary teacher near Sacramento and, after earning his MA and PhD in education at the University of California, Berkeley, he worked at California State University, Sacramento, for twenty years. There, he taught courses in education and conducted research on teacher retention, educational policy, and preservice teacher training programs. He also served as chair of the Department of Teacher Education for three years.

In 2008, Futernick helped found and direct the School Turnaround Center at WestEd, a national nonprofit educational research and service organization based in San Francisco. He and his colleagues helped school leaders across the nation improve student outcomes by strengthening teaching and learning conditions and targeted professional development programs for teachers and administrators. He conducted research on labor-management collaboration, and he coauthored several publications on this subject, including a chapter he wrote with Adam Urbanski for the book *The State Role in School Turnaround*.

He lives with his wife, Joy, in the Sierra foothills of California. He can be reached at kenfuternick.org.

Index

ABC Unified Federation of Teachers, 57,
59–60
ABC Unified School District (California),
72, 111, 117–118
behavioral norms for district leaders, 58
collaborative culture, 26
educator collaboration, 60–61
external collaboration experts, 59
guiding principles adopted, 58
hardest-to-staff schools, 58–59
informal conversations to address
problems, 34
labor-management collaboration, 57–61
Partnership with Administration and
Labor (P.A.L.), 60
principals and union site leaders
collaboration, 59
Proactive Problem Solvers (PROPS), 59
professional development and support
on collaboration by unions,
96
professional learning process, 95–96
retreats, 95
school-level partnerships between
unions and administrators, 37
social capital, 50
special education students, 59
student achievement, 61, 130
teacher unions striking, 57

teaching conditions surveys, 60
we don't let each other fail, 26
West Coast Labor Management Institute,
60, 72
Abrams, Samuel E., 158
academic achievement
professional development for teachers,
141
San Diego schools, 5–6
significant improvements in, 4
Academic Performance Index, 61
academic research, 12–14
accountability
education policies, 102
education reforms, 103
heightened, 76–77
leading with, 160
reciprocal, 137
teachers and teacher unions, 103
administrators
disengaged from teachers, 11
informal conversations addressing
problems, 34
layoff decisions, 147–148
personnel decisions, 147
professional development, xviii, 136,
138–139, 141
professional learning, 54–55
skepticism, 81

administrators (*continued*)
  support system to transition to
    partnership, 8–9
  teacher evaluation, 35, 139–140
  tools to help teachers succeed, 136
  top-down approach, 48
adversarial approach, 3–5
African Americans
  academic achievement, xvi–xvii
  Montgomery County Public Schools, xv
Alexander, Lamar, 156
Alter, Jonathan, 3
Alves, Tom, 27–28, 106, 123
American Federation of Teachers (AFT), x,
    12, 41, 63–64, 146, 152
  Race to the Top, 38
  shared vision statement, 16–17
  single-salary schedule improvements,
    149
American Institutes of Research, 6
Anrig, Greg, 32–33, 63
antiunion activity, 7–8
arbitration, 28
Argyris, Chris, 74, 94
art, xviii
art of talking together, 123
Asian Americans, xvi–xvii
Association of Supervisors and Administra-
    tors of Rochester (ASAR), 39
Atkinson, Tom, 97
authentic collaboration, xix, 11–12, 38

bargaining better, 105–110
Barnes, Ron, 58
Barth, Roland, 53
Basica, Nina, 39, 86
Berliner, David, 18
Bersin, Alan, 5, 6, 47–48, 78, 89
Bill & Melinda Gates Foundation and
    Common Core State Standards
    (CCSS), 65
Blanchard, Ken, 99
Bloomberg, Michael, 7
Blueprint for Great Schools report, 66, 111,
    133
*The Blueprint for Student Success in a
    Standards-Based System*, 5–6

both sides
  addressing differences constructively,
    26–29
  collaborating at all levels of education
    system, 36–41
  dependent on each other, 25–26
  fighting well with each other, 28
  joint ownership of decisions, 29–31
  joint responsibility for results, 31–33
Brady, Tom, 80–81, 110
Brown, Jerry, 68
Brown, Wendy, 155
Bryk, Tony, 50
Burke, Joseph, 98
Burnham Plan, 133
Bush, George W., 9, 155

California
  Blueprint for Great Schools report, 111, 133
  California Labor Management Initiative
    (LMI), 67, 72, 110
  The California Way, 111
  CalTURN, 72
  collaborative partnerships, 72
  Common Core State Standards (CCSS),
    37, 66, 110–112
  Digital Chalkboard, 68
  dispelling myths about collaboration,
    111–112
  educator effectiveness task force policies,
    67
  going slow before going fast, 111
  Labor Management Agreement, 37
  labor-management collaboration, 67, 110
  labor-management initiative, 133
  professional development, 68
  state-level collaboration, 37
  teacher evaluation, 35
  tenure laws, 145
California Department of Education, 72
California Labor Management Initiative
    (LMI), 67, 72, 110
Californians Dedicated to Education
    Foundation (CDEF), 68
The California Way, 111
CalTURN, 72
Canada, Geoffrey, 7–8

capacity building, 102–104
capacity for collaboration, 94–97
capitulation, 31
Career In Teaching Program, 55
career lattice program, 55
Center for American Progress, 145
Central Valley schools (California)
  academic achievement, 121
  WestEd, 100–102
change, resistance to, 73–77
Change Initiative, 81
changing narrative, 1–21
charter schools, 3, 7, 34, 86, 159
Chelsea public schools (Massachusetts),
  33, 123
Chicago schools
  adversity among educators, 10
  seven-day strike (2012), 77
Chicago Teachers Union, 10, 77
Chingos, Matthew M., 140
Christie, Chris, 97
Cincinnati Federation of Teachers, 61, 75
Cincinnati Public Schools, 45, 61–62, 112
  achievement gap, 32, 62
  autonomy of schools, 62
  collaboration and joint responsibilities,
    31–33
  collective bargaining agreements, 32
  Community Learning Centers, 33–34,
    62
  graduation rates, 32, 62
  Instructional Leadership Teams, 62
  labor-management collaboration, 61–63
  labor-management confrontation, 4
  peer assistance and review (PAR)
    programs, 61
  principals and teachers making
    operational and educational
    decisions, 45
  school-based committees, 61–62
  school board members, 62
  teacher selection, 75
  trust, 63
civility, 10, 51–52, 79, 93
Clark County School District interest-based
  bargaining (IBB), 106–107
Cohn, Carl, 10–11, 87

*Collaborating: Finding Common Ground for
  Multiparty Problems* (Gray), 24
collaboration
  after conflicts, 100
  Alan Bersin on, 6
  arguments against, 2
  authentic collaboration, xix, 11–12, 38, 76
  capitulation or collusion, 8, 31
  choosing over confrontation, xv–xvii
  collective bargaining, xi–xii
  Common Core State Standards (CCSS),
    63–68
  complexity, 24–25
  before conflicts, 100
  critics, 15
  deep, 23–24
  defining, 23–24
  developing capacity for, 94–97
  disagreements, 24
  discretionary emotional energy, 52
  discussion group, 117
  diversity of perspectives, 26–29
  educational policies and, 9
  educators, 15–16, 52–53
  essential features, 25–46
  exploring new ideas, 97–98
  fueling collusion, 79–80
  harmful actions, 101
  high school graduation rates
    (Cincinnati), 32
  implementing strategies to promote, 15
  inadequate funding, 85–86
  inside, 40
  introducing in small groups, 116
  labor-management collaboration, x–xi
  major opportunities for, x
  management and teacher unions, xvii–
    xviii, 8
  misconceptions about meaning of, 8
  misunderstanding, xix
  necessary but not sufficient, 17
  not a silver bullet, 17–19, 157
  not imposed from outside, 98
  obstacles to, 71–89
  opposition to, 80
  outside, 40–41
  overzealous leaders, 98

collaboration (*continued*)
  parties involved proposing, 98–99
  proponents, 116–117
  real, 7
  regional conference on, 117
  skeptics, 8–9, 30–31, 116–117
  skills, 94–97
  stakeholders, 23–24
  strong social capital and, 50
  supportive actions, 101
  support system absence, 8–9
  tactics, 113–133
  teachers, ix
  trust, 23, 50–51
  wide-ranging benefits, 49–53
  without trust, 99
collaborative bargaining, 12
collaborative cultures, 78
collaborative districts
  decisions affecting teaching and
    learning, 29–30
  management and union leaders, 117
  norms, 118–119
  role-alike meetings, 117
  setting their own agendas, 29
collaborative leadership and professional
    development, xviii
collaborative norms, 118–120
collaborative partnerships
  conflict, 78–79
  mandated reforms and, 86
  opposition to, 15–17
collective bargaining
  agreements that neither party wants, 42
  bargaining better, 105–110
  building genuine profession for
    teachers, xii
  changing negotiation process, xii
  collaboration, xi–xii, 42–43
  contentious, 105
  derailing efforts to collaborate, 42
  as dreaded ritual, 42
  expanding scope, xii, 143
  interest-based bargaining (IBB), xi,
    105–106
  limitations, 107
  living contracts, xii, 43, 107–109

  memoranda of understanding, 109
  more effective schools, xii
  nonbinding compacts, 109
  opposition to, 80
  professionalizing teaching, 42
  relationships between administrators
    and teachers, 42
  restricting scope, 83
  teachers, 13
  transfer rules, 147
  trust agreements, 109
  varying state rules for, 109
college- and career-ready standards
    conference, 15
Collins, Timothy, 81, 82, 98
collusion, 31
  myth of, 79–82
Columbus City School District, 30
Columbus Education Association, 30
Colvin, Richard Lee, 6
Common Core State Standards (CCSS), 41
  California, 37, 110–112
  collaboration, 63–68
  controversy over, 64
  critical thinking, 64
  education stakeholder groups, 63–64
  high-stakes testing, 110
  implementing, 125
  locally appropriate curricula, 64
  New York State, 65–66
  New York State United Teachers, 65
  opposition, 88
  problems implementing, 64–65
  professional development on, 68
  Race to the Top requirement, 65–66
  real-world problems and, 64
  sanctions with implementation of,
    65
  states, 66
  students opting out, 65
  teacher evaluation, 65
  teachers, 64–65, 68–69
  teacher unions, 88
communities of practice, 41
community leaders strategies for collabora-
    tion, 131–132
Community Learning Centers, 62

compensation systems
  alternative, 148–151
  merit pay systems, 150
  single-salary schedules, 148–150
conflict
  collaborative partnerships, 78–79
  engaging constructively in, 29
  safe, anger-free dialogue, 120–122
confrontation
  adversarial approach, 3–5
  can't work, 9–11
  choosing collaboration over, xv–xvii
  replacing with interest-based bargaining
    (IBB), xvi
consensus, myth of, 78–79
Consortium for Educational Change (CEC),
    41, 96, 117, 132–133
contracts, 42–43
Council of Chief State School Officers, 63
Council of Great City Schools, 64
courageous leadership, 160–161
Cox, Sharon, 53
Crucial Conversations (Patterson et al.), 120
Crucial Accountability, 120
Cullison, Bonnie, 137
Culver City Unified Schools, 60
  administrators and union leaders, 123
  collaborative culture, 26
  contract negotiation problems, 28–29
  districtwide culture of collaboration,
    117–118

Darling-Hammond, Linda, 68, 88, 139
Davis, Jocelyn R., 97
decisions, joint ownership of, 29–31
deep collaboration, 23–24
Delaware State Education Association, 132
de Prosse, Nancy, 81, 142
Dialogue: The Art of Thinking Together, 123
differences
  both sides addressing constructively,
    26–29
  key strategy for resolving, 28–29
  respect for, 27
Digital Chalkboard, 68
disagreements, 24, 27–28
discretionary emotional energy, 52

District Capacity Project (DCP), 96,
    124–125
district leaders
  face-to-face interactions with
    counterparts, 41
  joint ownership threatening, 30
  leading by example, 91
  Montgomery County Public Schools
    (MCPS), 53
  resistance to change, 74–77
  social capital, 50
district managers, xv
District Wide Educational Improvement
    Council (DWEIC), 31
Dubin, Jennifer, 30
Duditch, Steve, 83–84
DuFour, Richard, 26, 114–115
Duncan, Arne, 1–2, 9, 15, 66, 86–87, 150
Dweck, Carol, 93

Eckert, Jonathan, 31, 129
education
  debates over future of, 156
  industrial model, 143
  influential constituencies within, 15–17
  matters critical to, 27
  US ranking near the middle in reading,
    math, and science, 155–156
educational foundations, 43–44
educational outcomes, 25–46
educational systems catering to teachers,
    44
education leaders
  collaborative norms and monitoring
    progress, 118–120
  fear of loss of control, 75
  incivility costs, 93
  mean-spirited leadership assumptions,
    93
  questionable belief systems, 52
  Race to the Top funds, 88
  resisting change, 74
  starting with yourself, 114–116
  trust, 51
  what it will take to pursue collaboration,
    115
EducationNext, 16

education policies
  accountability, 102
  authentic collaboration, 38
  capacity building, 102
  collaboration and, 9
  district level, 102
  federal and state, 104
  labor-management conflict, 9
  misguided, 85–89
  overly prescriptive, misguided, or poorly
      implemented, 102
  poor implementation, 89
  teachers' role in, 104
  teacher unions role in, 83, 104
  those in authority over, 88–89
education reforms
  accountability, 103
  addressing problems together, 157
  collaboration tactics, 113–133
  courageous leadership, 160–161
  debates over future of, 156–157
  educators and, xi
  failures, ix
  Finland, 157–160
  firing teachers, 2
  go slow to go fast, 97–99, 159
  labor-management collaboration, x–xi
  management, 135–153
  new mindsets, 93–94
  new practices and policies, 92–93
  overt confrontation, 2
  policy makers and education officials, 86
  silver bullet solutions, 17–18
  strategies, xi, 1
  teacher unions, 16–17, 82–83, 135–153
  value-added, 85
Education Sector, 83, 84, 138, 146
Education Sector report, 130
education systems collaboration, 36–41
Education Week, 57, 64
educators
  administrative top-down approach, 48
  adversity among, 10
  collaboration, 36, 116–118
  fixed mindsets, 93
  improving relationships, 49
  off-site retreats, 122–123

resisting change, 8
trust, 52–53, 121
undiscussable issues, 34
values to guide work of, 101
Elementary and Secondary Education Act,
      156
Elmore, Richard, 137
Emanuel, Rahm, 10, 48
Emigholz, Christopher, 97
emotional energy, 52
empowering teachers, 151–153
Evans, Robert, 73–74

false promise of adversarial approach, 3–5
fear of loss of control, 75
fear of unknown, 76
Feinberg, Ken, 146
Ferriter, Mary, 123
Fierce, Inc., 120
fierce conversations, 29
Fierce Conversations, 120
fighting well with each other, 28
Finland
  achievement gap, 158
  basic education, 158
  capacity building, 160
  education, 18
  education reform, 157, 158–160
  education system improvements,
      102–103
  educators, 158
  international exams, 158–159
  schools, 158–159
  significant and strategic investments,
      159–160
  standardized testing, 158
  student learning, 158
  teachers, 159–160
  teaching, 158–159
  test less, learn more, 158
Finn, Chester, 88
Finnish National Board of Education, 158
Fitzgerald, Tim, 40, 42
fixed mindsets, 93
Fullan, Michael, 23, 40, 78, 102–103, 141, 160
funding for schools and school districts, 18
Futernick, Ken, x, xi

Gaer, Ray, 34, 59–60
Getting Teacher Evaluation Right (Darling-Hammond), 88, 139
Glass, Gene, 18
Goldstein, Dana, 85
go slow to go fast, 76, 97–99, 159
   California, 111
governance structures, 31
Gray, Barbara, 24–25, 27, 29
Greatness by Design report, 67, 111, 133
Green Dot Public Schools, 72
growth mindset, 93–94
Guggenheim, Davis, 3
Guin, Kacey, 140

Hamilton County Schools, 33
Harlem Children's Zone, 7
harmful actions, 101
Hartford school district (Connecticut), 79
Harvard Negotiation Project, 106
Heffernan, Margaret, 76
heightened accountability, 76–77
Helena public schools (Montana) Professional Compensation Alternative Plan (PCAP), 45–46
Henig, Jeffrey R., 69
Hereen, Dawn, 59
Hess, Frederick, 3, 4, 79–82
high school students, exposing to real-world careers, 125
Hill, Heather C., 141
Hillsborough County Public Schools
   collaboration, 77
   mentor teachers, 33
Holtzapple, Elizabeth, 62
Huffington Post, 68
human capital and student achievement, 49–50
The Human Side of School Change (Evans), 73
Humphrey, Daniel, 12

if only approach, 114–115
Illinois
   Consortium for Educational Change, 132–133
   formal state partnership structures, 37
improved educational outcomes, 25–46

inadequate funding, 85–86
incompetent teachers, 139, 144
industrial-era assumptions about teaching, 13
industrial-style unionizing, 143–144
Ingram, Alan, 81, 82
Innovation Schools (Massachusetts), 34, 125
Institute for Education Sciences, 141
Institute for Innovation in Teaching and Learning, 96
Instructional Leadership Teams, 62
interactions, spaces where they occur, 122–123
interest-based bargaining (IBB), 42–43, 95, 105–106
   bargaining, 43
   Clark County School District, 106–107
   innovating and problem solving, 106
   living contracts, 107–109
   replacing confrontational bargaining, xvi
   San Juan Unified School District, 106
Interest Based Problem Solving (IBPS) team, 32

Janey, Clifford, 5
Johnson, Lyndon B., 160
Johnson, Susan Moore, 42, 103
Joint Labor-Management Initiative, 98–99
joint ownership of decisions, 29–31
joint responsibility for results, 31–33
Jones, Don, 45
Just for the Kids, 43–44

Kaboolian, Linda, 10, 14, 107
Kerchner, Charles Taylor, 13–14, 82–83, 108
Keys to Excellence for Your Schools (KEYS), 113–114, 116
Klein, Joel, 2, 4, 7, 48, 78
Knapp, Marc, 6
knowledge workers, 13
Koppich, Julia E., 12–14, 108
Koppich, Julie E., 24, 27
Kosienski, Robert, 30, 31
Kristof, Nicholas, 17

labor
   collaboration within, 38–40

labor (*continued*)
    commitment to collaboration, 24
    management as adversary, 2
    teacher-related issues, 35
labor leaders, 34
labor-management collaboration, x–xi, xiii,
    xvii–xviii, xx
    ABC Unified School District, 57–61
    addressing differences, 26–29
    affecting teaching and learning, 33–35
    attracting and retaining teachers, 43–46
    bargaining contracts, 42–43
    California, 67, 110
    case-study research on, xx
    Cincinnati Public Schools, 61–63
    college- and career-ready standards
        conference, 15
    collusion, 79–82
    cordiality, 24
    dependent on each other, 25–26
    district level, 36
    education system and, 36–41
    first national conference on, xx
    formal grievance procedures, 33
    impact, 47–69
    individual school sites, 36–37
    joint ownership of decisions, 29–31
    joint responsibility for results, 31–33
    labor and management, 38–40
    Montgomery County Public Schools,
        53–57
    national conferences on, 15, 37–38
    national level, 36, 37–38
    outside collaboration, 40–41
    state level, 36, 37
    student learning, xiii, xviii, 49
    substance of conversation and quality of
        decisions, 24
    "Transforming the Teaching Profession"
        conference, 15
    urban school districts, xii
labor-management conflict, 9
labor-management confrontation, 4
Labor Management Initiative, xx, 37
labor-management partnerships
    difficulty maintaining, 157
    union critics seeing benefits of, 17

LaRose, Dave, 26, 28–29, 117–118, 123
Latinos
    academic achievement, xvi–xvii
    Montgomery County Public Schools, xv
Lawrence, Martha, 99
*Leading for Equity: The Pursuit of Excellence
    in Montgomery County Schools*, 1
lead teachers, 55, 62
Leana, Carrie, 49–50
learning
    collaborating on everything affecting,
        33–35
    innovating and solving problems
        affecting, 49
Linked Learning, 125
listening to each other, 28
living contracts, xii, 43, 152
    bargaining contract provisions, 108–109
    renegotiation and modification during
        term, 107
    Rochester City School District, 108
Long Beach Unified, 139
Los Angeles Times, 145
Luyet, Ronald J., 52, 95, 98

Malcolm Baldrige National Quality Award,
    xvii
management
    adversarial and dysfunctional, 38–39
    agenda for change with unions, 136
    building capacity of teachers, 137
    collaboration within, 36, 38–40
    collaborative districts discussions, 117
    collective bargaining, 42–43
    Columbus Education Association,
        30
    commitment to collaboration, 24
    courageous leadership, 161
    disagreements within, 40
    emotionally and politically risky issues,
        120
    labor as adversary, 25
    needed reforms, 135–153
    perceptions about themselves, 115
    resources for teachers, 142
    safe, anger-free dialogue, 120–122
    sharing power, 127, 136

supports for teachers, 137–138
teacher advocacy, 142–143
teacher-related issues, 35
teacher unions and, xvii–xviii, 28, 136–138
transparency, 137
manifesto for fixing schools, 2
Massachusetts
formal state partnership structures, 37
state labor-management initiative, 132
teacher evaluation, 35
Massachusetts Education Partnership
(MEP), 41, 117, 132
collaboration support, 96
District Capacity Project (DCP), 96,
124–125
Professional Learning Communities, 124
Teacher Leader positions, 125
Massachusetts Teachers Association
(MTA), 16, 81, 143, 144, 161
Mass 2020/National Council on
Time and Learning initiative
(Massachusetts), 34
McCarthy, John E., 37, 50, 60, 129, 143
McClellan, Sara, 51
McWalters, Peter, 110
memoranda of understanding, 109
Meriden Federation of Teachers, 30
Meriden public schools (Connecticut), 30
merit pay systems, 150
MetLife survey, 139
Mielke, Dave, 26, 28–29, 117–118, 123
Milwaukee Teachers' Education
Association, 152
mindsets, developing new, 92–94
misguided education policy, 85–89
Montana Education Association/ Montana
Federation of Teachers (MEA-
MFT), 45
Montgomery County Council of PTAs, 53
Montgomery County Education Association
(MCEA), 53, 55, 151
Montgomery County Public Schools
(MCPS), 112
academic achievement, xv, xvi–xvii, 57
alternative compensation systems, 150
Board of Education, 53
career lattice program, 55, 150

challenges to success, 54
collaborative norms and monitoring
progress, 118
collective bargaining agreement, 24
community-supported aspirational goal,
54
criticizing Rhee's strategies, 4
culture of blame, xvi
district leaders, 53
educational initiatives, 54
facing crisis as partners, xvi
graduation and college readiness goals,
56–57
improvements, 1
interest-based bargaining (IBB), xvi
labor-management collaboration, 53–57
labor-management confrontation, 4
Malcolm Baldrige National Quality
Award, xvii
new unionism, 53
peer assistance and review (PAR)
element, 54–55
population diversity, xv
Professional Growth System (PGS), 33,
54–55, 81, 139
quality of education, xvi
Race to the Top funds, 1–2
reading, xv
R.E.S.P.E.C.T., xvi, 118
seeds of collaboration, xvi
seniority regulations, 147
social capital among staff, 55
teacher evaluations, 54–55
teacher retention rates, 56
teacher unions, xvi, 54, 56
trust, 54
Viers Mill elementary school, 55–56
Mooney, Tom, 61
Murphy, Tim, 79
myth of collusion, 79–82
myth of consensus, 78–79

narrative, changing, 1–21
National Assessment of Educational
Progress (NAEP), 4, 68
Washington, DC schools, 5
what students actually know, 48

National Board Certification Support
Program, 55
National Center on Teacher Quality report,
148
National Education Association (NEA), 12,
38, 63, 64, 149, 152
Keys to Excellence for Your Schools
(KEYS), 113–114, 116
Race to the Top, x
shared vision statement, 16–17
National Governors Association, 63
national level labor-management collabo-
ration, 36, 37–38
National School Boards Association, 64
NEA Foundation, 41
Institute for Innovation in Teaching and
Learning, 96
online courses for educators'
collaborative skills, 114
New Haven School Change Initiative, 81
New Jersey Business and Industry Associa-
tion, 97
Newsweek, 3, 4
new unionism, 53, 143
New York City teachers merit pay systems,
150
New York magazine, 3
New York State
Board of Regents, 65
Common Core State Standards (CCSS),
65–66
difficulty implementing reforms, 37
Race to the Top program, 65, 88
New York State United Teachers, 65
New York Times, 7, 17
Nielsen, Larry, 45
No Child Left Behind (NCLB), 9, 38, 86–87
academic achievement, 155–156
nonbinding compacts, 109
norms and collaborative districts, 118–119

Obama, Barack, 9, 87, 149
obstacles to collaboration
misguided education policy, 85–89
myth of collusion, 79–82
myth of consensus, 78–79
resistance to change, 73–77

shortage of technical support, 84–85
skepticism about teacher unions, 82–84
off-site retreats, 122–123
Olmstead, Cynthia, 99
Organisation for Economic Co-operation
and Development (OECD), 158
Osmond, Pamela, 39–40, 86
outside collaboration, 40–41

parents' strategies for collaboration, 131–132
Parker, George, 39
Partnership with Administration and Labor
(P.A.L.), 60
Patterson, Kerry, 120
Pearson, Christine, 51, 93
pedal to the metal approach, 97
peer assistance and review (PAR) programs,
14, 31, 81, 95, 103–104, 146
Cincinnati Public Schools, 61
Performance Evaluation Reform Act
(PERA), 133
Performance Index, 61, 121
personal spaces promoting reflection and
dialogue, 122–123
Peterson, Bob, 152
Phillips, Vicki, 65
pitching it first, 116–118, 125
Plattsburg City School District
collaboration and joint responsibilities,
31–32
District Wide Educational Improvement
Council (DWEIC), 31
teacher advocacy, 142–143
policy makers
believing they know better than teachers,
89
courageous leadership, 161
Porath, Christine, 51, 75, 93
Portland schools (Maine) Professional
Learning Based Salary System
(PLBSS), 150–151
positive results, 124–126
poverty
schools and, 18–19
student achievement, xii, 61
Poway Teachers Association, 32
Poway Unified District, 32, 72, 111

principals
  professional development, 59
  strategies for collaboration, 129–130
  teacher evaluations, 87–88, 138–141
Proactive Problem Solvers (PROPS), 59
problems
  addressing together, 157
  seeking solutions to solvable, 124–126
  starting small, 124
Professional Compensation Alternative
    Plan (PCAP), 45–46
professional development
  administrators, 141
  collaborative leadership, xviii
  Common Core State Standards (CCSS),
    68
  good and poor, 141
  principals, 59
  Springfield Public Schools
    (Massachusetts), 142
  student academic achievement, 141
  teachers, 141–142
  union site leaders, 59–60
Professional Growth System (PGS), 54–55,
    81, 139
Professional Learning Based Salary System
    (PLBSS), 150–151
Professional Learning Communities, 124
Providence schools (Rhode Island), 80–81,
    109–110
public schools, x, xiii

Race to the Top (RTTP), 1–2, 35, 38, 143
  Common Core State Standards (CCSS)
    requirement, 65–66
  divisive strategy, 87
  labor-management conflict, 9
  merit pay systems, 149–150
  New York State, 65
  school performance, 87
  test-based evaluation, 38, 87–88, 144
Radical Collaboration (Tamm and Luyet), 52
Ravitch, Diane, 6, 47–48
reading and Montgomery County Public
    Schools, xv
real collaboration, 7
reciprocal accountability, 137

relational trust, 50
relationships
  among adults within school, 53
  building and maintaining, 95
  improving among educators, 49
  superintendents and union leaders, 127
  trust, 25, 99–102
Rennie Center, 98, 99, 124, 142
Rennie Center report, 81–82
resistance to change
  fear of loss of control, 75
  fear of unknown, 76
  heightened accountability, 76–77
  lingering resentments, 77
  threat to leaders' identity and
    competence, 74–75
R.E.S.P.E.C.T., xvi, 118
respect for differences, 27
responsibility, reciprocal and shared, 76–77
results, joint responsibility for, 31–33
retreats, 122–123
Rhee, Michelle, 1–5, 7, 39, 48, 78
Rico, Laura, 57
Rider, Deborah, 39
Riley, Thomas, 57
Rochester City School District
  Association of Supervisors and
    Administrators of Rochester
    (ASAR), 39
  living contracts, 108
  School-Level Living Contract
    Committees (SLLCC), 108
  transfer rules, 147
role-alike meetings, 117
Ronan, Mary, 45, 61, 62, 75, 79
Rosenberg, Sarah, 17
Rotz, Tracy, 129
Rubinstein, Saul A., 37, 50, 60, 129, 143

safe, anger-free dialogue, 120–122
Sahlberg, Pasi, 158, 159
San Diego schools
  academic achievements, 5–6
  adversity among educators, 10–11
  reform efforts, 5–7
  superintendent and teachers union, 5
  teacher resistance, 6

San Diego Unified School District, 78, 87
San Juan Teachers Association, 83
San Juan Unified School District, 27, 72,
    111, 123
  interest-based bargaining (IBB), 95, 106
  off-site check-in meetings, 34
  peer assistance and review (PAR)
    programs, 83
  teacher unions role in education policies,
    83–84
San Mateo Union High School District, 139
Sarjala, Jukka, 158
Saunders, Nathan, 39
Schneider, Barbara, 50
Scholastic, 64
school boards
  colluding with unions, 79
  committed to collaboration, 91
  disputes among members, 39
  elections and teacher unions, 129
  hiring superintendents, 31, 126–127
  how districts conduct business, 127
  labor-management partnerships, 132
  strategies for collaboration, 126–127
school districts
  benefits for students, 81
  collaboration before and after conflicts,
    100
  facilitators building collaborative
    capacity, 96–97
  firing incompetent teachers, 144–146
  funding, 18
  outside collaboration, 41
  partnerships networking with district
    leaders, 96
  peer assistance and review (PAR)
    programs, 14
  resentments, 77
  site visits to, 41
  strengthening teaching profession, 81
  teacher evaluation, 2
  tone for conducting business, 127
  value-added models (VAM), 87–88
  vision statements that put kids first, 44
School Improvement Grants, 35
School-Level Living Contract Committees
  (SLLCC), 108

school management, x–xi
school reform movements, 50
schools
  bargaining contract provisions, 108–109
  Community Learning Centers, 62
  conditions for good schools, 18–19
  focusing on students, 43–44
  funding, 18, 85–86
  how students are doing in all subjects,
    48–49
  lowest performing, 86
  more effective, xii
  organizing, 14
  poverty, 18–19
  relationships among adults within,
    53
  social capital absence, 52
  standardized tests, 48
school sites and labor-management
    collaboration, 36–37
school systems
  chronically dysfunctional, 73
  successful turnarounds, xx
School Turnaround Center, xx
science, less attention to, xviii
science, technology, engineering, and math
    (STEM) content, 30
Sellers, Julie, 45, 61, 62, 75
Senge, Peter, 123
seniority regulations, 146–148
shared decision making, ix
Shirley, Dennis, 51
Short, Jake, 31, 129
Sieu, Mary, 34, 59, 60
Signer, Mona M., 53
Silva, Elena, 17
Simon, Mark, 53, 150–151
Singapore's improvements in education
    system, 102–103
single-salary schedules, 148–149
skepticism about teacher unions, 82–84
Smiley, Candy, 32
Smith, Steve, 80–81, 110
Smuts, Gary, 26
social capital, 49, 52, 55, 63
social studies, less attention to, xviii
solutions to solvable problems, 124–126

Springfield Public Schools (Massachusetts)
home-grown approach to collaboration, 98–99
instructional leadership team (ILT), 81–82
Joint Labor Management Initiative, 98–99
Keys to Excellence in Your Schools (KEYS), 116
paying attention to own group, 116
professional development, 142
student achievement, 99
stakeholders
collaboration, 23–24
professional relationships, 51
strategies for collaboration, 126–133
trust, 51
standardized tests
concrete, measurable results, 47
English language arts and math, 48
Finland rejecting, 158
firing teachers, 4
moratorium on, 2
school performance, 48
student achievement, 4
teacher evaluation, 2, 35
Washington DC schools, 4–5
Starr, Joshua, 2
starting with yourself, 114–116
state level labor-management collaboration, 36, 37
state management organizations strategies for collaboration, 132–133
state-mandated tests, xii
states and Common Core State Standards (CCSS), 66
state union organizations strategies for collaboration, 132–133
status quo trap, 76
strategies for collaboration, 92
bargaining better, 105–110
capacity for collaboration, 94–97
community leaders, 131–132
education policy, 102–105
go slow to go fast strategy, 97–99
new mindsets, 92–94
parents, 131–132

principals, 129–130
school boards, 126–127
solutions to solvable problems, 124–126
stakeholders, 126–133
state management organizations, 132–133
state union organizations, 132–133
superintendents, 127–128
teachers, 130–131
trust, 99–102
union presidents, 128–129
union site representatives, 129–130
student achievement
human capital, 49–50
improving, xii, xviii
labor-management collaboration, xiii
poverty and, xii, 61
relationships among educators, 49
social capital, 49–50
students
adversarial approach outcomes, 4
disengagement, xix
more and better learning time, 15
more effective schools for, xii
StudentsFirst, 7
StudentsFirstNY, 7
success breeds success, 71, 124
superintendents
acting collectively, 127
collaborative working environment at offices, 128
hiring, 126–127
school boards and, 39, 128
strategies for collaboration, 127–128
threat to leaders' identity and competence, 74–75
union leaders and, 127–128
Sutherland, Paul, 14
system approach to work, 25–26

tactics for collaboration
committing to collaborative norms and monitoring progress, 118–120
Keys to Excellence for Your Schools (KEYS), 113–114
personal spaces to promote reflection and dialogue, 122–123

tactics for collaboration (*continued*)
pitching it first, 116–118
safe, anger-free dialogue, 120–122
starting with yourself, 114–116
Tamm, James W., 52, 95, 98
teacher evaluation, 34–35
administrators, 139–140
Common Core State Standards (CCSS), 65
feedback, 138, 140
high-stakes evaluation systems, 35
meaningful, 138–141
Montgomery County Public Schools (MCPS), 54–55
positive ratings, 139
qualified observers conducting, 139
standardized tests, 2, 4, 35, 87–88
teacher improvement, 140
tenure laws, 140
Teacher Leader positions, 125
teacher-related issues to collaborate on, 35
teachers
accountability, 103
advocacy, 142–143
alleged misconduct, 146
attracting and retaining, 43–46
building capacity, 137, 141–142
catering to, 44
committed to collaboration, 91
compensation systems, 148–151
disengaged from administrators, 11
disillusioned, cynical, and burned out, 44
education policies, 104–105
empowering, 151–153
engaging, 68–69
erosion of support for, 44
ineffective, 87–88
lead teachers, 55
living contracts, 152
merit pay, 4
norms and responsibilities among, 103
peer assistance and review (PAR) programs, 14, 103–104
preparing students for tests, xviii
professional development, 141–142
professional learning, 54–55

professional relationships between, 49–50
qualifications and capabilities of, 49–50
quality, 103
ranking effectiveness, 147–148
reluctance to collaborate, ix
resistance to change, 74–77
retention, 15
running for union office, 130–131
running school systems, 13
seniority regulations, 146–148
shortages, 44, 140
skepticism, 81, 131
strategies for collaboration, 130–131
teacher evaluation, 34–35
teacher selection, 75
teacher unions, 17, 83–84
teacher unions advocacy organizations, 39
teaching to the test, 86–87
tenure, 103
tenure laws, 144–146
tools to succeed, 136
transfer rules, 147
urban school districts, ix, 159
Teacher Union Reform Network (TURN), xvii, 3, 12, 27, 41, 72, 117
regional conferences, 96
teacher unions, x, xi
accountability, 103
adversarial and dysfunctional relations within, 38–39
advocacy organizations, 39
antiunion activity, 7–8
articulating what they are for, 143–144
call for change, 12–14
collaboration, xvii–xviii, 3, 36, 83, 96, 128–129
collective bargaining, 42–43
colluding with management, 39
Common Core State Standards (CCSS), 88
compensation systems, 148–151
confronting, 7–8
controversial policies, 136
criticisms of, 4, 16
declining support for, 2–3

defining mission narrowly, 144
disagreements within, 40
district managers battles, xv
education policies, 104–105
education reforms, 14–17, 82–83,
    143–144
empowering teachers, 151–153
enemies of change, 84
external labor market organization, 14
industrial-style unionizing, 143–144
informing management about actions,
    28
interests of, 80
internal organization, 39
labor-management partnerships, 17
local chapters autonomy, 136, 152
managers as adversaries, 144
members, 16, 39, 40, 128
merit pay systems, 150
needed reforms, 135–153
negative effect on schools, 16
opposing change, 81
opposition to, 15–17
participating in, 39–40
policies and programs not working for
    teachers, 152–153
political infighting, 39
professional development, 96
public discourse about teachers and
    teaching, 39
quality organization, 14
reforming, 12–13, 143–144
resolving disputes with management,
    28
San Diego superintendent, 5–6
school boards, 79, 129
school organization, 14
seniority protections for teachers,
    146–148
site leaders and professional
    development, 59–60
skepticism about, 30–31, 82–84
strategic directions, 39
superintendents and district leaders,
    128–129
tangible improvements, 82
teacher evaluation, 34–35

teacher quality and student achievement,
    84, 130
teachers, 129, 136, 152
tenure, 145
traditional issues for, 130
transparency, 137
working with management, 13
*The Teacher Wars: A History of America's
    Most Embattled Profession* (Gold-
    stein), 85
teaching
    collaborating on everything affecting,
        33–35
    feedback to improve, 138
    industrial-era assumptions about, 13
    innovating and solving problems
        affecting, 49
    strengthening, 43–46
Teaching and Learning Cooperative (TLC),
    32
technical support shortage, 84–85
tenure laws, 144–146
    teacher evaluation, 139–140
Thompson, Scott, 55
Time, 4
Toch, Thomas, 138
Toner, Paul, 16, 143, 144, 161
Torlakson, Tom, 66–67
"Transforming the Teaching Profession"
    conference, 15
trust, 27
    better relationships, 99–102
    civility, 51–52
    collaboration, 50–51, 99
    educators, 52–53, 121
    leaders, 51
    loss of, 29, 51–52
    Montgomery County Public Schools
        (MCPS), 54
    reducing transaction costs in
        organizations, 50
    stakeholders, 51
trust agreements, 109
Trust in Schools (Bryk and Schneider), 50

underperforming schools, 3, 109
union leaders

absence of support system, 8–9
balancing act, 80
bread and butter rewards, 11
collaborative districts, 117
courageous leadership, 161
emotionally and politically risky issues,
    120
interpreting change for members, 13
leading by example, 91
perceptions about themselves, 115
professional development, xviii
protecting their interests, 3
safe, anger-free dialogue, 120–122
social capital, 50
superintendents and, 127–128
threat to identity and competence, 74–75
understanding changing environment,
    13
union-management relationships and if
    only approach, 114–115
union site representatives strategies for
    collaboration, 129–130
United Mind Workers, xix
*United Mind Workers: Unions and Teaching
    in the Knowledge Society* (Kerchner,
    Koppich, and Weeres), 13
United Providence (UP!) Compact, 80,
    109–110
United States ranking near the middle
    in reading, math, and science,
    155–156
urban school districts
    improving student learning, xii
    labor-management collaboration, xii
    teachers, ix, 140
urban schools and teacher retention,
    159
Urbanski, Adam, ix–xiii, 12–13, 143,
    151

US Department of Education, 15, 109
    high-stakes teacher evaluation systems,
        35
US Education Department, xx
"us versus them" world, 25

Valdez, Dan, 77
value-added school reform, 85
value-added models (VAM), 87–88
values, 101
Vance, Paul, 5
Van Roekel, Dennis, 64–65, 149
Vargas, Edwin, 79
Vergara v. State of California, xx, 145
Viers Mill elementary school, 55–56
Vince, Scott, 51
VitalSmarts, 120

Waiting for Superman, 3, 4, 8
Washington, DC schools, 4–5
Washington Teachers Union, 39
Weast, Jerry, 1–2, 54, 56, 137
"We Can't Just Say 'No': Teachers Unions
    Must Lead Change," 143
Weeres, Joseph G., 13–14, 108
Weingarten, Randi, x, 64, 68
West, Martin, 3–4, 79–82
West Coast Labor Management Institute,
    26, 60, 72
WestEd, xx, 96–97, 121
    Central Valley schools (California),
        100–102
what's best for students value, xii
Willful Blindness (Heffernan), 76
Win-Win Labor-Management Collaboration
    (Kaboolian and Sutherland), xix,
    10, 14
Wyoming Association of School
    Administrators, 132